D1193804

The Spirituality
of the
Teaching Sister

The Spirituality
of the
Teaching Sister

BY REV. EDWARD F. KENRICK, Ph. D.

B. Herder Book Co.

15 & 17 SOUTH BROADWAY, ST. LOUIS 2, MO.

AND 2/3 DOUGHTY MEWS, LONDON, W.C.1

IMPRIMATUR:

✠ JOSEPH CARDINAL RITTER

ARCHBISHOP OF ST. LOUIS

FEBRUARY 23, 1962

SECOND PRINTING 1962

© 1962 BY B. HERDER BOOK CO.

LIBRARY OF CONGRESS CATALOG CARD NUMBER: 62-10508

PRINTED IN THE UNITED STATES OF AMERICA
BY VAIL-BALLOU PRESS, INC., BINGHAMTON, N. Y.

Preface

IN ASCETICAL THEOLOGY IT WOULD BE PLEASANT
to have an inevitable omega such as Father de Chardin awards
evolution, but development here has been hard won. That
spirituality which consecrated religious need to guide their
teaching apostolate, offers a prime example. Indeed, a keen
challenge faces our efforts to streamline asceticism that it might
keep pace with the increasingly vast and complex world of the
sister-educator.

Because the present writer has had the concomitant experiences of teaching school and delivering spiritual conferences
to teaching sisters, he can claim quite honestly a first-hand awareness of this need. And, parenthetically, those experiences may
excuse somewhat the use of the editorial "we" throughout these
pages; alternate verbal approaches seemed awkward.

With interest high in mapping a spirituality of the laity, in
defining one proper to the secular priest, and in determining
differences among religious priests, how unpardonable it is to
neglect the spirituality suited to modern-day sisters. Their

v

religious-academic life has its own definite contours worthy of special consideration and able to yield valuable insight. "The promptings of particular ascetical ideals," comments Lindworsky, "are justified only insofar as they really fit in with one's main vocation" (*The Psychology of Asceticism*, p. 21).

Just as the local general store became a supermarket, so academic life has grown much fuller. Religious life, too, in some ways has striven to be increasingly religious: more religious, insofar as ecclesiastical directives underscore loftier spiritual concepts and require additional ascetical training, and insofar as the exacting objectives of the Sister Formation Movement become explicit—spelled out in terms of time and effort and ability. But religious life has also become more academic: concern mounts over accreditation, curricula, pressures for faculty degrees, and an endless etcetera.

Quite rightfully, therefore, teaching sisters may well resent an unknowledgeable asceticism which might fetter them to any local general store genre of spirituality. Accordingly, this volume, in its second and third sections especially, has sought to avoid incurring any such censure; but it has been equally careful, principally in Part One, to avoid sacrificing basic classical principles which have always nurtured essential spiritual progress.

This has meant espousing in places a rather somber spirituality. And this necessarily so, because we mean to place the facts of twentieth-century religious teaching clearly in the open and wrestle with them at first hand. Any attempt today to reincarnate dead Victorian platitudes would lead to futile disenchantment. The present emphasis upon individuals, generated by Existentialism, has affected all areas of thought; asceticism must likewise respect this, for individualism stripped of erroneous accretions has ever represented sound spirituality. Authentic realism demands that particular specifics should supplement the general; a lean, hard asceticism—spirituality with a bite—will actually secure for our religious educators the most generous and up-to-date means of holiness.

Perhaps this area of spiritual theology has hitherto been marked by too much rhapsodizing. Not that there is not sound basis for rhapsodizing; there is, but the modern presentation ought to seek a clear awareness of, and establish safety trails for, the rugged terrain of the heights of sanctity in terms of the flesh and blood individual who is here and now facing concrete trials; trials factually detailed from the academic tasks of the religious communities in the soul-searching 'sixties.

The Church rejoices in the high caliber of those women who embrace the role of sister-educator. They represent precious and mature vocations; vocations not unthinkingly poured out by an age of faith over an earth wallowing in the spiritual; rather, they have been wrenched from the rationalistic, materialistic generation of the careful young men and women. Powerful graces and raw will-power had to overcome an attitude, everywhere so fashionable, of non-involvement. A deliberately developed, deep, strong love of Christ forged their dedication of self to the salvation of the souls of others. Now, Christ's mastery firmly fixed, they offer one prayer—may the following chapters facilitate that prayer—

> Let him easter in us, be a dayspring to the dimness of us, be a crimson-cresseted east.
> GERARD MANLEY HOPKINS, *Wreck of the Deutschland*

Contents

TO OUR MOTHER
AND
TO MY MOTHER

❧ 1 ❧

The Path of
Religious Training

1

Humility, Gateway to Union with God

OVER THE CENTURIES THE WRITERS WHO HAVE provided traditional spiritual reading have poured out oceans of ink on the subject of humility. And one cannot be long in religious life, without becoming aware that humility often appears as the topic of spiritual conferences. Likewise, rarely is it absent from exhortations delivered during retreat times.

Because of this, one reaction might be a feeling of weariness at any new mention of humility, or, taking refuge in a sort of passive resignation, we may let our eyes see it, but permit our hearts to wander far away. A much better, more sensible reaction, however, must conclude to the essential importance of the virtue, no matter how wearisome talk about it may seem. An intelligent teacher realizes this fact in a very practical way. Among all spiritual endeavors, the practice of humility constitutes the most profound instance of going against natural human inclinations; hence, it needs to be forcibly presented again and again.

The incorporation of the Nineteenth Amendment into the Constitution symbolized the birth of a whole new world for women in the United States; and only the hopelessly naïve could expect the feminist movement to have few repercussions upon convent life. At present, sisters administer a vast elementary and secondary school system and their own colleges as well, serving as college instructors and even as university professors. Their academic degrees include the Doctorate in Philosophy, and their writings may be found in popular and learned periodicals. They speak at communion breakfasts and address educational, scientific, and cultural organizations. One finds sisters holding responsible posts in civic groups and serving on government boards. All of these achievements and more round out a picture of the remarkable progress of the Catholic Church in our land.

Yet, educational achievement is not without its pitfalls; new heights require immunization to the rarefied atmosphere. Not all men's heads, goes the expression, and by the same token not all women's heads, are strong enough to move in high places. Educational success must not outdistance spirituality, nor should Christians grow forgetful of the admonition that a good conscience and a virtuous life are always to be preferred before knowledge. Let the gains of the years be surveyed in a humble spirit, thanking God for the accomplishments in which his grace has played so large a part. The inspired words of the Scriptures themselves caution us to accept triumph humbly: "Be careful not to forget the Lord, your God, by neglecting his commandments and decrees and statutes which I enjoin on you today: lest when you have . . . increased your herds and flocks, your silver and gold, and all your property, you then become haughty of heart and unmindful of the Lord, your God. . . . Otherwise you might say to yourselves, 'It is my own power and the strength of my own hand that has obtained for me this wealth'" (Deut. 8:11–17).

The greatness of humility is driven home by reference to humility's enemy, the vice of pride. In real life we generally do not meet with stark, naked pride as such, for it would thus lose that subtlety which renders it so deadly. Pride functions as something of a combining element in the human person and in the affairs of the market place: it weaves itself into the fabric of character along with character's good qualities; it participates in the events of every day along with worthwhile actions and praiseworthy motivations. Pride derives quite matter-of-factly and easily from qualities of nature implanted deep in each man and woman.

When these tendencies have grown to serious deordinations, marring the character of the sister who teaches, they will cause her to alienate and even to harm a great many people. What, then, must be the far-reaching influence of one who over the years teaches hundreds and even thousands? How alarmed we should become when we consider that a main object of pride is to repel people. This consequence diametrically opposes an essential purpose of the religious teacher, namely, the drawing of the young to the pursuit of truth and to the way of life which she herself stands for.

Harsh manners and domineering attitudes may succeed in maintaining the strictest discipline, but at how great a cost in equally precious values. If there is any validity to the oft-leveled charge that Catholic graduates lack an ability to think for themselves and to lead others in later real-life situations, one possible explanation would be to blame the domineering teacher. How can such an approach nourish a love of learning the Church in America so eagerly desires? How many religious vocations can be seeded in the hearts of the young, when the one who personifies that vocation conveys a public image devoid of any warmth, friendliness, and attractiveness?

Class sessions can become very ludicrous affairs when the personality of the one presiding is saturated with pride. Picture the absurdity of a course in modern poetry wherein no one can offer suggestions of possible meanings in the text without these suggestions being haughtily disdained should they vary one iota from the rigid and frozen preconceptions of the teacher. No less sad would be the current-events class or the current-events section of a history class which is taught by a proud teacher. To generate healthy and helpful class-discussions which cumulatively bare the complex aspects of important leading domestic and foreign issues, would appear to be an impossibility. Certainly pupils studying under pride-stained tutelage will never be fired with an interest in the civic events surrounding them, nor will they be zealous to right wrongs and make progress in vital areas of community life.

Pride invariably builds on a false foundation: an unsubstantiated notion of personal grandeur. Since a teacher cannot always be infallible in many areas, even in subjects taught repeatedly over the years, occasions arise in the classroom which clearly demonstrate this obvious fact. A well-balanced teacher simply anticipates these occasions, and when errors are made or an unexpected insight from a member of the audience puts the matter into a focus warranting slightly different conclusions, she adjusts quite serenely. The well-balanced religious analyzes the situation, sums the subject-matter up a bit differently for the students, and then moves on.

When pride reigns, however, the teacher is unwilling to do this; sometimes, because her pride runs deep, she is even unable to do it. Stripped to the rudiments, this means that what is not truth, is passed off as truth. Oftentimes, of course, a teacher's dissimulation escapes the students' notice; but the old saying, "You cannot fool all of the people all of the time," never had a more truthful nor a more accurate application. One need not draw out unmercifully the blushing consequences of this instance of pride.

"Horrible examples" delineating such excesses of this vice could undoubtedly give salutary warnings, but they happen rather seldom in reality. And that is a tribute to the sister-teacher; it is a tribute because actually her way of life might almost be accused of containing a built-in pride.

In conscience she has to be sensitive to the lofty dignity of the religious state, since a proper respect must always be secured for the precious values it represents. This is doubly a hazard when she must constantly deal with subordinates whom it is her duty

to train to venerate and love the Church. To fulfill this obligation alone, and simultaneously to preserve the essence and habiliments of humility, represents no mean achievement; but for
the sister who is also a teacher (a position of fuller and more precisely defined authority) there arise even more formidable pitfalls.

Just how does one spend the entire day working to keep
order in a bulging classroom and at the same time, with dexterous
self-effacement, radiate the externals of humility? Surely the
process of instructing and afterwards insisting that the material
be assimilated fully requires the strength of authority and the
vigor of inspired command. The process of teaching does not admit of constant weakness and indecision.

When, then, through the assistance of divine grace and determined self-discipline, the sister-educator practices wonderfully
the virtue of humility, is she not almost being asked to lead a
double life—like an artillery captain leading a charge, who must
simultaneously make a delicate pause to hear out the criticisms of
others?

This is not expected of leaders in any other area of activity.
Rather, it is clearly understood that leadership needs to possess
certain qualities, whether in the world of fine arts, industry, government, sociology, and so forth. In fact, the reaction accepted as
proper is that of praise upon finding requisite firmness and de-
cisiveness. Even in the realm of education, although admittedly
to a lesser extent, this is verified; except, for some inexplicable
reason, when the very same comments are predicated of a religious.

Some Catholic parents are unfair in their judgments—ig-
norantly and prejudicially so. They are quick to pocket every
embroidered story that a miffed Johnny or Mary brings home.
Out of focus, sister's actions seem petty to them; but taken in
context and in the proper perspective, these same actions are
seen as not simply captious instances of a sister's piques, but
quite necessary elements in the over-all youth training program;

essential, if irritating stones for the final mosaic which becomes at graduation the gracious and morally groomed young man or woman. Then the identical parents who had succumbed so quickly to superficial peeves, are entranced with what, in unconscious arrogance, they assume to be their own exclusive masterpiece.

Why have these considerations been aired? To make it clear that sister-teachers ought to be honestly sympathetic with each other's efforts to pursue the virtue of humility, and not be too demanding or in any way unforgiving of lapses. Everyone should assess beforehand the magnitude of the task, so that, unlike the imprudent builder of the house in the gospels, adequate materials may be brought forth and success may crown sincere efforts.

While spirituality seeks much loftier aims than does public relations, there is no contradiction in spirituality being public relations wise. Consciousness of public expectations, briefly indicated above, should make the teaching sister cautious in her manner of acting, and ever alert to season with gentleness and graciousness necessary discipline and basic academic authority, difficult though that may be. She should not do so merely to be well thought of, but to fulfill her fundamental responsibility of maintaining prudent circumspection, so that all viewers will meet a favorable public image of the Church of Christ.

In any academic institution, from kindergarten to university, a bedrock requirement for scholastic achievement is cooperation on the part of the individual religious, both with other faculty members and with the superior. To make possible such cooperation, each religious must have a certain docility and pliability of character permitting normal give and take and a reasonable amount of adjustability and resiliency.

However, the stiff and unbending qualities which mark pride incline such a religious teacher to judge that compromises or concessions are a reprehensible defeat reflecting unfavorably on personal prestige. Thus, anyone heavily endowed with pride rules out of court salutary and wholesome modes of thinking which so greatly facilitate accomplishment on the group level, and actually constitute a necessary lubricant for the wheels of academic progress. Oftentimes pride makes a religious too domineering to get along creditably with colleagues when joint action is being planned and executed; and, pointing the same qualities in another direction, too rebellious to give willing and wholehearted support to the leadership of the superior. An opinionated and unbending person, to face the sad fact of the matter, cannot work well with anyone but self.

Over the last few years a rash of novels have very tellingly depicted faculty life and academic politics. Admittedly caustic and cynical (but frequently delightful), they have drawn many amusing scenes of overt and subterranean conflict. Troubles of this kind crop up so inevitably they seem natural offshoots of the ivy scene. And not always will they just disappear because the actors in the scene are clothed with religious garb. To be shocked or bitter about these things reveals an unwarranted immaturity.

It may be wiser to stress the brighter side of the coin and concentrate on the amount of spirit, the dedication of purpose, and thoughtfulness of planning, which various faculty members have given to the ideas and ideals they have broached. No doubt about it, when one is knee deep in one's own educational convictions, a certain *élan* is imparted to the mode of presentation. At times, however, a rather Machiavellian touch intervenes to engineer the consent of the group in favor of a particular project. Even though the panacea may be a good one, human nature has to struggle to keep personal productions unadulterated by pride, and free and clear of the many pitfalls stemming from pride.

When personal ideas get out of hand because of a really headstrong pride, however, they harm the school and create difficulties for both superior and fellow-religious. Yet, in the final analysis, the greatest harm befalls the proud religious herself. Her conduct, superimposed on the unattractive aspects of personality already implied, gradually results in isolating her from the group, from its *esprit de corps*, and from the interests of the school. Bit by bit the proud person begins to feel the pangs of this loneliness, but since no solution is available other than a change in the person's own way of thinking and acting, no solution is realized. How can a solution be found when pride prevents any admission of the need for change or any willingness to make the effort?

Another factor of considerable importance, is that frequently there will be no promotions for the pride-ridden religious teacher. Most promotions in an educational system demand, at least theoretically, some sort of executive or administrative ability. One indispensable component of this ability is the talent to appreciate the over-all picture, which includes the acknowledgment of contributions made by others. Keeping everything in delicate balance and acknowledging the right of even conflicting points of view must be the task of the administrator. A proud person, however, top-heavy with the importance of self, self's thinking and self's way of doing, cannot do this.

Yet, often it happens that the religious who is denied promotion is superior in general intelligence, and in many other ways, to those who receive advancement. Realizing this, the proud person concludes bitterly that unfair treatment has been her only reward for long years of hard work.

Such an internal diet savored in loneliness often leads to despondency and depression, a very dangerous situation and one which inevitably throws open the soul to all sorts of temptations. Precisely for this reason, the proud person will from time to time face difficult struggles against impurity; difficult, because during them the proud religious has only the strength of an isolated, depressed self. Other temptations which follow in pride's wake could be listed and detailed, but perhaps we should stress the weakness of spirit which pride engenders when resistance is necessary.

Humility offers the necessary and the only corrective by revealing clearly to the soul God's rightful role and the soul's own obligation to recognize, submit to, and thankfully welcome that divine assistance. Even though many good qualities may be possessed, one is not necessarily safe; sometimes the greater those qualities the greater will be the temptation to become proud, unless a salutary humility intervenes. Hence, the warning of St. Jerome—those who attempt to build virtue while they lack humility are vainly trying to carry dust in a sieve. Without humility there cannot be real hope of perfection; God insists upon humility as an essential condition before he will shower us with his gifts and special graces. "How important humility is to the whole spiritual life! All comes to us through God's grace, but if we are proud, God can give us no special graces; for his own sake he cannot, because humility alone renders to him the glory that comes from his gifts; and for our own sakes he cannot, because graces without humility only injure us and are occasions of greater pride" (Meschler, *Three Fundamental Principles*, p. 130).

Pride often foils attempts at detection. The difficulty arises principally because pride can become intertwined with zeal, or at least with what cloaks itself to look like zeal. Yet, a rather unfailing test can be applied.

Zeal pursues good for the sake of the good itself; love of praise pursues the good for the publicity and regard it brings. Caution must prevail, however; these motives are not always clear-cut, for at times the proud person lacks full awareness of the extent to which his or her motivation has become tainted. Here, certain tasks can serve as a sort of threshing machine to separate the zeal from the pride. When a proud person is assigned tasks which are routine, simple, and unpublicized, then interest in the work will noticeably wane; the lack of praise will bring about slipshod workmanship, even downright evasion of duty; soon thereafter, irritation and depression commence to invade the proud soul. These signs indicate that much of the previous "zeal" was not unmixed with pride, and that, although there was willingness to work enthusiastically, the basic cause of the energetic efforts lay in pride's satisfaction over the consequent praise of self.

Schoolwork can provide instances of this phenomenon; simple things, part of the routine, whose connection with pride may not be apparent at first, yield under probing, until their relationship to pride is definitely established. To be moderator of the school basketball team can be a thoroughly enjoyable assignment. The school may have a traditionally fine record in this sport. Great interest on the part of the faculty, students, and the members of the civic community as a whole, center upon the fine showing of the team. So it is that the moderator, too, becomes an important central figure.

To have one's comments about the team sought after eagerly and listened to attentively as presenting important inside insights, is gratifying to average human nature. To be the one looked up to by all the players, and to some extent by all the students, can give one a taste of quasi hero-worship on a small but, nonetheless, delightful scale. One can work very hard at one's extracurricular activities under those benign circumstances.

Let us suppose that the same religious who worked with such apparent zeal in moderating the basketball team was reassigned to looking after the swimming team instead. It would be hard to find a better touchstone for the purest zeal. Generally, schools have not the slightest interest in the swimming team. Conditions under which meets are held are often repellent. Pools are few and the moderator finds herself traveling all over the metropolis for practice. And where can she find a sympathetic ear into which to pour all of this? Nowhere, because to others the needs of a swimming team are like a foreign land; of its geography and climate no one else has the slightest idea.

If the religious in question can maintain her interest here, can maintain the same level of hard work that marked her enthusiasm for basketball, there certainly seems little doubt that she is zealous and that no admixture of pride but genuine self-sacrificing zeal has ever been her propelling force.

These examples are overdrawn somewhat; issues are not this clear-cut in average experiences, but they do serve to make the point. And this point can be applied very realistically to a host of everyday school activities where the shadings are much more refined. It has a very valid function in separating zeal and pride, in unmasking, perhaps even to self, true motivations, and finally in measuring accurately some of the qualities which may have been fixed upon too readily as virtues.

The above simplification can yield another lesson too, in the realm of pride. Sometimes religious tend to associate themselves so closely with a particular activity which has been entrusted to them, that they become clearly and excessively possessive about it. The pronoun "my" begins to be used in any references to the activity and there takes place a personification of the dictum of Ralph Waldo Emerson that an institution be regarded as the lengthened shadow of a great man. And this, more often than not, overflows into a rather cavalier disregard for the extracurricular activities which others have.

Allied to that pride which thrives on love of praise, is vanity. Perhaps the definition of a vain person should be, "One whose love of praise blinds his or her judgment." Thus, a vain person conjures up a biased picture of her own abilities, which in turn creates a weakness of character that renders her susceptible to temptations presented in the wrappings of flattery, and which ultimately leads her activities in false and unsound directions. Vanity is a bottomless thing, never satisfied. More praise, and still more praise, is continuously required to remain pleased with self and to keep superficially happy. Just as those who require the stimulation or sedation of drugs or alcohol constantly need more, so also must the doses to appease vanity be increased. If they are increased, the victim becomes farther and farther removed from reality.

Popular belief has it that some groups are particularly vain; for example, orators and actors, because they are always before the public receiving applause, and barbers because they stand constantly in front of mirrors. Should not those who teach be included as well? They seem often to receive as much audience appreciation. And one cannot blame the teacher too much here; to be liked by the students and to receive some adulation is a good.

To the proper extent, popularity may even be a legitimate aim since it is a definite and valuable means of being an influence for good upon youth as well as a potent factor in transmitting knowledge. Where to draw the line presents the problem. Certainly popularity should not be sought for its own sake; still less for selfish, egocentric reasons. Yet even when it is gained quite blamelessly, quite deservedly, it remains very heady stuff. Hence, the religious who teaches has to be constantly on guard lest, first unwittingly and ultimately quite consciously, she submit to these notably attractive blandishments of pride.

Human nature is fallen human nature. Today's teacher can recall days on the other side of the desk when, along with other students, she conspired to play upon teacher's vanity. How skillfully time could be wasted or a test forgotten by introducing teacher's pet thesis through "loaded" questions. How easily the innocent allusion to some article the professor wrote, or some lecture she was scheduled to give, could melt the iciest shell of discipline, and turn the most difficult work period into a pleasant, easygoing half hour.

These occurrences, of course, are very human and perhaps wisdom makes room for such universal foibles and willingly accepts them. But when they are dreadfully magnified under the impetus of a fierce deepseated vanity, the story becomes a very different and a very sad one. As a really vain person grows more subject to delusions of grandeur, that person waxes self-expansive, self-assertive. Totally incapable of comprehending the foolish picture thus created, even a teaching religious, despite a generous background in learning and asceticism, may not notice the factual realities but only the daydreams of personal greatness.

When finally the realities of life assert themselves and blame and failure close in upon the poor unfortunate so unreasonably desiring praise, she is unable "to take it." Others have met and conquered similar hardships, but the proud person has built up such a tender hypersensitivity, such an infatuation with praise, that now, not only is the lack of praise unbearable, but positive contempt and outright censure can actually cause grief, despair, and even personal collapse.

Pride is often punished slowly; it can long lay concealed, by good fortune escaping minor crises. As long as it endures, however, virtue and strength of character skate on very thin ice; the mills of the gods grind slowly but they grind exceeding fine. Only tragic failure makes the proud person realize how the vice of pride has ruined everything it has touched, seeped into what was thought to be zeal, and contaminated what was felt to be virtue. Thoughts, words, and deeds had been done too often by self and for self; life had not been lived by God and for God. "Though you go as high as the eagle, and your nest be set among the stars, from there will I bring you down, says the Lord" (Abd. 1:4).

At this point the proud person craves the charity of neighbors as a cushion against the assaults of misfortune. In the past, however, what has been her own charity toward neighbor? "Very poor," reads the record. Pride rarely holds a high opinion of neighbor; rather it is marked by a disdainful haughtiness in dealing with neighbor. Sharp criticism and harsh judgment have been the rule. Indeed, because of so much preoccupation with self, there has not been much time for neighbor.

High opinion of neighbor derives from humility, a humility aware of the weakness and sinfulness of self. In this way the humble woman achieves generosity in her appraisal of the worth of neighbor. Humility impresses upon its devotees the truth that one cannot fully judge neighbor, even should her every action be seen, for her intention—the all-important factor—is not seen; one can only guess. How unfair, then, to sentence by guesswork. Our neighbor, humility further realizes, can be guilty of imperfection or sin only in proportion to the graces she has received. Another cannot possibly possess competent knowledge concerning the fullness or paucity of these graces. Finally, what over-all success or failure will be awarded our neighbor depends on the end result of life, something about which—since even pride does not lay claim to knowledge of the future—we are entirely ignorant. Neither, it is well to remember with fitting gravity, do we know what the final result of our own life will be.

Today is an ill-disposed time in history for the practice of humility; apart from pagan times, enthusiasm for it was never less. But we pay for our neglect of humility—we live in an "age of anxiety." Such has become our sociological appelation as well as the title and spirit of one of the well-received and admittedly symptomatic musical compositions of Leonard Bernstein. While other things undoubtedly contribute to this anxiety, the lack of humility is certainly a substantial factor.

Much of the anxiety derives from the omnipresent obsession to get ahead, to achieve a progressively ascendant worldly status. This has become a compulsion, and deep-seated conflicts are generated by the disparity between one's factual position and the status sought. Since the religious, too, belongs to the age of anxiety, her outlook can be marred by this climate of opinion. Too often people forget that this is so and somehow expect that entry into a convent automatically erases the world and presents humility on a silver platter. On the contrary, the religious faces a lifelong struggle against this worldliness.

Should the sister's struggle be unsuccessful, she is considerably worse off than those living in the world. For any religious, status seeking amounts to a fundamental cleavage in the innermost soul and creates a divided personality. She finds, although committed publicly, *ex officio* to a life of detachment from honors, power, and position, that these drives actually constitute a secret mainspring. How can such an utterly irreconcilable situation yield spiritual peace? In this matter religious are prisoners of their vocation, for corrosive anxiety renders impossible the wholesome, integrated personality of holiness; such a religious can never fulfill the pledged commitment of her vocation to humility.

Is it not accurate to state that the abandonment of humility represents a giving up in the spiritual life, a throwing in of the sponge vocation-wise, a sad departure from those ideals which initially sustained the entrance into religious life and then powered its necessary sacrifices? To withhold the practice of humility is an implicit confession that those original high purposes have not worked out.

Yet, despite the obstacles, despite the failures and disappointments, the unending quest for increasing humility must continue to engage the mind and heart of the follower of Christ. He remains ever the supreme example here. Most of our Lord's life, thirty of the thirty-three years, was consecrated to a hidden life, and humility is the gateway to the hidden life. Christ could have lived in palaces, could have assumed stupendous power, wealth, prestige; but he did not. He chose the hidden life of obscurity; his was the status of the laboring man, living in a plain home, working in a carpenter shop. For thirty years his divine identity was unknown to neighbors and to the world; his were the simple tasks of the day, and the routine concerns of a small village.

While the religious community, like the much larger world, offers some choice corners, some positions of power and prestige, the aims of a holy religious should reflect the life of Christ, who must ever remain her exemplar. A sincere desire to be the Master's disciple and companion shows a willingness to share his hidden life. That hidden life represents the very top of the spiritual ladder; an unattainable pinnacle, however, without the rungs of humility. Simple tasks, unimportant to the world, preserve the purity of motivation. Certainly they are not performed for praise—no one ever thinks twice about them; they cannot be done for pleasure—in themselves they are unpleasant; they have only one possible interest—God takes an interest in them. They elevate neither one's opinion of self nor the world's opinion of self. The religious is thus forced to work with God and for God, stripping the mind of distractions, enabling the heart to be truly detached. Worries about praise or blame, failure or success, advancement and prestige are simply nonexistent; life is truly hidden with Christ.

Yet, this hidden life readily yields the goal of all spiritual activity, namely, union with Christ. A mind freed from distractions centers easily on Christ; a heart lacking attachments polarizes in Christ. Since all else is removed, only Christ and self remain, rendering union a natural, logical necessity. To recapitulate this spiritual achievement: pride, the greatest obstacle, is eliminated; humility, the gateway to the hidden life, is fostered; and the hidden life fructifies in union. In the world, this is an unfailing formula for living the best possible life with Christ.

2

Patience, Our
Spiritual Stamina

YEARS AGO, THE BOTTLE OF PATENT MEDICINE
was an exciting thing on the American scene. This single bottle,
although small and cheap, seemed pregnant with infinite possibilities. As the scientific clinical aspect of medicine continued
to grow, however, most of these colorful claims were proved
false, and have now been discredited.

Today on the same American scene, through the introduc-
tion of the so-called miracle drugs, such as penicillin and strepto-
mycin, great claims have been again put forth; but this time
science calmly confirms these claims, which, although fabulous,
are, nonetheless, completely defensible and medically quite sound.
Reflecting upon the startling ability of the miracle drug to lighten
with radiant hope the bleak despair of sickness and to terminate
even illnesses which have faltered over many lingering years, the
religious who is struggling for perfect health of soul, cannot but
feel an ardent longing for some similar sort of miracle drug in the
order of asceticism.

Our reflections and our longing, happily, need not be vain;
in the available, although difficult-to-master virtue of patience,
we do possess a spiritual lifesaver, an over-all religious panacea.

Without hesitation we should classify patience as a miracle virtue; it can accomplish advancement in our spiritual life genuinely comparable to the proud boasts of the new miracle drugs—and in a higher, nobler realm. The good will which is the greatest possession of many religious whose apostolate is directed to the classroom, the deep desire they have for spiritual progress, and the willingness they show to accept the measures necessary to secure that goal, make them most deserving of help of this sort. Most deserving, because the life they lead has so many duties and so many distractions that, despite their good will and unselfish effort, they require a special boon if real sanctity is to be mastered.

In their recurrent resolve to serve God as perfectly as possible, good people, including religious teachers, often experience moments of high aspiration. At such moments, great promises are made to God, and are made with firmness. Especially, at what are termed the turning points of life, do we solemnly pledge our unlimited allegiance to Christ. At Commencement, the graduate may well do so; the mother of the family, perhaps, offered such a promise at her Nuptial Mass; in turn, the religious, under the sacred inspiration of ordination or profession, consecrated all of self to a future of flawless holiness. And when the religious first began her life work of teaching, that sacred consecration was vigorously and purposefully renewed.

With a startling suddenness, we realized clearly at that holy moment how wonderfully close we are to God. That moment knew only an overpowering compulsion—"for me to live is Christ." Fresh and strong in resolute love of God, we vowed, in spite of sorrows, or trials, or storms, an utterly unflagging Christlike service. But time marched on. As our backs felt the burden of everyday concerns, our determination, it must be honestly confessed, was seen to lag, our spirituality to cool.

This inherent obstacle to lofty perfection, this retrogression from such ideal heights seems so universal as to be almost commensurate with our fallen human nature. As solvent of such an

obstacle, patience plays its all-important role; here stands revealed its keystone quality—the cohesive support of all the other
virtues. Patience imparts the stamina of our spirituality. Without
stamina, an athlete could not last through the rigors and hardships inevitably entailed in an entire season of competitive sport.
Patience provides the spiritual athlete, tyro and veteran alike,
with the stamina, or staying power, necessary for the life-long
season of asceticism. We have promised to be perfect. On the
morning of that first day we walked into a classroom, we promised
Christ in our Communion thanksgiving we would be perfect. We
may not have used that wording, but in effect that was what we
did promise. Patience acts to keep us perfect. Despite the many
obstacles—which now we realize much more fully—strewing the
path of any teaching apostolate assigned to us, patience will
enable us to keep our promise.

When we seek perfection, just what is it we do seek? What
does it mean in down-to-earth, visible, tangible terms? Perfection
is the practice of charity, the loving of God for his own sake and
our neighbor as self because of this love. We may account perfect
anyone able to possess such charity and maintain it always at the
highest level.

But a twenty-four-hour-a-day conspiracy of persons, places,
and things watches eagerly to steal that charity from our hearts.
Only through the eternal vigilance of patience can the necessary,
preservative buffer which protects charity, be erected. Throughout the week we must deal with people who may be unreasonable,
demanding, even antagonistic. Paths of duty sometimes lead us
into projects originated by those who have given them more
energy than thought, and we find ourselves enmeshed in a morass
draining away our time and causing only irritation and frustration. We ourselves can sometimes sound the most dangerous
challenge to charity by our own temperamental tendencies, by
passions not thoroughly mastered, by pride disguised under many
masks.

Persons, places, and things sorely try and would overcome

our charity unless patience stood guard to receive the blows, thus leaving our charity either wholly untouched or but little damaged and substantially intact. For a charity that despised patience to remain inviolate, for an impatient person to keep unerringly to the plotted path of charity, would require a moral miracle unworthy of God's wisdom. We cannot preserve charity without patience, and since charity is the measure of perfection, those who would be perfect must do some hard thinking about their practice of the virtue of patience.

In relation to other virtues, patience serves in a similar fashion, stabilizing them, protecting them, and against the ubiquitous forces working for their downfall, bringing them to their full flowering. Despite the well-founded and practically unanimous conviction, subscribed to over the centuries by intelligent men, that virtue marks the sole road to earthly and heavenly happiness, few have ever thought that the road to virtue is smooth and open and easy; arduous would be more properly descriptive. Hence, those who would be virtuous must learn to "live laborious days."

Virtue demands constancy, but often within us our natural urgings are inconstant; virtue, by definition a habit, demands the endless repetition of the same actions, but sameness and repetition weary the spirit. Virtue demands a straining and striving that cannot relax; our human preferences, being quite the reverse, react rebelliously to this. Virtue demands spiritual poise, ascendant and aloof, enduring and unmoved by life's irritations and discontents; but our inferior passions, resenting any rein, clamor for spirited self-expression. Patience alone can fulfill the demands of the virtues, and only patience, as a consequence, can achieve their perfection. This is a universal situation and the pursuit of virtue anywhere will encounter the same context. One can truly state, however, that in the classroom these same ingredients are multiplied and are present in a fashion much more intense; thus, the greater need for patience.

The ability of patience to insulate all virtues, particularly charity, against our waverings and perturbations under duress, bestows and preserves a peace of soul which insures our sustained drive toward perfection. Should the battle seem to turn against us, patience checks any want of spiritual fiber and rallies our resolution. Patience resembles a master train-dispatcher overlooking the huge track-bed of a vast railroad empire, ordering all things with smooth, unerring perfection. In proportion to its difficulty, however, lies the unlimited achievement of patience; its possession constitutes an unfailing test of a person's virtue, above all of his charity, and a just measurement of his perfection. Always on stage, with scarcely an inactive moment, patience cannot be counterfeited. One can pretend patience for a moment, for an hour; but patience as a way of life—never—not without its actual possession.

Patience can levy great claims upon us because of our teaching vocation; indeed, of all the varied occupations available to human ingenuity, none offers so convincing a *prima facie* case for the practice of this virtue. Patience is inherent in the task of teaching. The personalities of the pupils and their large numbers can doubtless triple the amount of patience required, but the mere fact that teaching surrounds an adult with an adolescent world, means that he or she must always strive to bridge the gap existing between adulthood and adolescence. As teachers, our efforts are constant to adjust ourselves to a world not naturally our own. The need to revamp our way of thinking, speaking, acting and reacting is ever-present. If we do not admit that need, our classroom message and potential personal influence may as well be suspended in outer space.

Pupils possess their own hierarchy of values and we have to be aware of them; only in this way will the intellectual and spiritual values we seek to impart be presented in terms understandable to the adolescent outlook. To master the ability to think in their concepts and make this ability become almost second nature to us in the classroom is a long and difficult process. Yet, when we do so, our subject-matter doffs its adult habiliments and appears in trappings which the adolescent will welcome. Obviously, this disciplining of our minds and tongues is impossible without the greatest patience.

Patience also serves as a pedagogical good angel to guard us against the very human tendency to express disinterest or disdain at some of the pupils' "contributions." Various considerations, which in the absolute order are of little significance, can be of great weight to their younger minds.

Sound discipline has always been a prerequisite for effective teaching, but patience, in turn, is a prerequisite for discipline. To be without patience is to borrow considerable trouble in the discipline department. In any classroom, the raw material of disciplinary difficulties is present in varying degrees. Handling this material with patience marks the difference between a good disciplinarian and one who does not, on any sustained basis, control the class as well as it might be controlled.

Upon being confronted with incipient trouble, the teacher who has no patience may immediately lose control of her temper and explode in anger. This brings things to a head abruptly and can foster an ugly crisis; punishment is meted out, staying after school decreed, and children are sent in flocks to the principal's office. The problem has been instantaneously ignited; almost immediately it is troublesome. Had a habit of patience prevailed, the critical moment or so of exercising the virtue might have enabled teacher to ride the wave just a bit longer and then firmly and calmly sieze the opportune opening to effect the strategic containment of the difficulty, thus preventing a serious, overt disciplinary fracas.

In the heat of a tense situation the pupil often becomes flustered and rash; particularly, he is afraid to "back down" publicly and lose caste in the eyes of classmates; so he continues to push himself and becomes obdurate. The patient teacher, without surrendering to weakness or sacrificing principle, maintains self-control and wields a calm, confident strength. This permits her shrewdly to open the door to the pupil for a graceful retreat and retraction, for which the pupil is actually most anxious.

Rarely do students want to go as far as passion and embarrassment force them; this is readily admitted afterwards. An adolescent inability to cope with the predicament, and fear generated by the nervousness of the situation, are often basically at fault. Tactful teaching diplomacy rightfully earns a fine reputation for the teacher who possesses it, and the student group pays it the tribute of lasting respect.

Surely it is superfluous to emphasize at length the great patience (fortitude in large portions may be more accurate) needed to face the fearful fact that our students retain but little knowledge despite all our struggles. Young teachers especially, when they have recovered from the shock of correcting their first set of tests, can use all available patience; but it remains ever a need for the most veteran test-giver.

Patience is also needed when equally lamentable answers are offered in the classroom itself, even after we have given repeated, meticulous, and lengthy explanations of the points to be known. Patience is also called for to stimulate questions from diffident pupils or to encourage those who are shy to participate in group discussions. Under patient guidance, absurd questions and shallow observations can at times be drawn into channels which may yield at least some oblique illumination of the material at hand. Resentment and exasperation which would be rather fatal to our efforts are thus checked. The peculiar patterns of juvenile thought are kindly probed, and a painstaking answer exposes some helpful nexus to the pertinent truths. That baby step forward, the basic ingredient of the learning process, has been secured.

Occasionally, the teaching religious can help pupils who are burdened with problems whose roots are entirely outside the classroom or learning areas. Extraction of these roots, however, constitutes an exercise in consummate tact and patience. While such pupils, according to their lights, will not be deliberately untruthful, they are capable of a good deal of misleading, circumvention, and essential omission. Bearing patiently with their tortuous efforts to unburden themselves, will finally gain the fullest trust and confidence from them. Only then, clearly and without emotional concealment, can they bare the whole truth which must be had. Only then can guidance be offered successfully to them.

As a special virtue patience opposes itself to those twin trials of everyone's existence, anger and sadness. Patience directs itself particularly against the beginnings of anger: vexations which gradually make us lose our tempers, annoyances which make us unreasonable and disagreeable. Anger's progress was well illustrated by an old-time movie comedian, famous for what was called the "slow burn." While the audience noted with delight each nuance, his expression changed from smiles, to frowns, to grimaces, to anger, to more anger—until finally he would explode in a terrific outburst of temper. With remarkable insight, he expressed visibly how the passion of anger overcomes us. His performance illustrated also, very tellingly, the only defense against anger—resistance at the outset. Right at the beginning, patience checks this passion of our lower nature; because of patience, anger never has a chance to get started. Since anger will receive considerable attention in our later pages, contenting ourselves here with the very trite observation that the classroom, as was already indicated, is a favorite target for the attacks of anger and gives the virtue thereby a very busy time indeed, we may move on to dwell more fully on sadness.

"Drive away sadness far from thee," Holy Scripture warns us, "for sadness hath killed many, and there is no profit in it" (Ecclus. 30:24-25, Douay version). Fleeting moments of sadness, perforating life, as well as heavy burdens of sadness occasioned by particular personal, family, or community tragedy, must be accounted integral parts of human experience in this vale of tears, and must be understood and accepted in a Christian spirit. Far removed from such genuine sorrow, however, is a subjective predilection for endless sadness which aimlessly dissipates our energy, hopelessly wastes our time, and leaves us to languish in that fruitless and unavailing grief proper to those who have no hope. Sadness of this latter sort, wrongful and harmful, gradually builds itself to the proportions of an enervating vice corruptive of all spiritual effort.

Stripped to its essentials, such sadness can rightly be attributed to selfishness; a selfishness which nurtures sadness and, in turn, receives nutriment from it—the unbroken process of a vicious circle. Over-concentration on self, repeatedly bewailing self's plight, sentimentally weighing the extent of self's affliction, mournfully brooding over self's future, all such attitudes deepen the wound of sadness in the sensitive part of the soul and finally open the tear-valves of self-pity to further moisten this self-created well of bottomless sorrow.

When this happens to us, self and sadness gradually become the alpha and omega of our consciousness, with the result that our normal interest in, and zest for, the religious vocation, begins to wane and may even disappear. Sympathetic concern for needy souls consigned to our ministrations no longer holds our attention, for nothing can break through our completely self-centered thoughts. Our abilities and their potential lie fallow—unnoticed by us, of no avail to others. We turn away from all but self, blotting out the beauty of sky and stars, the warmth of sunshine and landscape, the joy of smiles and laughter. The lovely progress of grace etching peace and happiness upon the face of humanity, the shining inspiration of holy hearts so humbly hallowing all— these things which make life sing, receive no second glance, meet only an unseeing eye.

Dwelling exclusively on self, sadness forgets friends and even God. Friends, pleasant in manner and genuinely interested in us, our link to needful recreation and our reminder of invigorating, joyous experiences, can withdraw us from our self-imposed sadness. But no! We prefer to nurse feelings of self-pity in solitude, to mold ourselves into clay martyrs, to tickle our vanity and inflate our ego with spurious notions of self-sacrifice.

Our conduct becomes even more reprehensible when we extend such an attitude to our divine Friend, blinding ourselves to the presence of God who created heaven and earth and to whom all sorrow is subject, neglecting the presence of Christ who warms the grace-laden breast with infinite peace and matchless contentment. Mary's outstretched arms, the arms of the most devoted of mothers, are permitted to close upon empty air; the prayerful watchfulness of the angels and saints, is ungratefully ignored. How can sadness be maintained in a milieu, our milieu, brimming with such heavenly happiness?

Sadness multiplies sadness, pyramiding mere molehills to giant mountains of oppressive sorrow. Anyone who has had occasion to use a stove recalls the experience of thinking that the gas jet was left burning. Walking down the street, we advert to this. Gradually, we picture a pot boiling over, a ceiling burning, until, bit by bit, we have drawn the dreadful vision of a whole house in flames. Sadness causes that same process in our souls. Beginning with some triviality, some slight, offered perhaps unwittingly, some petty injury of which no one but ourselves was even conscious, sadness fills the soul with petulant self-love, ignites it in the imagination and memory, until the picture becomes that of a soul inflamed with melancholy.

"Slights" of one sort or another seem always to be cropping up on the educational scene, and, if we foolishly mull them over in sadness, we can go a long way toward making life unliveable for ourselves. When the school term gets fully under way, things move very quickly and with such variety and scope that it would be a moral miracle were everything perfectly coordinated. Many misunderstandings arise. If we exercise some patience, the facts gradually become clear and we conclude wisely that we need not take umbrage. If we have no patience, acting recklessly on the spur of the moment, fires will be kindled on all sides; and in our own heart a large bonfire of sadness will burn.

Trivialities can sometimes set teachers at each other's throats. Such a hazard is the interclassroom phone system in many schools. A combination of classroom noise and static can cause two religious to be quite shocked at what each other said. Patience here is rudimentary common sense.

Dealings with the school office offer various examples. Such is the multitude of reports of one sort or another made out by the teachers, that a percentage of them are somehow misplaced. When a sensitive teacher receives a chiding memorandum for not handing in some particular report, although actually hers was among the first filed, unless patience intervenes a bitter misunderstanding can result.

At times necessity dictates the employment of students as messengers between faculty members. If we believed all the messages so conveyed, there would be no peace in the school. Patience wisely remembers the imaginative genius of the young and waits to straighten things out quietly with the teacher involved.

In many schools the principal periodically addresses the faculty, and here again many obstacles are encountered to the preservation of patience in the soul. What psychologists term the fallacy of self-reference often has a field day in this situation, and a number of religious cannot attend such gatherings without going away with the deep conviction that everything said was a veiled attack on themselves. Sprinkled with a little humility, patience ought to solve this, too.

These rather elementary examples could be multiplied endlessly in the complex pattern of activity to which a religious teacher is committed. The components would be nearly the same, however, and certainly the lesson to be learned is identical—the need of patience to prevent our torturing ourselves and harmfully saturating our souls in demoralizing sadness.

Inasmuch as we have described sadness as a state nurtured in loneliness of soul, it may be well to refresh our realization of the amount of loneliness inherent in the life of a religious dedicated to the academic apostolate. It is true that other apostolates face greater loneliness, but the loneliness of the academic life sometimes goes unnoticed.

A number of young religious spend hours taking courses in university or college. The study for these courses and the library work which has to be done in conjunction with them, mean many hours of loneliness. To prepare well the classes that one is teaching likewise requires a considerable amount of time spent alone. Again, the processes of preparing examinations and tests and then grading them, while sometimes admitting of group endeavor, are carried out mainly by the teacher alone. Even in the classroom one finds a certain loneliness; this may seem a strange point to make, since the religious is surrounded by students in the classroom, and yet, although they are present, they are not companions. Essentially, as teacher, the religious is alone in the work of teaching; and this despite the friendliest of relationships with the members of the class.

When these items, and others as well, are combined with the times spent in obligatory silence, in personal prayer, in liturgical services, and so forth, they add up to a good deal of being alone. Consequently, if a religious has any tendency to sadness and permits that tendency to go unchecked, ample opportunity is present for sadness to grow very formidable in the soul. Should this take place and the vice of sadness master our interior life, all of our spiritual exercises lose their former attractiveness; our taste for the spiritual, previously so keen, turns to ashes in bitterness of soul; virtue no longer possesses its flavor and inner satisfaction. Our spiritual fiber rots from within. "Like a moth in clothing, or a maggot in wood, sorrow gnaws at the human heart" (Prov. 25:20). We have lost the will to fight for perfection.

Yet, constantly present within such a soul is a deep, eager drive for escape, a discord that keeps fermenting, an oppression yearning to be free. These powerful urges render the person who has abandoned self to sadness a large and easy target for temptation. The Fathers used to caution their disciples that a sad heart is the plaything of Satan. Quite easily Satan can tempt it to gloom and despair or to illicit worldly pleasures.

This points up the necessity of being patient with ourselves as well as with others. Adapting the old adage, we can say that patience should begin at home, for it is essential that we be patient with ourselves, too. A quasi-humorous anecdote may illustrate this more succinctly than many-worded paragraphs. One Sunday a certain priest decided to speak on the virtue of patience and as he spoke rejoiced at how well the beginning of the talk had gone. Then, some children in the front pews began to shift about and murmur. As the sermon on patience continued, the children also continued, and the voice from the pulpit grew noticeably louder. Next, the preacher cautioned the children, not without some chagrin at their misconduct, and again returned to the sermon. Instead of improving, the children became worse; the flush mounting beneath the Roman collar became darker. Finally, the priest himself grew so impatient at their impatience, he simply had to make the sign of the cross, and, lest he utter vigorous thoughts, indecorous in the temple of God, terminate the talk on patience.

Despite all of our efforts to remain patient, we can count on times when we will be unsuccessful, times when we will make mistakes, times when our imperfections will burst forth, times even perhaps—though certainly they should not be counted on— when we will fall into sin. Even at such times, indeed especially at such times, we must remain patient with self. Discouragement, panic, and despair do not improve the situation; such reactions are more often traceable to egotism, to pride wounded by our fallibility, rather than to deep-seated love of God, which, when genuine, bears the seal of peaceful trust in him. At such moments we need to learn the cool patience of the courageous words of Sir Andrew Barton:

> I am hurt, but I am not slain;
> I'll lay me down and bleed awhile,
> And then I'll rise and fight again.

One who compartmentalizes the spiritual life and assigns varying degrees to each division, could be accused of arbitrary presumption. Yet, were it done, great importance would be given to the life of prayer, since nothing is more vital to progress in holiness. Prayer stokes the fires powering all the meritorious activities throughout each single day of the life-long religious vocation. A prayerful day means a day spent in union with God; prayerfulness can be recognized as the hallmark of those serving as effective instruments of his wonderful providence. Moments of prayer, above all other moments, are the sweetest to the devout religious; during them, the soul rests alone with Christ, savoring him with the deepest insight, drawing close to him in the most loving fashion. Patience, however, can legitimately claim credit for establishing and protecting this oasis wherein our soul drinks hungrily the divine truths of the Beloved. Patience provides this oasis, conquering a desert which stretches everywhere its sands of cares, tasks, anxieties, and distractions.

In general, "practice of the presence of God" designates the prayerful approach of the religious to the duties of the day; a practice arising from the sincere conviction that such duties are best performed with Christ as companion. His presence in our consciousness supplies the link between earth and heaven. His presence keeps that link unbroken throughout a day crisscrossed by sundry assignments, some large, some trivial, all of them distracting. Hand in hand with Chirst, how easily we transfer from our own hand to his, all the "prayers, works and sufferings" of each day, whose only purpose is to please him. There can be no sustained practice of the presence of God, however, without the hard work of patience, which keeps clear the center of the soul. In that center rests the hallowing divine presence, and patience dutifully locks out the intrusions of an outside world ever eager to invade that sanctuary.

Even during religious exercises which physically separate us from school and kindred concerns, only patience insures that same separation on the psychological level. Were it not for patience, those concerns would flood and submerge our attempts to concentrate exclusively upon heavenly considerations. Despite the quiet prayerful atmosphere of our chapel, the welcome assistance of patience is needed to ward off thoughts, desires, and recollections which seek to draw us away from the object at hand—the dedicated worship of God.

Above all else, contemplative mental prayer, the crown and sweetness of our prayer life, needs support from the virtue of patience. Its very existence presupposes patience; patience forms the cloister of the heart and enforces there the rule of enclosure. Since prayer should be, and in fact must be, the expression of our whole life, without recollection of spirit as a way of life, contemplative prayer cannot be a reality. Anyone who goes through fifteen hours of the day, her mind bubbling over with distractions, emotions distraught and uncontrolled, a feather in the wind of environment, does not suddenly become a new second person at the sixteenth hour, devoted to prayer. Unless patience has won recollection throughout the day, a recollected mind and heart are not lifted to God in prayer. Recollection has ever been the *conditio sine qua non* of mental prayer, and patience remains still the *conditio sine qua non* of recollection.

Our navy honors a tradition that no one ever visits the captain's quarters on shipboard unless sent for. Laying down the same rule to all distraction, patience preserves the innermost quarters of the soul so that in tranquil quiet we may turn to God in prayer. Our greatest asset in prayer is the union with God that patience has safeguarded outside the moments of prayer. Thus, contemplative effort becomes but a matter of continuation and augmentation, not a new and strange task foreign to our personality.

Thus, we have seen the uses of patience. In general, it preserves charity, perfects all our virtues, and supplies the enduring stamina so essential if we are to surmount the difficulties constantly challenging our spiritual efforts. As a special virtue, patience enables us to vanquish two particular difficulties, sadness and anger, which threaten our spiritually fertile peace of soul. Their lesser manifestations, irritations and vexations, are likewise quelled by patience, and we are kept alert and steadfast against the inroads of temptation. Our prayer life, too, in all forms and especially in the lofty realm of contemplation, owes much to patience. These are the good offices revealing the universal role of patience in our asceticism, documenting its unusual importance, establishing its right to be termed a "miracle virtue." Having laid this groundwork, we can quote the words of Benjamin Franklin, and very properly apply them to that most sublime vocation to which the religious has dedicated life itself: "He that can have patience can have what he will."

3

Obedience, Keystone of Spiritual and School Success

FOR OVER A DECADE NOW THE CHURCH HAS DI-rected careful attention to what has become a rather pressing question, namely, in the light of prevalent conditions of twentieth-century society do we need a fresh examination and a possible revamping of certain aspects of life in religious communities? In the United States, Notre Dame, Indiana, has played host to such conferences, and the dignity and importance of them have been enhanced by the presence there of high Vatican authorities. Similar meetings of the heads of different religious groups had already been held at Rome, and even before that, seminars in France were busily probing the same question.

Many of the rules and constitutions which bind religious living in the twentieth century draw their origins from medieval, and even earlier times. The practice of virtue and the execution of spiritual exercises, as enshrined in these documents, still retain the flavor of those bygone days. There is, in consequence, an understandable concern over the possibility that some adjustments have become necessary. While the same objectives must be sought, the *modus agendi* employed to obtain these objectives has to take into account the different world in which the community today

35

exists, and through a wise adaptability achieve an easier, yet greater, efficiency.

All ascetical theologians would agree, in the twentieth century as well as in the thirteenth, that obedience must be the heart and soul of any religious community, must be the touchstone of its spiritual success, and the only possible path to individual ascetical perfection. No religious, and no religious community, can ever achieve gains in any virtue, if this key virtue be spurned. A community without obedience, although patched together with external trappings, cannot exist without internal chaos. Against any community contemptuous of obedience, Pascal's cutting judgment of the group at Port Royal must be leveled: "Pure as angels, proud as devils."

So basic to spiritual advancement is the virtue of obedience, that it is emphasized universally in the training given to religious of every community. Obedience receives constant stress in the spiritual reading the religious has done over the years and in the many retreat conferences she has attended. As a result, if any quality ought to be found in a religious, it is obedience.

When a sister lacks obedience, she can rightly be charged with being a strange kind of religious. The presence of such a person in the community means that all of the efforts of the Order or Congregation, all of the ascetical conferences, and all of the spiritual reading have failed. Confronted with a failure of these proportions, what hope remains? The only available judgment concludes that here is a poor religious, and that probably little can be done in the future to change her—the disease is difficult to cure.

Having said this clearly and strongly, it should not be interpreted as any sign of laxness, in assessing the value of obedience, to note that certain factors in the modern world have to be considered in order to form our attitude toward the present-day practice of obedience.

One characteristic of the modern world which occasions deep concern among the leaders of religious communities is the breakdown of reverence and respect due to all authority, a breakdown which sociologically-minded historians have so amply documented. In this environment, neglectful of the Fourth Commandment, modern youth has grown up, and so have those who are now members of religious communities. As a result, when as youthful postulants they placed their hand on the doorknob of the entrance to religious life, the formative effects of years spent in a world little honoring obedience could not be expected, instantly and magically, to disappear. The present-day religious must squarely face the fact that during those pre-community years she was exposed to a great deal of prejudice against the virtue of obedience. This, of course, was not done deliberately or consciously, but the degree of advertence simply is not pertinent. Quite pertinent, however, is the fact that as a consequence, the modern religious career needs to begin by "unlearning" a great deal about obedience. Of all the virtues to be studied and practiced, we bring to obedience the least understanding, the least docility.

This in turn gives rise to some practical consequences. When, for example, we think that superiors have been mistreating us, we ought to go very slow in accepting such a conclusion. Such suspicions are best put aside unless the evidence is clear; otherwise, we begin to adopt the attitude of visiting teams toward referees. Stop and consider how much better placed a superior is to see and understand community situations. Usually the superior possesses more information, envisions a larger context, and grasps connections with relevant aspects we may be utterly unaware of. Further, the office of superior carries with it the habit of decisions; many problems have been faced and solved; experience and tradition are easily drawn upon. In addition, its occupant also enjoys some grace of office and may put forth a rightful claim to special graces in the carrying out of the many and difficult duties which, under God, she has accepted.

The little esteem in which the world today holds obedience is aggravated and becomes doubly dangerous because of the role the religious superior is forced to play in modern times. Never before in the history of the Church has the position of religious superior been as complex as it is today: financial responsibilities have pyramided until one needs the joint skills of accountant and purchasing agent; some problems require legal knowledge; paper work alone has grown mountainous; frequently, activities of the group are involved in many organizations outside the actual community; institutions have become enmeshed in a network of relations with civil, diocesan, national, and professional bodies. To deprive such a burdened superior of legitimate obedience is crippling and consummately uncharitable.

We should always look upon superiors with a sympathetic, understanding heart; indeed, to be truthful, deep in that heart we are conscious of our own weaknesses and our own need to receive the same consideration. Unquestionably, superiors are fallible; we might find it enlightening to examine how precisely definition narrows even papal infallibility. You will never serve under an infallible superior, and when you in turn become superior, neither will you be infallible. On the merely human level, how true are the words of the poet:

> Who'er thinks a perfect thing to see
> Thinks what ne'er was, nor is, nor e'er will be.

On occasions when mistakes are made, they are best quickly forgotten; no profit accrues from hoarding injuries or supposed injuries. Looking back over any semester, no teacher can herself boast a hundred per cent average. A classroom would resemble Dante's inferno if every slip was stored up by the pupils in bitterness of heart.

Realistic thinking, then, forces the conclusion that somewhere along the path of life a superior will err in our regard. Well-balanced and truly spiritual religious can laugh this off. To do so at times may, true enough, take considerable effort, but a religious of high caliber does it. A good indication of how well a religious has developed spiritually can be discerned in the ability to live with episodes of this sort and simply make them a component of the routine; even though generally they happen rather seldom.

The alternative to this balanced and spiritual reaction is sulking. Other words and phrases may be used to probe its nuances, but in the final analysis it is precisely that—the old and often-relived story of Achilles sulking in his hut. What a loss to friends and country and how childish, the familiar story reminds us. A sulking religious in quite the same fashion makes life miserable for self, and for those living about her, and, to some degree, she generally succeeds in hurting a conscientious superior, too.

The crime which shatters the sensitivity of the sulking religious is, "I have been injured." Not the extent of the injury, but that "I" have been injured, demands that it be regarded as so important. Pushing things further, it is important because I am so important. To forget it, would be to forget me. One must not forget me; the superior needs to be taught a lesson. The future must show clearly that no superior can again do this with impunity. A blueprint for the careful scrutiny of all superiors has been provided—any superior doing this must count on facing these consequences.

Years ago, as we pondered the question whether or not we possessed a religious vocation, all the literature we read and all the advice we received made a cardinal point of the will of God. If it was God's will, then we were doing the right thing in asking admittance to a community. The will of God was what we had to seek then and throughout our entire religious life. One asks here the same fundamental question, where is the will of God in the conduct of a sulking religious? Has the sulking religious supplanted the will of God and made self the last end?

Obedience fundamentally involves a relationship between ourselves and God. For our religious vocation to mean anything, it must mean that we have committed ourselves to doing God's will. To do God's will is to be obedient to God. God's method, in the present dispensation, employs creatures to obtain his ends;

in the sacraments creatures are used (for example, water, oil, bread, and wine). God's creature, our neighbor, is given to us as the normal means whereby we manifest our love for God. In the same way God also employs superiors for his ends; in fact by means of them, God measures our willingness to obey him. If we do not obey our superiors, it would be illogical for us to maintain that we would obey God himself. That the superior comes to us as God's representative, receives obedience because of God's delegated authority and out of love for God, has ever been the basis of Christian obedience. Obedience, any differently conceived, can be built only on straw.

Unless this is thoroughly understood, we see in the superior only the human person and merely tolerate direction as a necessary, unavoidable evil, to be "put up with." Unable to see beyond the superior's natural abilities and deficiencies, we consider them the very unsupernatural controlling influence. Were the superior highly intelligent and pleasant, obedience would flow freely; were the opposite the case, obedience would be denied or extracted under duress. Since God is changeless, obedience to his commands must consequently be unvaried. Since we feel no concern that God chose the element of wine in one sacrament, and water in another, we should be equally unconcerned to find a superior tall or short, young or old, smiling or melancholic. The virtue of obedience does not direct itself to the superior, but toward God; paradoxically, we may even say that true obedience ignores the superior. This is the naked, rational theology of the virtue of obedience in its proper ascetical framework.

We shall find it best to be quite frank in the matter of obedience, quite honest with ourselves. In the long run, it pays to speak plainly and acknowledge the difficulty attendant upon being an obedient person. In the matter of obedience the natural does not suffice; the supernatural is needed. We require a strong faith and unceasingly we must bring the faith to our obedience. Faith marks the starting point of obedience, seasons its manifestations, illumines its final end. When obedience does not maintain itself on the high level of faith, it gradually sinks to the low level of naturalism. Practically speaking, one cannot maintain a middle course for long; either obedience is, with effort, raised up, or under its own heaviness sinks down.

Should obedience sink to the level of the natural, what happens? What happens is this. We are held to endure many hardships under obedience; nature revolts against hardships. Under obedience, always we find some inequity, some people are going to have to carry out assignments more difficult than others. To arrange things otherwise in any concrete, human, group endeavor, from a sand-lot ball team to the President's cabinet, seems impossible; again nature revolts against any apparent inequity. On the natural level, what will take place? There will be injured feelings voiced in grumblings, grumblings which will eventually reach out and focus on real or imagined defects of the superior. Such grumblings become conversational and infectious; if unchecked, they sow community discord. When we find ourselves in a conversational group, often without noticing it we are carried along by the verbal momentum; even the sound and fair-minded can be trapped so that they too contribute to building a straw-man superior. Any superior is defenseless against this trial *in absentia*, with the injured plaintiff also volunteering to act as judge. When the "bleeding hearts" parade before us the pageant of their awful woes inflicted by tyrannical authority, we must keep tongue in cheek. Often the superior's side of the story will never be known; merciful secrecy surrounds that office and conceals the bigness of our blunders. Remember the story of the stuttering boy who told all who would listen how unjust his debating coach had been, rejecting him just because he happened to be too tall.

If our obedience does not draw on faith, if it operates only on natural power, it will be sadly delinquent. Weaknesses of temperament and flaws of disposition are natural things, and in our obedience only the addition of the strength of faith can overcome them. Those with hypersensitive temperaments, who bruise easily, need to be eternally vigilant over their judgments and emotions; those pronouncedly high-strung must beware of exploding, using the superior as fuse. We must remember, for our own peace of soul, that the teaching life is lived under very high tension. When the semester's moments of battle fatigue periodically flash by, we have to beware of articulating our views of what's wrong with the world in general and the community in particular. An ancient Jewish sacrifice consisted of figuratively loading all the sins of society on a goat and then driving the animal out of the city gates. At times of seasonal hazards in the school year, the superior becomes the most likely candidate for scapegoat. In the Roman Empire, when anything went wrong, the Christians were blamed; as an early Apologist put it, if the Tiber overflowed its banks, the chant would go up, "The Christians to the lions." If we have had a hard day or impossible week, and at its conclusion a pupil in class sneezes the wrong way, we should not yell out loud and clear to each and all, "The superior to the lions."

Obedience can also help eliminate throwing others to the lions by acting quickly to check possible rivalries within the community, and by quelling any incipient inordinate ambition. In the eyes of obedience all community positions are equally important. Certainly, when done under obedience they are equally important for the development of our spiritual perfection. Task A, which has been given to us by legitimate authority, constitutes the labor God wishes us to offer him. If we go ahead and do Task B, omitting Task A, the inspiration we may claim to follow rests on very shaky grounds; we are omitting God's will and following self-will. Self-will, as even the spiritual beginner can readily point out, raises, perhaps, the greatest obstacle to perfection. Obedience offers the very weapon best calculated to check self-love, the greatest safeguard for our spiritual efforts. Washing dishes under obedience gains more for the welfare of our souls than founding a thousand institutions in defiant disobedience. When superiors restricted St. Alphonsus' visits to church, he prayed: "Very well, O good Jesus, it is better, through obedience, to remain at a distance from thee than, contrary to obedience, to enjoy thy presence." We can easily delude ourselves and chase rainbows in our spiritual strivings, but we never delude ourselves by following an obedience which marks the straight, pure path to perfection. This virtue has the priceless faculty of transforming the most commonplace actions of our life. In the words of St. Theresa: "Obedience is the most prompt and also the most effectual means of arriving at perfection."

While our obedience, to be worthy of our religious vocation, has to be a supernatural and not just a natural virtue, nonetheless, there are considerations apart from the supernatural order which may serve to demonstrate its importance. Most religious communities embrace the active life; they have been established to achieve certain ends which contribute to the salvation of souls and the spread of God's kingdom on this earth.

To secure the efficiency requisite to accomplish successfully the objectives a particular community has assumed, the community must demand obedience of its members. Specifically, after undertaking certain concrete tasks, the community has a responsibility to fulfill the obligation of completing those tasks well. In this matter the good name of the community, and in proportion the good names of those who belong to it, are at stake. Obedience here takes on the coloration of loyalty to the group; disobedience becomes disloyalty, a betrayal of our fellow religious and of our Institute.

Community commitments represent a shared burden; it is the community's burden, but all have to shoulder it together. When one, or a number of persons, are delinquent through disobedience, it means that the burden becomes unnecessarily and unjustly heavy for others. When statistically there is found minus tens in the efforts of A, B, and C, generally plus tens have to be added to the efforts of X, Y, and Z. Quite obviously this is a bad situation, with unfortunate implications for life within the community and for the peace and charity and joy which should characterize that life.

This team spirit nourished by obedience, so fundamental to the success of any of the activities pursued by a religious community, is particularly necessary when the activity concerns itself with the staffing and administration of a school. A coordinated program, implied by the very nature of a school, marks the only way to secure that full spiritual and intellectual training to which our students have a right. Without obedient faculty members, no coordination of the over-all program, or of anything else, can exist. What a chaos would result, were teachers to disregard their curriculum or fail to keep the requisite scholastic records. While this must be immediately apparent to any thinking person, it is similarly true that in many other areas the same near-chaos would also occur, if instead of cooperation there is disobedience. One need not go into lengthy detail here. Indeed, it would be superfluous to do so. Every teacher knows quite well that it is true and can easily summon from memory many sustaining examples.

In schoolwork, too, obedience has a rather unique aspect. The religious teacher, although under obedience always, does, quite properly, enjoy a reasonable amount of autonomy. No one can legitimately dictate to the teacher the marks she will give, the relationship her individual personality will evolve with the members of her classes, or the stresses placed on certain aspects of the course which she has found helpful in imparting to the pupils a mastery of the body of material which over the years she has studied and taught.

A percentage of the activity of a religious whose active life is lived in the schools goes unsupervised. There is some supervision, of course, and there should be. But it is simply a physical impossibility for a superior to be with a multitude of teachers in every class and at every extracurricular activity throughout the entire day. For that reason a *spirit of obedience* ought to be developed in the teacher. With a spirit of obedience to safeguard the religious teacher, the natural autonomy of some aspects of the teacher's life and its unsupervised areas will be carried out well. All will be accomplished in substantial obedience to the general norms which have been supplied by proper school authority. Without that spirit, obedience quickly degenerates into something rather helpless, for which there are no remedies but the most drastic. In the last analysis, only this spirit of obedience will carry out adequately the mind of the superior and make a reality of the rules and standards to which the school has already been pledged.

Treatises on the subject of obedience generally urge upon their readers that, in practicing it, response made to the commands of superiors should be marked by a laudable cheerfulness. Again, in schoolwork this would seem to be especially needful. Outside the actual teaching of classes and the usual extracurricular activities, novel, uncharted tasks may occasionally arise, and they require much time and effort on the part of those assigned to them. Sometimes they require substantial sacrifice. At times, assignments of this type are of such a nature that a superior does not feel justified in assigning them, or at least does not want to assign them simply as something that must be done under strict obedience. The vehicle of suggestion or of invitation here seems appropriate to the superior, who considers them "over and above the call of duty."

For the superior even to consider assigning novel projects she must at the outset have the encouragement of good will and cheerfulness on the part of the prospective agent of their execution. Otherwise the superior would just as leave put aside the project entirely. Precisely for this reason the cheerfulness is invaluable; it makes possible the undertaking and achievement of school projects which will yield additional benefits to the students. Often the decisive factor in the determination of the superior to go ahead with such pioneering has been the ability to rely on this type of obedience. To phrase it another way, when the individual members of the community and the community as a whole are permeated with cheerful obedience, the school is able to do much more and do it more effectively in a real atmosphere of cooperation and charity and happiness.

On the other hand, dire consequences afflict any school community where obedience among the religious is but a grudging compliance able to be extracted only when unavoidable. Obedience of this kind has the effect of chaining the school to an unvaried, established routine with no receptivity to educational advances and no vision for the future. In fact, such half-hearted obedience hampers the implementation of even that routine. Obedience which completely lacks cheerfulness oftentimes is not obedience at all.

A new activity entrusted to that type of obedience usually falters and dies because the faculty member in charge generates no enthusiasm for it. For a while the moderator and the students go through the motions of working on the project; then they give it up. Thus, the religious becomes freed from a task to which she gave only lip-service obedience; an obedience, we may say, which enabled her to be disobedient legally.

Strange attitudes toward obedience are sometimes encountered among religious. A few seem to adopt a sort of occupational or professional attitude toward it; they consider it from the viewpoint occasionally encountered in policemen or firemen or those holding industrial positions calling for a certain amount of what might loosely be termed obedience. "Obedience" becomes a somewhat cynical and calloused policy of doing whatever strict law binds one to. Apparently, it is felt that anyone going beyond a fixed boundary is a bit of a Don Quixote.

One automatically equates such a point of view with a rather low concept of spirituality, and yet often this is not so. Some of these religious are genuinely concerned with spirituality, and in the areas of prayer, virtue, and mortification make strong sallies to advance along that hard road. Surely though, an hour or so of prayerful analysis should enable them to perceive a glaring contradiction here.

In considering religious who, despite sincere interest in spiritual progress, possess a false conception of obedience, the weakness of their position can be seen in reference to the three classes St. Ignatius speaks of in the *Spiritual Exercises*. The first class, he tells us, wish perfection but will not use the necessary means to obtain that perfection. His second category embraces those desirous of perfection who do not use either all or the best of the available means. This would be true of the religious whom we are discussing; they do not exploit the opportunities offered by obedience as fully as they might. And, whatever means they are using, praiseworthy as these means undoubtedly are, they certainly are not using the best means. The best available means are always those directly in front of us, those which flow naturally from the situation in which God's governance of the world, and of the community, and of ourselves has placed us.

Obedience constitutes a vital factor in the spirituality of every religious, and it can yield very great advances. There is no self-delusion or sham here. The more lofty and self-sacrificing our practice of it becomes, the more will we become a truly holy religious.

There is another class—and this is not one of those listed by St. Ignatius—whose attitude toward obedience goes to the opposite extreme. It is not, however, the opposite extreme of virtue, but only of attitude. In fact, one may question just how much virtue it possesses at all; although it certainly lives to the fullest all the externals of obedience.

This type of character, found in religious life, faces quite different dangers in the pursuit of a rather misguided notion of obedience. Their personal disposition is such that, unconsciously perhaps, they make of obedience a vehicle of escape; it becomes a prop for their innate weakness. They welcome obedience as a refuge from sharing any responsibilities; they are only too glad to be relieved of having to make decisions or having to reason anything out for themselves. These religious lull themselves into a false contentment in their abdication of taking the slightest initiative. Such an approach to "obedience" only produces a limp, immature personality, and encourages authority to grow disproportionately into authoritarianism. Rarely do religious, thus conceiving obedience, "grow up" spiritually or even naturally, because they lack the courage to face life. A collection of such helpless people is of little assistance to a superior. Rubber-stamp automatons simply leave the superior unaided, especially in more important matters; the pretense of "obedience" is a worthless excuse.

It should be made clear that psychological predispositions are entirely distinct from the actual virtue of obedience; whatever our character, temperament, or dispositions, all can be utilized to build up the virtue. Obedience is quite compatible with a strong, decisive personality; in fact, obedience shines forth most appealingly in a vigorous personality. One purpose of the virtue is to train, to channel our natural assets of character, not to destroy them. The superior deserves to be assisted by able, obedient subordinates who can aptly manage delegated responsibilities and who can be trusted to solve difficult problems the superior has not time for. To utilize the brains and talents of all is certainly the goal of any intelligent superior. Even in matters of honest disagreement, when subordinates present divergent or contrasting views, the wise superior gratefully respects them. In their obedience, however, these subordinates will present such views with detachment, with humility, and with a ready willingness to leave the final decision to the superior. Although perhaps still interiorly convinced that the alternate plan would work better, the obedient religious strives to carry out the superior's ultimate decision as cheerfully and as perfectly as possible.

Through apprenticeship in obedience, future superiors must first learn how to obey, so that later they will know how to command. One who has never obeyed well will never command well, either. Both factors will be known by the community, and both will be resented. True obedience makes us obey for the love of God; that same love of God is expressed in commanding. The new superior follows God's will to command, just as previously she followed God's will to obey. Roles are reversed, but obedience to God's will for love of God, remains the common denominator.

Our best sample both of how to command and how to obey may be found in the life of Christ. Our obedience should be joined to his. Christ's mission on earth was to do his Father's will; we have the same mission and we should fulfill it in union with Christ. In order that this means of union with Christ may be realized to the fullest, we ought always to accompany the actual externals of the exercise of the virtue with interior acts of obedience. Regrettably, it is possible for a person never to disobey and yet be merely a mechanical, unthinking machine carrying out directions. What precious graces may be lost, accordingly, unless interior dispositions of humble obedience offer all in the spirit of loving sacrifice to Christ. If motivation is vital for all our actions, it is especially necessary that we guard always the proper motivation in acts done under obedience; thus, obedience will promote our union with God. Here we have the full, beautiful doctrine of obedience; it is unfair to ourselves and to our possible degrees of spiritual progress and happiness, to accept anything less.

Thus, we gain a conscious, happy obedience, tranquilizing and heartening the soul. The obedient person is at peace. In her *Dialogue* St. Catherine has this apotheosis to obedience:

> Oh how sweet and glorious is this virtue, which contains all the rest. . . . She is a queen whose consort will feel not trouble, but only peace and quiet; and waves of the stormy sea cannot hurt her, nor can any tempest reach the interior of the soul in which she dwells. . . . Oh! blessed obedience! thou voyagest without fatigue, and reachest without danger the port of salvation . . . thou walk'st erect, without bending for thy heart is sincere and not false, loving generously and truly my creatures, thou art a sunrise drawing after thee the light of Divine grace. . . .

4

Fortitude, Its
Role and Results

SINCE FORTITUDE, OR MORAL COURAGE, STRENGTH-
ens the soul in the pursuit of "arduous good" (a phrase aptly
descriptive as well of the labors of teaching), a point of inter-
section is easily established between the practice of that virtue
and the daily routine of the sister-teacher. In her school, too
often she finds personnel shortages, overcrowded classrooms,
anemic budgets, and sundry other handicaps; all of which everyone in general laments sincerely enough, but only sister in particular lives with it day after day.

To the teaching religious, however, of deeper concern than
these externals are the classroom consequences of the current
breakdown of traditional attitudes toward school discipline and
the repercussions in the home of today's unlimited attention to
pleasure—seeking with its variety of distractions to lure youth
away from anything difficult or burdensome, such as study. The
religious is concerned, too, because the vocation of teaching has
been changing; school has become, or has been made, a much
more complex affair, and teaching religious are now occupied
with an increasing number of duties beyond the actual teaching
itself. Caught between the cross-currents of administrative am-

bition and a budget prohibiting requisite office and non-teaching help, teaching religious have experienced some rather dizzy whirls. Indeed, such religious require little persuasion that they can use the valuable support of fortitude in this pursuit of "arduous good."

No longer is it possible to take for granted things their predecessors could; automatic reactions previously assured by a mere twist of teacher's tongue, have long ceased to be automatic. The spirit of humble willingness and docile trust does not lie ready-made and waiting in today's classroom; it must be won. More than ever, discipline represents an achievement, a measurement of professional prowess and often of fortitude as well. In lower grammar grades and higher college years this would be much less true, but in the space between the fortitude link is unmistakably needed. While the requisites of discipline vary widely with specific contexts, nonetheless, where the discipline is woefully inadequate, more fortitude would generally help.

Consistent academic excellence also has a relationship to fortitude. Such results depend upon the work assignments the students carry out, but unless a school deals exclusively with scholarship material, teachers regularly encounter reluctance, ranging at times to recalcitrance, when heavy tasks are broached. Unreasonable demands, of course, constitute poor pedagogy; however, apart from them, if our current public commitment to excellence is to be implemented, hard work must be the rule. Nevertheless, to make it the rule involves a struggle, sometimes obvious, sometimes implied, always psychologically perceptible and in need of some fortitude. Other factors can doubtless prompt a teacher's failure to obtain adequate work from a group, but that failure can at times involve a lack of fortitude.

Every school imposes regulations, which may be either quite demanding or not at all taxing. Whatever they be, it is axiomatic that they should be enforced. To promulgate rules and then do nothing about their infraction is psychologically unsound, morally harmful, and a great disservice to the school. But this indefatigable upholding of discipline and scholarship means struggles, troubles, tensions, and requires a goodly supply of fortitude. Modern-day students in growing percentages do not accept rebukes with good grace nor do they accept low marks or long assignments with docility, in the firm conviction that teacher knows best.

A protracted diet of whining and wheedling on the part of even a few pupils can get on a teacher's nerves, wear her down, and tempt her to compromise. Fortitude here has to *sustain* difficulties—fortitude of a high caliber. In sustaining rather than attacking, the teacher actually experiences the difficulties at first hand. And, what is hardest, she also knows they will have to be suffered for still more time and in the same concrete realistic fashion. There is no room for rosy illusions. The fortitude of the teaching religious is nothing momentary; days become weeks, then months, until almost the entire year is encompassed. In September she experiences the difficulties which will be present in larger editions in May. It is not, figuratively speaking, the momentary blow which causes acute suffering but rather the cumulative weight of past blows plus the wry anticipation of their unceasing continuance.

Religious who are in teaching work have to insulate themselves against such dangers. Experience shows that the subconscious can work very subtly upon a fatigued spirit. When people are tired and harassed, as certainly happens in cycles throughout the school year, they are sorely tempted to give ground where they should not and to surrender positions which afterwards will have to be recaptured. Without fortitude, a harmful defeatism can precolor all attempts at solution. The consequent relaxation has always a tendency to increase, and the ultimate thrust is toward the weakening of authority. In our day, perhaps educators have not enjoyed a sufficient realization of fortitude's importance in the academic blueprint; certainly they do not seem to be fully appreciative of the extent to which many of our current classroom ills are traceable to the absence or fainthearted application of this moral virtue.

When fortitude settles problems, they are settled according to principle, without any surrender to sentimentality. In truth, the heart sometimes does have its reasons, as Pascal counsels, where the mind has none, but should the heart grow unreasonable the sentimental results are usually disastrous. Fortitude avoids, as well, any settling of problems purely with an eye to popularity; the right solution may not always be a popular one, but in the long run only the right solution really does solve. Those who would bypass the virtue by deferring or omitting that right solution ultimately live to regret their action.

Despite any hampering difficulties, fortitude pledges a clear-cut obedience to all duties, the unpleasant as well as the pleasant, the small as well as the large. Any double standard of performance is rigidly eschewed; followers of the virtue fulfill obligations as a matter of principle, not for pragmatic reasons. We are thus afforded protection against potential weaknesses sometimes hidden away inside the heart. Among the various aberrations which can creep into life, none is more despicable in religion than the incongruous ability to work well only in the right setting for the right people for the wrong end. Since such an attitude is incompatible with fortitude, our devotion to the virtue can happily set our minds at rest on that score.

Fortitude similarly disdains the seeking out of all the leisure that traffic will bear; rather it searches to "fill the unforgiving minute with sixty seconds worth of distance run." Complexities of administering the modern school do not permit a delimitation of faculty tasks with the automatic exactness possible through the assembly-line technique of a factory. Of necessity there have to be vague, indistinct areas, and, as a consequence, what might be anyone's job could easily enough belong to no one.

During wartime an amusing magazine cartoon showed the

desks of two naval officers, one piled high, the other empty. Seated at the empty desk, the smiling officer remarked, "It's easy, I just mark everything 'Lieutenant Smith.' " Fortitude prompts us, while certainly not becoming Lieutenant Smiths, to make a willing, fair-minded decision to give help where legitimately we can and should. The "artful dodgers" of Dickens' novel provided much in the way of entertainment; little in the way of accomplishment.

In these hazy circumstances the only possible criterion of applied spirituality must be the simple spirit of willingness. Oftentimes one cannot estimate what help should be offered; it is quite relative. A few minutes attention may clear away a challenging problem, and those few minutes will have contributed mightily to school success. On the other hand, one may accidentally run across something requiring great expenditure of time and effort; while not very important, it is something which cannot be bypassed in conscience. Fortitude provides a dutiful sensitivity toward such unmarked areas of work, quietly pocketing the labor and deftly righting the situation. Of their nature these contributions frequently go unnoticed and our unselfish solution receives no plaudits. Nonetheless, it is precisely this "human touch," although only a handful or even only one of the students may benefit, which prevents our institutions from becoming impersonal transmission belts of identically stamped educational units.

Up to this point we have examined the relationship of fortitude to difficult tasks, yet greater still is the concern of the virtue with fears and dangers. Fortitude strengthens our soul in the pursuit of an arduous good; but fears and dangers would deter us from that pursuit; hence, fortitude enables us to overcome them. Fears and dangers can be very personal and very common. All of us judge certain things fearful and dangerous; at the same time, some of us may be fearful in the face of that which others scarcely notice. A general discussion of fortitude can treat only its role in combating obstacles shared by all.

Often we hear it said of a person, "I admire him because he has the courage of his convictions." What we actually admire here is the virtue of fortitude. Such persons have overcome perhaps the most common of all fears—human respect, hesitation to state opinions or to practice convictions because of what people might think. The quest for perfection is undertaken by many fine religions, but, alas, how many lack that intensity of fortitude capable of transforming them into really great religious, saints or borderline saints?

All ascetical writers emphasized the need of fortitude for beginners in religion—a sound, necessary stress, yet one possibly obscuring its continuing need. In any group, even a religious community, the effort to progress beyond the common level of achievement postulates a certain fearlessness.

Those who observe every fine point of the rule unconsciously indict others who possess a more easygoing conception of its provisions. One whose conversation maintains such charity as never to participate when group conversations grow somewhat loose may be thought irksome. To be notably punctilious in the matter of silence and the minutiae of obedience occasionally generates the suspicion of scrupulosity. Severe efforts in the practice of prayer and mortification can make one the cynosure of neighboring eyes, a target for considerable comment. To act in a manner somewhat different, at least in degree, requires a strength of fortitude able to withstand human respect. Since the level of our religious life has not yet reached universal heroic sanctity, the assistance of this virtue remains essential for those whose sights are trained on the spiritual summits.

Quite early in her convent career St. Theresa of Lisieux had to overcome human respect and faulty friendship. The ensuing incident is inspiring in itself, illustrative of the psychology involved in any such efforts, and encouraging in its demonstration of the unexpectedly happy results. During her novitiate, Theresa had formed a close friendship with another sister and they had received permission to converse together on spiritual subjects. What resulted, St. Theresa tells us in her own words:

> . . . it came home to me with sorrow that our conversations did not attain the desired end; and I saw clearly that I must either speak out fearlessly, or put an end altogether to what resembled mere worldly talk. I begged our Lord to inspire me with words at once kind and convincing, or better still to speak himself in my stead. At our next meeting the poor little sister saw well from the outset that my manner had changed, and blushing deeply she sat down beside me. I told her tenderly what was in my mind. . . . She humbly acknowledged herself in the wrong and admitted that what I had said was quite true; then, begging as a favor that I would always point out her faults, she promised to begin a new life. From that day our love for one another became wholly supernatural and in us were fulfilled the words of the Holy Ghost: "A brother that is helped by his brother is like a strong city" (*Autobiography*, pp. 210–211).

The age of the cold war and the hydrogen bomb in which we live has incubated much emotion and tension. Too often, current opinions sear with the flaming quality of passions; scorching overtones in the very air we breathe have made it difficult to retain cool self-possession and a sweet reasonableness of viewpoint; nor has it become popular or easy to do so. Those endowed with fortitude are not mere followers of the crowd; their opinions do not change color with the color of the walls of a momentary environment. Telling people what they wish to hear may be pleasant; to speak, when necessary, in a kindly fashion of honest differences of opinion requires more courage. Mr. Pickwick's advice, to shout with the mob and, positing a number of mobs, to shout with the largest, may avail in politics; it is not the workaday philosophy of the followers of fortitude. Fortitude decides debatable issues to the best of the abilities that God has implanted and that training has developed, and then stands on its own two feet.

These thoughts are not without pertinence for our own relationships within the community itself. Fortitude brings a definitely wholesome attitude to those inevitable disagreements which periodically plague human associations this side of paradise. Gently and courteously, our virtue draws such disagreements into the open and tries to give them full airing by discussing them in a friendly, fair-minded spirit. Doing this frequently goes far toward illuminating how closely allied in reality are apparently conflicting points of view; in such a fashion previous estrangements can sometimes be reconciled. Even should the disagreements persist, fortitude's wise forethought and charitable procedure has at least destroyed the context necessary for envies, jealousies, hidden resentments, and lasting bitterness. Settle it and forget it, suggests fortitude's salutary approach.

Borrowing some of the virtue ourselves, we may make bold to speak rather plainly here. Bitter, harmful disagreements sometime arise between superiors and subordinates. Any opinion voiced by a superior by reason of position seems very important to us; every word of a superior, it has been said, weighs a ton. What otherwise might be received lightly in a spirit of jest, becomes, in the case of a superior, something subjected to minute analysis, stretched this way and that by unbounded interpretative genius.

Likewise, the superior's ex officio preoccupation with maintaining due respect and upholding disciplined good order can sometimes impair the freedom of friendliness and create an atmosphere of brittle tautness. Fancies and suspicions yielded to by either party can, at times, hopelessly and dangerously distort actual situations, which, were they truly known and calmly understood, would quickly remove any basis for friction.

Unless such cases involve exceptional personalities, an honest vis-à-vis talking-out of things offers a very salutary procedure. To do so, however, postulates the possession of fortitude on the part of both: a fearful, weak superior, hypersensitive because of her own failings, is afraid of such meetings; on the other hand, the subordinate, understandably enough perhaps, must overcome some degree of natural fear before approaching a superior.

Similar factors are involved in community planning and institutional policy. There can be no doubt that the greater responsibility here belongs to the superior; yet wisdom, tradition, and parallel provisions of Church Law frown on a go-it-alone obsession. Wise administrators find it helpful to delegate some responsibilty and to utilize available counsel. Again, only a superior strengthened by fortitude does this well, and only a courageous subordinate can cooperate with maximum disinterest and truthfulness.

Perhaps in this respect the children of this world can teach the children of light. Captains of industry have long since done away with the armies of yes-men, rubber-stamp counsellors. They have realized that to receive back only their own opinions has deprived them of the very brain power and industrial know-how that with great care and expense they had assembled for the welfare of their business.

While labor unions and industrial companies are not governed by the vow of obedience, their interest in happy, cooperative teamwork between labor and management follows both justice and charity. Accordingly, much time and thought have been devoted to the processing of grievances and personnel relations; whole departments have been established to deal exclusively with these considerations and no one has questioned their great value or denied the increased accomplishment they have made possible.

Naturally, such departments cannot be reproduced in the religious community; to do so would be sheer nonsense. Yet, unquestionably, the basic concept underlying these moves on the part of industry finds root in a clear knowledge of human nature and a wholesome understanding of the problems generated in any community. In religious life we are a community and we have human nature. Fortitude, exercised as recommended, will go far in advancing the achievement of our community and the work with which it is entrusted.

Fears and dangers, unless controlled by fortitude, can infiltrate all areas of our vocation, can prevent us from blazing important educational trails, introducing worthwhile religious projects, or accepting community positions of heavy responsibility. How unpleasant to see a religious moving through the wonderful opportunities of our precious vocation with leaden feet and palsied spirit because of nullifying petty fears. That religious has never really grown up, has remained for a lifetime unable to face responsibilities in an adult fashion; cloistering, in this instance, seems to have been the perpetuation of a state of adolescence.

Our learning, our piety, all our talents, need to be supplemented by fortitude if they are to be activated to the fullest possible extent, if their splendid potential is to be realized. Like a bridge, fortitude elevates our talents to a position of real leadership; steeling the fiber of the soul, grafting a holy daring that inspires, instilling a leadership that is contagious. Initiative launching forth and stamina persevering to success are the happy yield of fortitude.

Although retaining humility of spirit, fortitude nonetheless wisely comprehends that if we do not have confidence in ourselves no one else will have confidence in us—a sad thing for our cause, the cause of Christ. Pushing aside any misgivings, fortitude accepts difficult assignments, takes on new enterprises with a steady hand and fearless eye. While acknowledging there will be mistakes, its serviceable rejoinder reminds that those who never made mistakes never made anything. Set determination, unflinching effort, an oaken-hearted stoutness fires the ever-forward motion of the virtue. As Kipling wrote:

> If you can force your heart and nerve and sinew
> To serve you long after they are gone,
> And so hold on when there is nothing in you
> Except the will, which cries to you "Hold on,"

then you have fortitude.

We should never forget that we belong to a Church without fear and rich in the fullness of fortitude; a Church formally instituted at the descent of the Spirit of fortitude and which continues with that same Spirit as its very soul. To forget this would be to turn our back on all history. History has witnessed our emergence from the catacombs, our firmness before the savagery of the Barbarians, our resiliency despite insidious and overt heresy, our fighting spirit now on the rack of Communist persecution. Were our asceticism to neglect fortitude, we would be unworthy of the Church which it is our vocation to serve.

Basic to all of fortitude's activities against fears, dangers, difficulties, and the like, lies its final purpose, the removal of any impediments which may either impair the proper functioning of reason or so disturb the will that it is unable to follow reason's dictates. As a result, firmness prevails in moments when impediments make it most difficult to preserve the constancy of soul necessary to act in a reasonable manner.

St. Thomas stresses this; too much so, may be his reader's first reaction. However, reflection, as usual, reveals his wisdom. What he drives home to us with unmistakable clarity is that fortitude is a reasonable virtue, and that only within the framework of reason can it legitimately operate.

Drawing to the end of this chapter we would like to echo St. Thomas by likewise insisting, lest the whole meaning of our words be misconstrued, that all we have presented must be received in the broad context of right reason. To receive it otherwise would vitiate the traditional and only defensible understanding of fortitude; the one solely intended here.

Thus, rashness in any shape or form must be ruled vigorously out. Such precaution precludes any twisting of the virtue to defend the launching of obviously inane or even harmful projects. Fortitude places no opposition to salutary fears which should be honored when persuasive temptations, dangerous occasions of sin, or even sin itself threaten; a praiseworthy *via media* between groundless fear and sheer folly is its goal. Reason also readily admits that some labors should be avoided; for example, those which may ruin our health, harm our Institute, or jeopardize our vocation. Nor can the vain, the proud, or the captious lay valid claim upon fortitude to champion their stubbornness or their truculence. Any appeal to fortitude on their part, in order to cloak pet peeves, mere dislikes, and vulgar exhibitionism, must receive short shift; the reasonableness of the virtue diametrically opposes them. Like all other virtues, fortitude is governed always by prudence, charity, and the limitations of one's state in life.

Herein shines the beauty of character fortitude implants in the willing soul; a combination of strength and gentility, of power and restraint, of courage and prudence, a leadership knowing when to be properly assertative, when to rest inert in masterly inactivity. Ever quick to act, fortitude yet pauses humbly and not reluctantly to acknowledge limitations; persistent, it is yet open to change, to reap the lessons of life.

Fortitude to be fortitude must be strong, but with the strength of holiness; holiness is its blood and its breath. Because in externalization it can be grandiose and sublime, it needs the deepest internal wellsprings. Fortitude's delicate steel is wielded with the cool sureness of the master surgeon, but retains all the tenderness of a nursing sister. Among the very saints themselves, who doubtless possessed fortitude, a fully graphic picturization of this virtue seems ever elusive. Constantly, one's thoughts return to Christ; only there does the mind and heart rest content in the fulfillment sought; to Christ, who could say, "All power is given to me in heaven and on earth," and about whom it could be said, "The bruised reed he shall not crush nor the burning wax extinguish"; Christ near and dear to the hearts of mankind; the hero-Christ close to his companions, their fearless and lovable leader.

Then I saw mankind's Lord
Swiftly come with courage, for he willed to mount me. . . .
Then he stripped himself, the young hero, that was God Almighty.
Strong and firm-hearted he mounted the mean gibbet;
Noble-hearted in the sight of many he would set free mankind.
(*Dream of the Rood*)

5

Spiritual Reading, Environment of the Soul

IT GOES WITHOUT SAYING THAT FOR CENTURIES devout religious have been striving to live a life of the spirit just as pleasing to God as they could make it. For us to have such an objective, consequently, is not at all new. We do have at present, though, new difficulties, special modern obstacles, to that traditional goal. Contemporary obstacles and difficulties lend a particular importance to certain aspects of ascetical training; one such aspect is spiritual reading. Our predecessors in religious life needed spiritual reading, but, in all honesty, they did not need it nearly as much as do we.

In our own decade, revolutions in the media of mass communications, magazines, movies, papers, radio, and television, have been more swiftly moving and far-reaching than upheavals of the past. No religious community, as a result, can build a wall so high that the siren song of the world does not threaten. Worldly values and examples and principles have always been a danger, but never before have they been so ubiquitous and insistent. Today, worldliness peeps in at us from every side, and only exceptional faithfulness to our spiritual reading will serve as an adequate counterweight.

Mass media of communications have attained an unparalleled persuasiveness in their presentation of the message of the world. The eye and ear are charmed; pictures, style, synopsis, and every other conceivable mechanism of artistry are tellingly employed. All this offers a challenge, for it can impart a distaste for quiet, tame, spiritual reading. By contrast, spiritual reading can be thought unattractive, not sufficiently high-paced; it may be found dull, boring, slow-going, and difficult. We must beware lest we permit ourselves to become bewitched, and as a result lose all desire of and taste for spiritual reading which, by superficial comparison, may seem both uninviting and unsatisfactory. Any initial unfaithfulness to spiritual reading later renders the practice more difficult; any ennui or carelessness will greatly weaken its over-all influence. We need spiritual reading badly today to maintain our sensitivity to sin, our vigilance against distractions, our alertness to temptations, and our recognition of worldliness. Only such consecrated reading properly nourishes our intellect, stores helpfully our memory, protects our imagination, strengthens our will, and renders truth beautiful to our souls and forceful in our lives. Only spiritual reading can brush aside the goals the world esteems. It rekindles within us those supernatural motives which are our mainspring. Unless our views are kept spiritual by our reading, the views of the world gradually become predominant even in the life of the consecrated religious.

"The world is too much with us," tells more than a poet's fancy; it is a fact to be faced. Sadly, the world stands ever at hand to win us to its ways; happily, so does spiritual reading. We do not always have at hand devotions and sermons presenting heavenly values; we do not always have at hand lofty principles exemplified by living saints; but spiritual reading is always available, and always in that reading we can find right principles, heroic examples, and sound stimulus to devotion.

Upon those religious who are engaged in the teaching apostolate, spiritual reading has special claims. One such claim

is drawn from the fact that most of us number religion among
the subjects we teach. This subject, contrary to popular belief,
ranks high among those most difficult to present attractively in
a classroom.

The pitfalls of teaching theology (to denominate it accurately) are inherent. In teaching the doctrinal part of the religion course, because our essential duty concerns the accurate
formulation of what must be believed, it can happen that these
truths emerge cold and austere. In teaching the moral part, on
the other hand, one has to trace the minimum which satisfies
the letter of the law, and this, too, sometimes portrays religion
in a fashion less than inspiring. We are able to avert such pitfalls
and achieve a more stimulating and worthwhile presentation in
proportion to the fullness of our spiritual reading.

That religion textbooks are necessarily rather limited affairs, no one knows better than those whose daily vehicle they
are. The warmth and richness that these texts but hint at can
be savored only through our own additional reading. How beautifully, for example, has the doctrine of the Mystical Body been
expounded in dozens of fine spiritual books. Also, through our
familiarity with such reading, the unfathomable riches contained
in the sacrifice of the Mass come to light and become real motivating forces. This same assistance is likewise available in
treatises dealing with the Person of Christ, the vocation of Our
Lady, the mystery of grace, and so forth. These examples are
capable of endless multiplication. In varying degrees, all that we
must discuss in class is elaborated already in works of spiritual
reading which are easily available to us.

So it is that the amount we do of this reading has a very
direct bearing upon the ability and inspiration we will manifest
in the religion class. By this means we acquire a depth of understanding of doctrinal truth and an awareness of its delicate
nuances. A firm and full and moving presentation is thus en-
sured. All the interest and fire which we ourselves have gained
will be found to be contagious; insights which would not other-

wise be available will be imparted; more than ever our pupils will be influenced. Not only knowledge will be their lot, but there will be present a love of what is known. From that love will spring action. Theology will be lived—the true definition of religion. They will not only have a religion course, they will possess the virtue of religion.

We have said that a banal by-product of the moral part of the class may be a mentality of legalism or minimism. Since the necessary concern is with the line of demarcation setting off sin and with the establishment of what minimum fulfills the law, things are at a rather low ebb, spiritually speaking. Students have a right to know these things and deserve to be taught them. Yet, how to do so and still keep casuistry from becoming a state of mind (an inferior approach to Christian living), is a serious, unavoidable problem.

An admirable step in the direction of solution is afforded by our spiritual reading. When the material of this reading forms the context of what we are teaching and provides us with a refreshing outlook, the loftier ascetical note will be present from time to time to counteract the above limitations. Moral theology will periodically be supplemented by ascetical theology.

This requires a sustained allegiance to such reading; otherwise, it will not be sufficient or wholly successful. Simply to announce some inspiring spiritual considerations at the beginning or end of the course, will not achieve much. Spirituality needs to infiltrate the whole course; before it can do so, however, it has to become part of the mind of the teacher, and only day-to-day faithfulness to spiritual reading can accomplish this. No distortion, or artificiality, or superimposition should be permitted to sabotage the course. Even in the proper and exact teaching of moral theology, lofty banners must be raised for the pupils to follow as they battle in the world for Christ's victory. This attitude, infinitely superior to one exclusively concerned with avoiding any wrongdoing, instills a holy and positive desire to build up the Mystical Body of Christ and secure the reign of

Christ the King over the length and breadth of the universe.

Even from the pedagogical point of view, quite apart from considerations of religion itself, reading of this sort offers a happy assistance. Any class in any subject receives additional interest and enlightenment from apt anecdotes, arresting incidents, happy insights, and deep intellectual penetration of the matter at hand. A conscious effort is made to observe this in planning history, literature, and other courses; we must not forget it when we turn to religion. Here the parallel service is provided by spiritual reading, an admirable equivalent of the additional preparatory reading the teacher has done to present history, literature, and other subjects in the greatest possible dimensions.

A further claim of spiritual reading upon religious whose task it is to teach, derives from the nature of that apostolate as it is generally practiced by the communities so engaged. Heavy schedules and crowded classrooms seem the rule rather than the exception, especially in the large urban centers. So pronounced is this that the teacher, unless she takes definite precautions, will find that a routine of this sort can markedly weigh down her spirit. Only a struggle will keep the spirit fresh. Care needs to be taken lest things degenerate into a seemingly endless tug-of-war with too many duties; a war in which the spiritual nature and the spiritual ends of the religious vocation may be lost sight of.

Spiritual reading is all-important here in setting before our eyes the reason for our sacrifices, in recalling and renewing our supernatural motivation, and in repeatedly reminding us that we have aimed at an achievement far nobler than simply getting the greatest number of pupils through the greatest number of examinations. Our controlling objective in dealing with youth is to help them to save their immortal souls through living the life of grace fully. The desire to enrich them with a proper competence in the various intellectual disciplines is in no way contradicted; we certainly want to do that, and to this end should devote the substance of our time, but always we must have in view a much wider objective.

The exigencies of the teaching apostolate can also play havoc with the spirit of recollection and the atmosphere of silence of soul, which should distinguish a person dedicated to religious life. Any religious properly aware of her vocation always tries to lead a deep interior life. Yet, teaching is a task which dissipates recollection and militates against attempts to establish control over the mental faculties. Memories of ideas studied privately or brought up in class, repeatedly assert themselves; almost mechanically the mind reviews the questions which arose and the subsequent groping for the correct answers. The brain at times resembles a squirrel's cage as all these thoughts chase one another around in circles. Anyone who has had occasion to try to pray immediately after the mental exertion of preparing a class, or the physical and mental exertion of teaching one, knows only too well how very difficult it is to anchor these faculties in the presence of God and then maintain them absorbed in union with him.

Spiritual reading will not totally avert such difficulties, but at least it will minimize them. It creates the possibility of shifting the mental faculties into other channels of thought, those that concern themselves with the things of God. When this is done, it is easier for the mind to become recollected; it is a beginning which gravitates toward interior union with God. In other words, instead of the difficult task of attempting to arrest the intense activity of the faculties at the outset, there is hope of successfully sidetracking them into material gradually conducive to prayer and recollection.

A kindred concern here is the hardship sometimes felt in observing the community silences enjoined by their role. Much of this, too, can be traced to dissipation of soul. The faculties lack that tranquillity requisite for the easy and even joyful observance of this necessary and helpful staple in our ascetical way of life. For the mind which is engaged in teaching but has not taken means to nurture itself on the golden grain of spiritual reading, these times once again tend to become a review period for the material we have studied, or a re-examination of the way we have handled the intellectual problems of the classroom.

When spiritual reading is a faithful practice, however, we are better able to check the natural tendencies of the imagination, memory, and intellect, and make times of silence welcome opportunities to ruminate over and probe further, in the helpful atmosphere of the presence of God, the wonderful truths stored from that reading. Moments of silence and solitude incubate the seeds sown in the time of spiritual reading; now they spring forth in full flower.

Because of the tensions and demands of the teaching routine, should things go wrong or should we feel harsh treatment has been our lot, there is a temptation to grow disheartened or cynical. Our shining idealism may become somewhat shopworn and the glorious vision of the everyday working Church as the Spouse of Christ may grow dim. Here, spiritual reading serves as a wonderful tonic, reviving and reinvigorating our pristine enthusiasms. The many beautiful treatises on the Church which we have read, can keep us inspired, and even amidst the clouds of here and now, stimulate our love for the Mystical Body and recall our holy pride at the lofty place we hold therein. We stand in good stead then, should the demands of ecclesiastical needs or discipline ask us to face trials or master our sensitive natures, which are so easily bruised.

Previously we emphasized the strong appeal the world's voice has in modern times—couched in all the attractiveness and insistence of mass communications. The decision of the young religious to leave the world was a firm, effective one. Years passed without the slightest regret. In time, however, some of us begin to experience a reawakening of our curiosity about the world. We wonder how conditions now are. What customs have changed? Are things as bad morally as hearsay leads us to be-

lieve? Certain events transpire about which we grow eager—
for no legitimate reason—to obtain more information. Like Lot's
wife, we are tempted to look back upon the world, its events
and personalities, and re-examine its maxims.

Again, this may be considered a particular difficulty for religious teachers. When one teaches literature or those divisions
of history touching upon current events, surely problems of this
sort have to be expected. Professional competence in these fields
demands some knowledge of the happenings in, and the literature of, the modern world.

How to distinguish between duty and worldliness poses
subtle difficulties. Certainly, carelessness in this matter can be
most unhelpful, the first step to rashness. If rashness is persisted
in, the mind becomes dissipated and the full attraction of the
world's presentation of its values is felt; "duty" may soon become simply a pretext for reading what is wrong and harmful.
Indeed, some items of current literature present dangers so grave
that one would rarely be justified in reading them. Since they
constitute serious moral hazards for people living in the world,
how much more a danger are they to those vowed to a life of
chastity.

Problems of this type arise when the religious must be
simultaneously engaged in studies for a degree. Many things to
be done increases the danger—a danger which in some cases
may jeopardize a spirit already tempted by discontent because
of a fear that the cumulative tasks may prove too much.

The natural restlessness and disinclination of the mental
faculties to accommodate themselves to the silence and the
peace of religious life are augmented when large amounts of
rather worldly and even dangerous reading is done. Yet assignments we must prepare in order to pass our examinations successfully may involve such borderline material. Where do we
draw the proper line, how shall we allot our time, how scale our
values? All has become very complex. Unless there has been
much well-assimilated spiritual reading, this situation is almost

a booby trap for the religious. The soul avoids spiritual dryness and a lukewarmness toward the life of grace, only if there has been a long, strong record of fidelity to spiritual reading.

Spiritual reading preserves our sensitivity to these dangers. It enables us to keep within proper bounds an intellectual interest in our fields and it will continue to provide a proper background. As a result, our judgments in this area remain morally and ascetically sound; a gradual erosion of standards has been prevented.

Quite naturally, the more deeply we have drunk of spiritual reading, the less we are tempted to seek after unnecessary worldly information. Our interest has been centered firmly in the things of our vocation; they have filled our mind and heart; no vacuum has been left for the world to enter. Should the mind reach out for the things of the world, their inferiority is clearly perceived; they compare poorly with the treasures already stored. Any flirtation with tinseled falsehoods will be temporary and uninfluential.

Neglect of spiritual reading, on the other hand, will prompt us to open wider the avenues of the world. At this point the religious may take definite measures to secure increasing contact with, and finally to yearn for, actual experience of the world. Unconsciously perhaps, we begin to compare the contrasting appeals of world and cloister, reassessing what each offers, reviewing the decision that had decided for Christ. Then a real crisis arises; we may succumb to false values, looking upon the community as boring and dissatisfying; the husks of corn may appear strongly attractive. Ultimately, there is the possibility of concluding that we have made the wrong choice; we may take back our dedication of self to the spiritual. We may leave the cloister and hazard our chances to capture the seemingly alluring prizes of life outside. In this way vocations have been lost. Possibly we exaggerate the importance of spiritual reading, but there seems little doubt that any honest examination will confirm the fact that here it definitely plays a substantial role.

It may be well to add a paragraph or so devoted to reading closely allied to spiritual reading—namely, the habit of reading a Catholic magazine which comments upon and evaluates current events and current literature. Such a habit can be motivated by a very sound spirituality and be of real service to that spirituality. It enables us to cope with any current developments which affect the subjects we teach; what is significant is clearly indicated as new movements and incidents are reviewed in the light of Catholic principles; novelties in the literary world are clearly labeled, while the worthwhile is praised.

Also, a good Catholic review obviates any wrong attitude toward pupils who raise these matters in class. We can guide them prudently, stressing any necessary restraints, and stimulate scholarly curiosity in an intelligent, educated fashion, which will salvage their love of reading, their desire to investigate, and their praiseworthy efforts to be legitimately *au courant*.

More than ever these qualities need to be preserved in our students and striven for when they are not present. The age of automation is already upon us, but the perceptible beginnings are as nothing in comparison with what lies ahead, directly ahead —this is not a matter of the distant future. Those we teach today will have all the problems of the "new leisure" tomorrow. If they are to use this "new leisure" well, they must be prepared. Having thus aroused in them the habit of reading, may we not also attempt to render them the additional service of directing some of it to the spiritual?

It can readily be admitted that many of the arguments for spiritual reading can also be advanced for the need of mental prayer. While mental prayer remains essential in our spiritual lives, to meditate or contemplate when there has been no spiritual reading attempts to build a fire without any fuel; only the mind steeped in matters of supernatural faith can be easily elevated to God in prayer. Should spiritual reading be neglected, the memory and imagination feed instead upon the affairs of the City of Man; then, our meditation becomes filled with distrac-

tions which will derail our efforts onto mundane bypaths. Quite
naturally our mind dwells on the thoughts that have been stored
there; very normal laws of psychology govern its operations.
Although he seeks the elevation of the mind, God does not
change or distort our nature. It would be against nature and its
laws to suppose that God would enrich with lofty affective prayer
a soul whose neglect of spiritual reading has prevented it from
being receptive at time of prayer. Should our mental prayer seem
a failure, should there be something apparently wrong with it,
we ought to examine our spiritual reading. "Seek in reading,"
says St. Bernard, "and you shall find in meditation."

Spiritual reading affects not only our mental prayer, its
scope is much broader. Spiritual reading colors our whole outlook, our work, our judgments of the people we meet, our attitudes toward the problems we face. St. Paul admonished us:
"Let that mind be in you which is in Christ Jesus"; spiritual
reading forms that *mens Christi*. That mind, if we possess it,
does not remain hidden, but makes itself evident from time to
time in our speech, our actions, our evaluations. If, on the contrary, the "mind of Christ" is not firmly established in us by
means of our spiritual reading, its absence will not go unper-
ceived. Those under our charge will conclude in confusion that
our mentality echoes the mind of the world, and they will lament
that we are not better fitted to blaze the trail to a better world
for those whose vocation keeps them living in the world. Spiritual
reading also makes its contribution toward life in the religious
community. It renders palatable to our personalities the life of
retirement, and shrouds our spirit in calm recollection to fill
the moments of silence. In a word, by spiritual reading we are
prepared for, and adapted to, the life we have freely chosen.

Since this is so, our spiritual reading should include some
treatment of principles of the spiritual life. Since sanctity is a
science as well as an art, under God's grace we achieve sanctity
by the intelligent adherence to fundamental rules which the
Church has traditionally taught in the realm of ascetical the-

ology. The soul, be it ever so willing, requires the guidance of clear, correct, orderly spiritual principles. Reading of this type supplies spiritual direction of a sort, showing us our need of mortification and the kind best suited to our activities. We learn how to build up the virtues, especially the ones pertinent to the tendencies of our own temperament. Spiritual reading gives help to those problems of how best to purify our motivation and conquer distractions and temptations. This reading also helps us in our efforts to acquire self-knowledge; indeed, the master writers in this field go beyond mere knowledge, they inspire our will to practice asceticism. Allied to such reading, too, is our effort to understand the beautiful dogmas of our religion and the wonderful liturgy in which they are enshrined.

In addition to the theoretical principles, spiritual reading details their actualization in the lives of the saints. These men and women are the great Christian heroes and heroines given to us for our example. By the lesson of their lives, God tells us in effect, "Go and do thou likewise." They are "proof positive" for us that it can be done, that Christ's teachings are not too hard or too lofty, but that under grace his teachings can flourish fully in human lives. This does not mean we must try to mimic every detail in our own lives; saints have performed very unusual and extraordinary things through specially given graces. It does mean, however, that we follow the main outlines of their lives, the underlying spiritual principles. With the saints as guides before our mind's eye, the truths of the gospels take flesh in persons who have dwelt upon the same earth as ourselves. We ought to mention here that the writing of saints' lives in accordance with the norms of current historiography is only a fairly modern development; medieval and even earlier writers had their own particular estimate of the scope and tasks of hagiography. It is understandable that the saints' lives written many years ago reveal the preconceptions of those times.

Of all spiritual reading the very best remains the reading of the Sacred Scriptures themselves. Those sacred pages, Pope

Leo XIII stressed in his encyclical on biblical studies, *Providentissimus Deus*, were written wholly and entirely under the inspiration of the Holy Ghost. God intends Holy Scripture as a means to bring us to him. Will not its reading, then, achieve God's intention? How often in the Scriptures has he repeated that his word is effectual, that it will never return empty. St. Jerome, the Father of scriptural studies, wrote to his pupil, Paula:

> Tell me whether you know of anything more sacred than this sacred mystery, anything more delightful than the pleasure found therein? What food, what honey could be sweeter than to learn of God's providence, to enter into his shrine and look into the mind of the Creator, to listen to the Lord's words at which the wise of this world laugh, but which really are full of spiritual teaching? . . . Our delight is to meditate on the Law of the Lord day and night, to knock at his door when shut, to receive our food from the Trinity of Persons, and, under the guidance of the Lord, trample under foot the swelling tumults of this world.
>
> (*Epist.* 30:13)

Prudence must attend our reading of the Scriptures; certain sections of the Historical Books possess an oriental realism and other sections have deep, involved truths requiring of the reader the most humble faith as well as years of linguistic and theological training. The New Testament more than all else should be our delight; it has been richly indulgenced by the Church. Return again and again to the gospels to imprint upon your hearts the words and actions of Christ, our Teacher and Exemplar, who is true God. From time to time this can be supplemented by reference to the standard lives of Christ. Neither should a religious neglect to foster a deep devotion to the Mother of Christ. It is unthinkable that the true followers of Mary would not love to read about her.

In choosing our books, a taste for the spiritual classics is a very sound one. These have stood the test of time; they have been spiritual best-sellers over the centuries. No finer *vade mecum* can be found in planning and systematizing spiritual reading than Tanquery's *The Spiritual Life;* the volumes of Pourrat's *Christian Spirituality* will provide a valuable historical approach. For the sake of variety and freshness of outlook we may find it helpful to take up modern works which articulate holiness in the light of our own times. Here it is wise to select authors of admirable reputation; or, in the case of newcomers, to utilize the safeguard of an authoritative review, lest we waste our time as the newcomer may have wasted his. Works which are sensational, rankly sentimental, faddish, should not delay us; when so many diamonds abound, how foolish to be allured by colored glass.

Of course human personalities differ and will have different tastes in the matter of spiritual reading. Some will require reading along a particular line, others will like books of a different stress. It should not be, however, just a matter of what we like; we must make the effort to conform our likes to our needs. Backgrounds and abilities likewise differ, and spiritual reading should be chosen accordingly.

Not only what we read but how we read is of serious importance. It is praiseworthy to begin all spiritual reading with a prayer, no matter how brief. Very helpful, too, is the practice of placing oneself at the outset in the presence of God. Folly marks the approach of those who make of spiritual reading a sort of marathon to pile up a record number of books read; books read but in haste, in dissipation of spirit, with the mere glancing contact of the dilettante. Wisdom weighs the reading with mature reflection, with a calm interior spirit. The spiritual message, thus permitted to sink into the soul, may prompt the interspersion of ejaculatory prayer. There are those who urge us to raise the mind to meditation during parts of the reading; this, however, should not block altogether a steady progress in spiritual reading.

Our spiritual reading ought to be our delight; it should radiate happiness in the soul. This is the *tranquillitas,* tranquillity or peace, which is ours at the moment of spiritual reading. Deep joy floods our consciousness:

> We realize in reading how bound up we are with God; how good he is, how sweet, how solicitous, how rich, ample, and overflowing. We are glad to renounce the world, to mortify the flesh, to humble and annihilate ourselves. We regret nothing that we have given up; but rather, in the music of the gentle refrain which arises from the words of the Prophets, the evangelists, and the saints, we despise and loathe everything which is not God or related to him. This is the "sweetness" of God's word which is so often referred to by the Psalmist, "How sweet are thy words on my palate!—more than honey to my mouth!"
>
> (HEDLEY, *Retreat*, p. 374)

6

Fundamentals Which
Never Grow Old

ONE OF THE FINE FLOWERINGS ON THE SPIRITUAL
landscape of America has been the enlightened interest in the
liturgical movement. Its achievement has been to give our spirituality both a sound and broad basis: sound, by rooting our
efforts in the bedrock dogma of the Church so sublimely expressed in the prayer and sacrament and sacrifice of the Spouse
of Christ; broad, by accepting all implications of that creed and
cult in their seemingly infinite application to the daily affairs of
the whole human race as well as the innermost workings of the
individual soul.

In his encyclical *Mediator Dei*, Pope Pius XII praised the
accomplishments of the liturgical movement and urged an even
fuller acceptation of its hallowing potentialities in our own lives.
Yet, from the pontifical throne, a note of warning also sounded,
one necessitated by an overenthusiastic handful (the common
bane of all good movements) who, unhappily, have circulated
the impression that any personal or subjective piety, because it
might not be immediately connected with the liturgy, should be
written off as meaningless and worthless. Strong emphasis may
be found in the papal document to the effect that all religious

exercises, even those quite separate from liturgical ceremonies, can be highly praiseworthy; their commendation over the centuries by classic writers on asceticism indicates their indispensable assistance in the pursuit of perfection.

Such private and personal exercises of piety possess great value in exposing dangers which threaten our individual spiritual lives. When carried out in the sensible fashion advocated by ascetical theology, these non-liturgical practices constitute an effective safeguard by properly channeling our religious aspirations, and are undoubtedly successful in positively promoting a strong virtue. Tending to increase our fervor, stimulating as they do our generosity, these practices prod on our reluctant human nature to an ardent and arduous imitation of Christ. Between them and the liturgy rises no high wall of separation; rather, both are supplementary and complementary, merging in heavenly harmony for the good of the individual and the advancement of the Kingdom of God.

With this prelude borne in mind, it would seem fruitful to devote our attention to a detailed examination of a few of these spiritual exercises. The detail cannot be exhaustive, of course, in this brief space, and, to avoid disappointment, it should be understood at the outset that these explanations are not offered in the vain expectancy of transforming such exercises into something new and novel. Our simple aim is merely to provide a refresher course in some aspects of our ascetical "basic training."

While this "refresher course" may be studied at any time of the school year—one can hope not without some profit— perhaps the time likely to prove most appropriate occurs when the year has partially run its course; for example, those dreary weeks crawling toward graduation, or the dark days before the Easter vacation. Since, however, the condition of the soul need not follow nature's seasons, we might also turn our attention to matters of this sort when the inner weather of the spirit seems threatening or overcast, when the cumulative strains of duty appear to have tightened us unduly, when somber shadows have somehow settled about the heart.

On such occasions the absence of our customary cheerfulness and alacrity of soul may cause our spiritual exercises to hang heavy upon us and to become drab, onerous, and barren. Yet, these very exercises are meant to be our support and sustenance precisely at such moments. Their re-examination and re-evaluation may succeed in restoring them to favor, and may turn them even more effectively to our spiritual benefit.

A good beginning can be made by recollecting that an examination of conscience constitutes a necessary staple in the daily spiritual diet. Because this examination has grown up with us from the very beginning of our life in religion and because in itself it appears to be a rather simple thing, we always face the danger of taking it too much for granted and, as a consequence, perform it with little thought, little zeal, and little confidence. Failure to perform this exercise well hamstrings our good will and actually misdirects much of our effort.

This sometimes happens in the case of religious whose active apostolate is an academic one; a rather lax attitude is somehow developed. Their reasoning, while seldom made explicit, seems to hold that the teaching day has been too full and variegated in its details to be amenable to any such scrutiny; it would be like attempting to tie together the tendrils of an octopus. This thought is aided and abetted by a very simple one—the teacher is much too tired at the end of the daily routine; it is enough to go through the motions of an examination of conscience; a once-over-lightly survey has to suffice. An approach of this sort, incidentally, remains entirely unmindful of the fact that teachers, in the estimate of their students, have notorious reputations for being creatures of habit. In consequence, many may be badly in need of this nightly check lest grooves of character, which would be better avoided, be worn and become utterly fixed.

Although the modern world moves in swiftness and turmoil, nonetheless, it puts a great premium upon foresight and efficiency. A person who sings commercially or one for whom the making of speeches constitutes an important item in the workaday world, will record his songs or speeches, and the results will be diligently studied. Any slight deficiencies are ruthlessly exposed and methodically tabulated. Whys and wherefores are then probed, ways and means worked out for the future elimination of whatever militates against a perfect rendition. Surely one's own struggle to serve God well outranks in importance the world's concern for a flawless virtuoso performance. Spiritual performances of a consecrated religious deserve careful review at the end of each day spent in living the most important of all vocations.

Of its nature, religious life accents this examination of conscience. With the eternal sameness of each day's routine, the repetition of the same things among the same people in the same surroundings, a sister can be gripped by an ennervating ennui, a listless disregard for her activities, and a feeling of sheer boredom cloying all thoughts, smoldering and smothering all aspirations. This vice the monastic writers subjected to their periodic strictures under the term *accedia*. We find St. John Climacus writing: "Accedia is a remissness of soul, an ennervation of mind, a neglect of religious practice, a distaste for our vocation . . . languid at the psalms, infirm at prayer, cold toward ministrations, sluggish toward tasks. . . ." Nothing serves more effectively as a check against falling into such a state than the daily examination of conscience, which is quick to detect its beginnings and prompt to dissipate its threats by a carefully formulated vigilance guarding against such subtle entrapment. "One must cultivate one's garden," the French aphorism reminds us; of all gardens the garden of the soul requires most cultivation, but it also offers the richest yield.

Should the examination reveal a day streaked with failure, the religious needs to beware lest reactions of disheartening discouragement totally oppress her. That, unfortunately, would render the last condition of the soul worse than the first; an error placing heavy penalties upon even the best intentions. Rather, in a spirit of calm and becoming resignation to the goodness of God and to the unpleasant personal facts of the case, the religious may humbly learn an invaluable lesson—the weakness of self alone. This will lead the soul to dwell with particular intensity on the strength of God. Such fundamental confidence, once it has been attained, looks courageously toward the dawn of a better tomorrow in hopeful anticipation of heaven's generous graces.

When by good fortune this examination turns up encouraging results—repeated performances of virtuous acts, unmistakable advances in self-conquest—the better part of wisdom suggests passing quickly over such accomplishments. While it may undoubtedly be sweet to so center the memory and imagination, it may not be helpful. Lest sentiments of vainglory be stimulated, the gold stars won in the daily strife should be immediately handed over to God; let him receive the plaudits. Following this approach faithfully makes it easy to offer heartfelt thanks to God for his many known helps and also for the many, many unknown helps received throughout the entire day.

Another exam, the particular exam, concerns itself with whatever appears to be the particular fault, the greatest obstacle, the sword of Damocles menacing all spiritual progress. Damocles, enamored of wealth and power, envied anyone so blessed, and convinced himself that such people enjoyed a complete heaven on earth. How radically his views changed after a sage ruler, hearing of Damocles' pronouncements, showered wealth, power, and all their accouterments upon him. This ruler arranged to have Damocles seated at the royal banquet table; at his finger tips rested all he could desire; literally, the ruler cradled Damocles in the lap of luxury. Yet, Damocles had never before been so unhappy, for a terrible sword remained always poised above his head, suspended by only a single horsehair. That threat, as may well be imagined, spoiled all his other surroundings; luxury, power, opulence lost all appeal, were reduced to nothing because of this menacing sword.

Pursuing this analogy in terms of the spiritual life, a religious, although possessed of splendid personal qualities and virtuous tendencies, although surrounded by devout practices and opportunities for grace, may find that there still lurks in her essential character a suspended sword nullifying, or at least capable of nullifying, the fine spiritual banquet. Our particular exam directs itself day in and day out to the gradual elimination of the particular fault, weakness, passion, or tendency which constitutes the sword poised against our entire asceticism. The particular exam is the intelligent activization of our realization that this one flaw could hold back our progress, menace our moral safety, and sterilize our opportunities for increasing sanctifying grace.

One phenomenon of the life shared by religious who staff schools and their students, which generates vast amusement to all, except perhaps the individual specifically victimized, is the popular pastime of awarding nicknames to anyone who presides over a classroom, whether that classroom be housed in a world-centered university or the local grammar school. Although a source of merriment, nonetheless, a rather deep psychology sometimes lurks in these nicknames; they are capable of focusing unerringly upon a predominant characteristic of the teacher. That they are successful and gain wide circulation, derives from the fact that the stress placed by the nickname upon some aspect of personality is immediately recognized by all who know that teacher.

Yet, strangely enough, it sometimes happens that the very one of whom it is predicated, has to have its pertinence explained —a rather delicate task. Does not this tell volumes about the blindness of teachers in their estimate of the make-up of their own selves? Certainly it illustrates the wisdom of a particular exam dedicated to the search for the dominant fault or that special tendency which looms large in the personality. Further, the extent to which such a characteristic can color one's manner of thinking and of acting is rather well exposed. Filtered through a particular exam, a soul may find valuable spiritual implications for its development.

When one is known throughout the school as "Old Rough and Ready," she ought to probe her soul to see whether some improvement might be in order by way of increased gentleness, kindness, and patience. "*La Favorita*" may be awarded the religious whose chief teaching vice consists in playing favorites in the classroom. This deordination departs badly from the practice of essential justice. In such a case, objective standards are shuffled and reshuffled until a chosen few manage always to emerge with the lion's share of all laurels. Or it may involve a blatant inconsistency between announced policy and the factual application of those standards to the students as a whole. Things of this nature are rather important in the minds of students and wield a great influence in shaping the measure of success which a teacher will achieve in stimulating enthusiasm for the material taught and in securing the diligence necessary to master it. They will affect adversely also the attractiveness the religious should present as a beacon lighting the path of virtue.

All intelligent teachers agree that standards of intellectual accomplishment must be observed if any school is to fulfill adequately the purpose of its existence. Inevitably, this seems to mean that a percentage of the youths must fall by the wayside. Quite legitimately and often with quite salutary results, the conscientious teacher will mete out failing marks to this percentage of the students. On the other hand, when a certain religious finds herself referred to as "They Shall Not Pass," it is quite possible that she is too rigid in this respect. She may have to admit that the feeling, shared by faculty members as well as students, that she has been oversevere and overdemanding, has a basis in fact. Unless she is able to see this herself and do something about it, discouragement and bitterness may result in the hearts of the youngsters.

Another academic title that comes to mind, "The Happy Wanderer," reveals worlds about the teaching methods which even well-intentioned instructors may fall into. Again, there surely have to be some distractions and digressions in a classroom to make life livable for teacher and student alike, but that is a situation totally different from failure to cover the requisite matter. Substantial failure to treat the allotted material of a course deprives students of what is quite essential to their needs. State-recognized examinations constitute an important rung in the ladder to graduation, but how, under such circumstances, can the students be expected to pass them? Future college or university matriculation is also a weighty factor which must be considered. A matter of serious injustice here concerns religious teachers. Surprisingly, it sometimes happens that otherwise quite virtuous persons develop lax consciences about this aspect of the academic apostolate.

Thus, to a degree, traits popularly associated with us, nick-names, widespread reactions to either ourselves or our methods in dealing with students both in class and outside of class, do provide insights into the manner of persons we are. Some of these considerations in themselves may not be especially vital, but there seems little doubt that they possess value in sometimes opening a door to some essential spiritual point which may well warrant, at least for a while, regular scrutiny in our day to day spiritual exam.

So essential do the acknowledged masters of the spiritual life (for example, St. Ignatius Loyola) consider this particular exam, that they vigorously cautioned against the lamentable folly of any underestimation of its role. Clear expressions of a similar conviction can be discovered in the writings of accomplished and sage men of the world. They are aware, just as keenly as the saints, of its power to mold strong and noble characters, winning and arresting personalities. An interesting proof of this awaits the reader of Benjamin Franklin's famous *Autobiography*.

Both Franklin and St. Ignatius, in fact, so wholeheartedly went at the particular exam, their tabulations nearly required the services of a bookkeeper. Charts were drawn and scrupulously filled; every move made by the particular fault was registered; a strict account was kept of all the victories and every defeat. While doubtless burdensome and somewhat mechanical, such rigorous adherence to the particular exam can point to successes which no one can gainsay. How well its fundamental ratio was expressed by the writer of the *Imitation:* "If each year I rooted out one fault, I should be a perfect man."

Another *must* in the daily spiritual routine is visits to the Blessed Sacrament. Particularly evident should be the necessity and especially dear should be the fruits to those religious whose Institute has deployed them in the very active life of teaching. No task becomes more mentally absorbing; like a lodestar the quest for knowledge and the attempt to clarify and impart that knowledge, draws to itself all the faculties of the soul—intellect, memory, imagination, and will power. Teaching almost automatically narrows the span of our consciousness. Rugged indeed becomes the effort to preserve an awareness of the presence of God in those circumstances marking the everyday *modus agendi* of the sincere, truly learned, capable teacher.

What spiritual refreshment our visits to the Blessed Sacrament offer. Just as the desert traveler, wilted by blazing whiteness of sun upon sand, toil-worn by hours of taxing, monotonous travel, feels his heart leap in exultation when a clear, sparkling spring of cold water is at hand, so does the religious teacher experience spiritual retrenchment at the wellspring of the tabernacle. During those briefly snatched moments with our Emmanuel, and especially during golden half-hours or even hours, which a most blessed providence sometimes awards, we recall and even anticipate our heavenly goal. Here in quiet, peaceful perspective we can examine the fundamental purposes of our active life. There has not yet been devised a more excellent antidote against becoming estranged because of a multiplicity of duties, or slipping dangerously into judging and functioning on a merely natural level.

The apostles must have found their deepest happiness in the constant presence of their beloved Master. Amazingly, for them casual conversations could be the vehicle of petitions or thanksgiving to God. Looking upon Jesus how could they not love him; watching him, listening to him, praying with him, adoration could not long be withheld. Yet, in the tabernacle, Jesus remains as truly present to his convent followers who strive to dedicate to him their talents and their time. To visit that tabernacle is to be with Christ. In that companionship, lies the deepest happiness for true apostles. Fast united to his Eucharistic presence, their self-forgetful, adoring prayer wells up from glad hearts.

What wonder, the central point, the greatest event of all history, our altar holds—almighty and eternal God has taken flesh and dwelt amongst us. Why has he done so, why is he with us now? To redeem us and to perpetuate the fruits of that redemption. The Son of God actively adores the Father for us, and in our behalf continues to offer all his infinite merits. To draw near to him means to converse with a faithful friend, to love a spotless spouse, to unite mind and heart to God.

In the course of our visits to the Blessed Sacrament one is urged by the saints to recall that Christ is present in the tabernacle as on a throne of love and mercy, dispensing his graces and offering his love. The word "throne," in earlier centuries when kingships were so universal, conjured up a warm hope in the human bosom. Kingship symbolized hope—if one could but reach the throne of the king, all things needful would be gained. History recites that the suffering, the defeated, always felt that if only they could reach the throne and seek the king to ask their boon, all would be righted. If this hope has been fulfilled through the goodness and mercy of an earthly throne, if human power and finite limitations have so rejoiced the eager expectations of the heart, how glorious our sacred anticipation as we prostrate before Christ the King whose power is infinitely loving and whose love is infinitely powerful. Here awaits a divine King desirous of lavishing upon us the redemptive graces entitling us to share that eternal kingdom.

Biographers frequently picture great saints in fervent prayer before the Blessed Sacrament, and saints' own written testimonies recount that in these visits they found fountains gushing forth Christ's love and mercy. While St. Margret Mary Alocoque was paying a visit to the Blessed Sacrament, Jesus showed her his heart enthroned in flames, crowned with thorns, and surmounted by a cross. He then addressed to her these words: "Behold this heart which has loved men so much."

One would be hard-pressed to recall any saint whose life did not record great fidelity to daily Eucharistic visits. In the presence of the Blessed Sacrament many of the saints conceived and formulated their most significant achievements. Although Mother Cabrini's career was so filled with external activity that the Vice-Postulator of the cause confessed, "In the whole Catholic hagiography there is probably no other saint in which there are so few signs of mystical experience," her enraptured visits to the Blessed Sacrament offered convincing proof of an intense interior life.

Another great help in our religious life comes through the practice of spiritual communion. It would be well to join this spiritual communion to our visit to the Blessed Sacrament, making it the pinnacle of that visit. St. Thomas Aquinas defines spiritual communion as an ardent desire to receive Christ in the Eucharist and to embrace him lovingly as if we had actually received the sacred host (cf. III, q. 80, a. 1). Hence, although the chapel remains the ideal setting for this exercise, nonetheless, no reason obtains why it cannot be made in any other place.

As a general rule our zeal flames highest at the moment of our reception of communion in the Mass. At that moment, surrounded as we are by the strength of Christ and joined in union with him, we can achieve a supernatural ardor which we can

bring to the day's tasks. We almost look forward to every trial
as to so many opportunities to draw closer to a crucified Master
and to demonstrate to him the depth of our affection. Making
a spiritual communion at one of the darker moments of the day
helps us to recapture the zeal which burned within us when we
received sacramental communion at Mass. Despite the oppression
of burdensome problems and stinging irritations in the course
of our activities, our spiritual communion supplies the invaluable
awareness of the strength and love of Christ. Just as a soldier on
the battlefield finds his spirits buoyed up instantly when a great
general comes and stands beside him, so the captains of Christ's
army, the devout religious, serve best when, through spiritual
communion, they summon their supreme Commander to their
side.

One most personal practice, mortification, should never be
absent from the life of any serious-minded religious. Every treatise on asceticism wholeheartedly urges this practice, and invariably the second nocturnes of the breviary, which recount the
spiritual exploits of the saints, report this same concern for
mortification. Factually, in our own circle of acquaintances, whenever sound reason has pressed a judgment that X is possessed of
real holiness, there has always been parallel evidence of real
mortification; and, *de jure*, it would be our rightful anticipation
that this would have to be so. No spiritual advance in any direction, not even a general advance, can be gained without it.
Whether we seek to elevate our prayer-life, or to increase our
charity, or to become more zealous, to be successful we must
include mortification.

Anyone who has tried hard to be charitable in all of her
dealings with others, knows how formidable a task has been
chosen. It requires a constant watch over self; not yielding to
anger, suppressing the cutting remark, reining the harsh judgment, even within her own mind. These things constitute an exacting record of self-control, of relentless struggle with lower
nature and its uncharitable proclivities. Clearly, mortification

needs to be an integral part of all of this. To practice the demanding routine of charity and to be simultaneously unmortified, would postulate a personality more divided than Dr. Jekyll–Mr. Hyde.

Zeal, in the spiritual life, is the foundation upon which worthwhile achievements are built; without zeal, ascetically speaking, we could not even get up, stand on our feet, and be ready to begin. But, again, the basic mechanics of zeal simply represent a series of present mortifications and the fruits of past mortifications. By definition, zeal overcomes self, overcomes the difficulties inherent in the duty at hand; it calls for the identical qualities requisite in all mortification. No wayward person can muster the determination necessary to overcome self and carry on the works of zeal; neither can she possess the courage and stamina so essential to their fulfillment.

Without question, our life in religion confronts us with what might be termed a "built-in" mortification. This is, perhaps, all too evident when the religious life includes many hours spent in the classroom. Whoever begins the day with a resolution to perform all duties as perfectly as possible, and then succeeds in such a resolution, can feel quite certain as the day ends that a rather large quota of mortification has been filled.

The fact remains, however, that not all of us go through the day quite so perfectly. The reason for the lack of perfection may be found in the lack of mortification. Mortification does not work automatically; it is either something we are conscious of and practiced in, or it is not "carried off" when the occasion for its exercise arises. Without methodically formed habit, we do not, as a matter of course, check a rising temper when student efforts go awry. The regular ability to accept additional school tasks which are unforeseen and crop up at inconvenient moments, is not developed out of thin air by a sudden inspiration that here is an opportunity to mortify ourselves. The acceptance of mortification as a way of life has to exist first.

We ought to make it an ironclad rule to practice some additional voluntary mortification daily. It can be of a very minor nature; that is not significant. What is significant is that we have consciously paid allegiance to the principle that the spiritual life needs mortification. When we are not only aware of this fact but deeply convinced of it, then the routine mortifications, which are indeed part of school and community life, will be accepted, their obstacles hurdled; otherwise, there results an attitude of bypassing what mortification we can and grudgingly sliding through what we cannot.

This represents only common sense as well as sound ascetical theology, for if our life is to be lived supernaturally, the weaknesses of fallen human nature have to be overcome. We must take some initiative in this matter because, left to itself, nature will seek only the level of nature; its placid adaptability will accept only the unavoidable, and a routine of compromise will destroy the efficacy even of the inescapable. What cannot be avoided thus becomes deprived of the influx of our intellect and will—which is essential for its doing our souls any good. Any religious who dismisses this hard but necessary practice, under the delusion that religious life plus its academic apostolate makes it superfluous, lives in a fool's paradise.

In recent decades there has been a considerable playing down of physical mortification. This may be a good thing—to an extent. Physical mortification does not always offer the highest type of mortification, and in our age of tensions with its high incidence of neurotic reaction, great caution should be observed in undertaking the physical variety. That we have sinned in the past through excesses and formalism, is certainly true. To all that we can say a hearty "amen," but our assent need not prevent insistence on the fundamental need of some physical mortification. Physical mortification, in a general way, lays the groundwork for higher mortifications, and we can take it as axiomatic that if there is none on the physical level, there will be none on any level.

Once this salutary caveat has been stipulated, however, we

can move on to grant that the best mortification, deserving of our best efforts, concerns the disciplining of the higher faculties and the smooth regulation of our interior life. While this traditional approach of Catholic asceticism should be abided by in all walks of life, it has special pertinence for the religious engaged in teaching. For this reason: the teaching process involves much study and an imaginative presentation for the classroom, with the result that the faculties employed are kept in ferment. All through our waking day, unless we are unusually fortunate, the memory constantly drags up things from the well of consciousness; the imagination, if unguarded, begins to run wild. Likewise, temptations to *curiositas* arise in the intellect, the classic word *curiositas* denoting any unnecessary search after vain and useless information or even dangerous and harmful knowledge. We will be unable to escape these pitfalls unless we maintain a mortification of the mind and will, the memory and imagination.

Interior mortification reveals its importance especially in prayer. It should be self-evident that success will be barred from mental prayer by bringing to it unmortified mental faculties; only distractions and wanderings will, quite logically, result. How can the senses determinedly turn to God and the higher faculties remain there in union with him, unless they have been thoroughly disciplined? And if this is the price we pay for unmortified faculties, even when our meditation has been structured for us and its operating level a matter of discursive prayer, how can the lofty heights of contemplation be even considered under such circumstances? Our earliest community instructions on mental prayer, prayer looking forward to its culmination in contemplation, correctly insisted that we would never attain much progress without the protection and nourishment of mortification. And it was made plain also that to keep pace, mortification, in time, would have to be of a rather arduous nature. We cannot ask God to reward indolence and neglect by pouring forth upon a soul of this type his very richest graces. That would be to place ourselves in the position of acting quite un-reasonably, and then expecting the movements of divine grace to conform to our own lack of wisdom.

In turn, the fruitfulness of our prayer, the tenacity of our adherence to the rigors of zeal, and the unfailing practice of our charity under constant difficulties, all bear witness to our mortification and yield a praiseworthy appraisal of how effective it has been. To put it succinctly, if we are going to remain close to Christ throughout the long day of our teaching apostolate with its kaleidoscopic activity, by means of our prayerfulness, charity, and zeal, we first have to mortify ourselves. Long ago, and repeatedly, that point was made strongly to us; the principle has never changed, nor will it change. Here and now we can again remind ourselves how essential to our spiritual life is mortification.

This little review of fundamentals must draw to a close. The fundamentals are familiar, have become a part of us. They are habits that Mother Church early taught her children of predilection when at her knee they first learned to lisp the eternal words of religious life. As the centuries evolve they will continue to be learned and relearned by those who will come to follow in our footsteps.

Sometimes it happens in the world that a child likes to taste all of life, to experiment with the novel and the strange, to counterbalance the parental teaching. Often, that same child in old age, with a bitter taste in the soul, sadly repents the folly of having departed to erring bypaths. Then, it is realized that in childhood truth was held unprized and that a vain course was run. May God preserve us from such error; may we treasure always our traditional religious exercises. Honoring them now by faithful observance, we shall finally rejoice to see how splendidly they have honored us.

The Shadows
of the World

7

Death, Somber
but Salutary

EVERY LANGUAGE IN THE WORLD CONTAINS THE
word "death," the most pregnant of all words regardless of the
variation in different lands of its spelling or accent. Death has
been on the tongue of every man who breathes. Every living
person has at sometime pondered death. It is a touch of sharp
sorrow which makes the whole world kin; it is the only thing
that matters, for it marks our final triumph over matter; it is
the most timely, for it conquers time and frees us for eternity; it
bridges earth and heaven; it is the last step by which man walks
to God. Death is the most important thing in life.

The Catholic family, on the occasion of the loss of a loved
one, experiences great consolation from the solemn exequies of
the Church, and not rarely do the non-Catholics in attendance
comment on how comforting and compensating the moving
liturgy has been. This should not be considered strange or surprising, for the realism of the Church has always recognized that
the thought of death can be a very salutary one for the Christian. Traditionally, meditation upon the fact of death has been
a staple of the prayer of the religious community, and each of

95

us should find in such meditation a strong reservoir of ascetic motivation and spiritual formation.

Meditation upon death strongly counteracts our innate tendency to self-importance, a temptation so universal that its origins are easily traceable to the sin of our first parents which stained human nature. Death can be a means of flooding the soul with images productive of humility, for at the thought of death, the great leveler, how quickly human greatness fades. The most opaque pride trembles before the judgment seat of God; in the white heat of that flawless justice, all human accomplishment melts to a terrifying littleness. Even the worldly poet, after recounting the deeds of fame of the great ones of the earth, poses the ironic question: "But where are the snows of yesteryear?"

This is a pertinent question to ponder for religious engaged in teaching work. It is not true to say that a teaching religious lives two lives, one as a teacher and the other as a religious, for both become joined, part of each other, synchronized into a single life devoted to God. But the teaching life, in its own right, comprises an entire world with particular tasks, varying degrees of authority, a hierarchy of positions, a scale of possible promotions, and so forth. Unless the religious is careful she can become sealed up in this elaborate world, forgetful of the fact that she is first a religious. Almost inherent in the educational milieu is a pull of ambition, a concern with pride of place, more intense than one normally finds in other areas of endeavor of religious congregations. Caught up, as willy-nilly we have to be to some extent, in the educational machinery, such temptations are bound to confront us, and in all honesty we have to recognize them and struggle against them.

A religious community charged with the responsibility of a school or many schools is obliged in conscience to develop a staff of qualified teachers and competent administrators. Academic strength needs, then, to be deployed in such a fashion that positions demanding greater accomplishment are assigned to those who have made the most progress in earning subject credits and who have demonstrated high-level, pedagogical skill. In consequence, a hierarchy of position does exist. This situation can divide members of a community, pitting them one against the other, or individuals against groups. The educational world with its necessary apparatus, thus presents a real challenge to the world of religious life, a struggle, it might be termed, between the natural and the supernatural.

A healthy awareness of death, through our spiritual reading, prayers, and meditation, can offer invaluable assistance here, for the more we think only about life, the more we will be tempted to limit ourselves to this educational world. The final fact of death enables us to broaden our horizon to the measurements it should have, those of the supernatural world which embrace eternity and the happiness of heaven.

Unless these necessary aspects are constantly before the mind's eye of the religious, she may well slip into a spirit of harmful competition born of ambition. It is not far-fetched, in view of the above considerations, to argue that our spiritual concern with death, our keeping it always as a frame of reference for our evaluations and our activities, will prove a means of needed grace to the teaching community. Death makes the difference. If religious, upon completing this life, were just to dissolve into thin air and be no more, it might be reasonable to give ambition full sway, to push ourselves forward for the choicest plums available, to make self-advancement the legitimate goal of our work. Death reminds us that the real rewards which we must ever seek, rewards to which our holy vocation has committed us independent of teaching work or of anything else, come after this life.

Death asks embarrassing questions of the ambitious. To what does endless promotion lead? Only to the door of death. We may have known religious who devoted their lifetime to worldly advancement. They are dead now; they will be dead for a long time—all eternity. At some future time we will also die. Then, it will not make the slightest difference what position we held in the educational hierarchy. Death will reward us according to the simple measurement we learned in the first days of our novitiate—how well we served God and humbly did his will in whatever niche he placed us.

This citizenship of two worlds can play hob with our interior life. We begin to find that we do not have time for the interior life, and so it is short-changed. This may so affect our values, that religious life is deprived of its rightful importance in our basic thinking. Death again can be helpful here, as silently it pleads for a supernaturalizing of all things, and an emphasizing of the dimensions of eternity; it removes any doubt that progress, educational or otherwise, is dependent upon grace.

If we are disloyal to fundamental spiritual presuppositions, little is gained by, or added to, our teaching. We may just as well spend our lives as schoolteachers in the world. Reflection upon the last moments of our lives, should remind us that the justification for dedicated teaching is that it flows from interior charity, and is, hence, an apostolic activity, an extension of that charity built by the interior life.

When a person spends most of the day presiding over a classroom, another temptation, the temptation of self-importance and proud authoritarianism can be most seductive. Because authority is a cardinal principle, a teaching necessity, how easily do we expand that authority and our own importance; and how effortlessly do the four walls of the classroom soon expand to the four winds. All the world is his or her classroom can quite unconsciously become the schoolteacher's version of the saying, "All the world's his oyster." Death makes us realize, however, that the four winds will sometimes cease, that our classroom walls will be one day contracted to the narrow confines of a simple coffin. Meditation, such as this, soon neutralizes or eliminates the allurement to self-importance and forces upon us an awfully realistic humility.

This humility constitutes a warning, too, that, as his sinful creatures, we owe God acts of reparation. Because we are so busily preoccupied with our workaday concerns, it is difficult, unless some special, forceful reminder presses us, to keep ourselves imbued with any spirit of reparation. Simulation of the atmosphere of life's last moment implants in the soul sincere and fruitful feelings of repentance. If there is any time when we will realize this need, it is at the time of death. Our efforts to foresee and savor that moment gain for us—to be utilized when we can do something about it—a true spirit of repentance.

Reparation, in truth, goes against the grain of fallen human nature surrounded by the ease and luxuriousness of a modern materialistic civilization. But under the sway of the forthcoming fact of death, it becomes both feasible and practicable. Then, we become reconciled to the beneficent necessities of the spiritual life—penance, discipline, self-denial, and abnegation, the unpalatable and generally unwelcome ingredients of reparation. Consciousness of death involves consciousness of the life after death, and, in consequence, an awareness of the time we will have to spend in Purgatory. To lessen our sufferings there, we should be willing to grant the importance of reparation and wisely write off beforehand our unpaid spiritual debts.

A simple, though quite ancient spiritual aid which has served religious communities well over the centuries, is the practice of attempting to live each day as though it were to be the last, as though death would come with the sunset. The twentieth century, eager to be considered sophisticated, may be inclined to scorn this, but if the practice is received in childlike simplicity and faith, it can effectually help us to live better. Biographies of a number of the saints offer ample proof that they used it, abided by it, and were able because of it, unsophisticated though it may be, to take great steps along the road to sanctity. When we practice it in this same spirit, we may also confidently believe that similar progress will be achieved in our own lives. Its keystone, of course, remains the recognition of the importance of death.

One would need to be Pollyanna, indeed, would even have

to be unjust, to maintain that irritations inherent in the academic life simply amount to nothing. The plain fact is that at times they add up to a great deal; periodically they cast quite a pall over one's spirits. Shakespeare has lamented through the mouth of one of his characters, "How sharper than a serpent's tooth it is to have a thankless child." That sharpness remains unchanged when the thankless child is not only an ungrateful pupil with no regard for our efforts in his behalf, but one who shows instead only recurrent, unintelligible resentment and hostility. Such students exist, and they can provide the religious with deeply bitter moments. To gloss over or airily dismiss the impact of these moments, is being a little less than fair to any teacher who has to live with them.

We know that, in general, youth cooperates with a wise and veteran teacher, but despite even an amalgam of all possible good qualities in a single teacher, there are times and people who combine to indulge in insolence and in serious misconduct. Here we meet a bona fide trial. These experiences, bad enough in themselves, take on a heightened obnoxiousness should we happen at the time to be unwell because of colds, upset stomachs, or the understandable affliction of strained, overwrought nerves. Little wonder, then, that we can be almost overwhelmed with feelings about the futility of it all.

These limited, at-random samplings, serve to illustrate quite honestly some of the unpleasant realities the religious teacher occasionally faces, and they clearly establish a genuine title to sympathy. Recognition of the realities, however, does not preclude a plea that we try to place them in the context of death and eternity in an effort to make them lose much of their ability to wound us.

Any anxieties which may be troubling and confusing our lives will be noticeably softened as we prayerfully ponder death. Against the backdrop of a small unit of time, tasks that appear beyond our strength, problems that seem devoid of solution, loom gigantic and forbidding. When measured against death, however, we see that the tasks and problems must all end, must all pass away; at the moment of death, how tiny and insignificant will they appear in retrospect. Although our daily routine may be studded with irritations and hardships, would they not seem relatively easy to bear were we to contrast them with the last agony? May we not valiantly endure them now as a sound preparation for the moment of that last struggle of the departing Christian soul?

In the lives of our fellow religious behind the iron curtain, death looms daily as a very pressing reality; in their lives our current hardships would find a glad welcome, could those religious at the same time share our spiritual opportunities. How easily, amidst the blandishments of American freedom and prosperity, do we forget this plight of our fellow religious. The incontestable fact is that they have been fiercely and unmercifully persecuted; untold numbers of them have died for the faith, and still more of them will die.

A keen, lively sympathy for them can be an occasion of grace, an impetus toward holiness. To put ourselves in their stead as we meditate on death cannot fail to stimulate us to serve Christ with growing dedication. Were we in their circumstances, how very serious we would be about the slightest duty of our holy vocation, how priceless to us would be each Mass, how diligent would be our confessions, how enraptured our thanksgivings after communion. What notable progress there would be in our attention and devotion at prayer, particularly when we have the opportunity to kneel before Christ present in the tabernacle. Let us count our blessings. In the dark shadows of their tryst with death, we can easily discover much sunshine surrounding whatever we consider to be our own troubles.

From time to time failure must be found in our own lives, and it certainly should not be unexpected. What is unexpected is that we may capitulate to the failure and grow discouraged. What is failure? Can we accurately know until death has put the whole human puzzle together in a completed picture? Beyond the great divide the perspective may well be different. Perspectives alter pictures. Some of our apparent failures may prove to have been our best successes. Who but God knows the pattern of his divine plan for each human person? Leaving Calvary, the Jews and Romans mocked the failure of Christ; reversing that verdict, the centuries have confessed with bowed head, "Thou hast triumphed, O Galilean."

Such a true perspective for appraising the events of a single day or an entire life can be maintained through our devout praying of the liturgy of the Mass for the Dead. Some are disappointed on those mornings when they find that the priest is offering a requiem Mass; they would prefer to follow the Mass of the Day which they have experienced personally as more helpful to devotion and more inspiring in the development of holiness of life. No one should gainsay this admirable attachment to the liturgy of the day; it is well that the Mass of the Day is generally offered, but it would be a mistake to lose sight of the deep riches contained in the requiem liturgy.

Surely the black vestments clothing the priest and the black cloth shrouding the altar, suggest a somber, moving quality; an intangible suggestion of endless finality which somehow induces a most serious, otherworldly outlook in the hearts of the worshipers. The four last things—death, judgment, heaven, and hell—hover over us. Within the awesome aura of the requiem liturgy, frivolity and worldliness seem shallow and shabby. How freely our belief is given as the prayers of the Proper urge upon us that it is appointed once to every man to die and that after death comes the judgment. Heaven and hell loom large in that perspective. We silently yield an "amen" as the beautiful contrasts enunciated by the Preface reaffirm the wisdom of our dedication of this passing life to the enduring life after death.

Human nature, strangely enough, sometimes welcomes death. Now, we might shrink from death because we are in the fullness of our powers, in the vigor of still early life, but the day must come when those faculties will falter, when our activity will be made static in the vacuum of chronic sickness, when, in the terminology of gereatrics, we become potential debtors instead of potential donors to society—then we will confess our inadequacy. We will not shrink from death then, we will be resigned. Even the quiet hope that God will take us to himself will find articulation in our secret heart, and at the close of life, as the taper slowly sputters out and there is silent darkness, we feel contentment.

When the patriarch Jacob had grown old and feeble, he dreaded the thought of making the arduous and perilous journey into Egypt. Things changed instantly, however, when he learned that his beloved Joseph awaited him there. Then, he could not go with sufficient eagerness; no speed satisfied. Upon his arrival, Joseph descended from the royal chariot and embraced him, and Jacob spoke these words: "Now I shall die with joy because I have seen thy face." The Christian soul may wince at the perils of death's journey until he thinks of Jesus coming to meet him, to welcome him home, then he, too, feels the happy eagerness of Jacob. He remembers the words Jesus spoke to the sister of Lazarus, "I am the resurrection and the life; he who believes in me, even if he die, shall live; and whoever lives and believes in me, shall never die" (John 11:25–26).

A good indication of what will be the degree of eternal beatitude we are to enjoy in the next life is our possession in this life of the theological virtue of charity. Meditation upon death should help us to increase this charity. Sad as the thought may momentarily be, we must admit the inevitable eventuality, that at one time either we will gather about the grave of our fellow religious, or they will gather about ours. At that moment how painful will be the remembrance of any past unkindness on our part, how bitter the remorse for any help, ungiven, that we might have offered to those of our family in religion. How minute then will seem the suspected injury once felt so keenly, how infinitesimal the alleged fault which once provoked us so. In some communities it is the custom during November, the month of the poor souls, for each religious to pray for some particular departed soul who once lived in the community. Is it not shortsighted to wait until death? Is it not a contradiction to refuse now what is done so eagerly then? It should not require death to wring from us a kindness and charity which would be so appreciated in life. Now is the acceptable time.

While the thought of death can offer consolation to the true follower of Christ, it is not without its note of warning, either. In the Middle Ages there was a proverb: "The cowl does not make the monk," which the twentieth century might restate: "The religious habit does not in itself guarantee salvation." The religious may be prone to forget, because of the happy circumstance of being surrounded by the community's supernatural life, that the grace of final perseverance is a special gift of God. Even the most holy, as the Council of Orange stated firmly, need the constant assistance of God to persevere. Sanctifying grace does not destroy the weakness of human nature; the human person is still subjected to concupiscence. St. Peter, the one chosen by the Redeemer to strengthen and to lead all others, realized this. From the poignance of personal misfortune, how truthfully could he warn us, "Be sober, be watchful! For your adversary the devil, as a roaring lion, goes about seeking someone to devour" (I Pet. 5:8). No one of us can prearrange the circumstances which will surround the moment of our death. No one of us, without a special revelation from God, can be sure of the gift of final perseverance.

In the circumstances of current-day events, we would be rash indeed to act as though we had some guarantee that death would overtake us only in the far distant future. To live, as presently we do, in an age of atomic and hydrogen bombs, daily to drink in the frightening atmosphere of new threats from hostile nations, repeatedly to find newspaper headlines telling of brinks of war, compels any thinking person to be mindful of the reality of death. Science and history have forced death to the forefront of today's world stage. Hopefully, deaths of this sort may never eventuate; it seems unthinkable that they should. But hard facts certainly present them as a possibility not to be ignored. We ought daily to beseech God's mercy, so that whenever death does strike, we will be well prepared, and so that in his continuing goodness to us, our Heavenly Father may vouchsafe the gift of final perseverance.

Among the posts that can be given to a priest is that of chaplain to the State Prison. Often, chaplains testify that their hardest duty is to walk "the last mile" with a criminal condemned to die. As they strive to console the doomed man and to prepare his soul for its departure from this life, they grasp intensely what a very horrible thing can be the death of a single human being. That death, until the tightly tense instant of execution is swiftly over, grips the other prisoners in grim fear:

> Like things of stone in a valley lone,
> Quiet they sat and dumb:
> But each man's heart beat thick and quick
> Like a madman on a drum.

In his *Ballad of Reading Gaol,* Oscar Wilde continues with poetic exaggeration, but an exaggeration capturing what can be the terror of death:

> There is no chapel on the day
> On which they hang a man:
> The chaplain's heart is far too sick,
> Or his face is far too wan,
> Or there is that written in his eyes
> Which none should look upon.

But death can be a beautiful thing, too. For the religious, who has served God well, it should be beautiful. Nowhere has the death of a religious been more tellingly described than in the famous letter of St. Cuthbert wherein he pictures the death of Bede. The beloved father of the monastery, Cuthbert's letter stated, had been slowly sinking; his weakness was more apparent and his speech grew labored, yet he was calmly cheerful. He went about his work of teaching and continued to dictate his translation of the Gospel of St. John. In a playful fashion, he urged the novices to be quick to learn, for he knew not how long he had to live. At the beginning of the day on which he was finally to die, his scribe told him there was still one more chapter left to translate. Bede answered, "Take thy pen and write quickly." At the ninth hour Bede asked the priests of the monastery to assemble around his bedside. Bede then made his good-bys, giving to each something of the little treasures he had preserved round about him. "I have lived long," he recalled, "and my merciful Judge has well disposed my life. The time of my departure is at hand, for my soul longs to behold the Christ, my King, in his beauty."

Now, as the evening grew dark, and his scribe alone remained, he worked heroically that he might finish. The novice spoke: "There is still one sentence, dear master, which is not written down." Bede answered, "Well then, write it." For a space the pen continued on. "Now it is finished," sighed the boy. "Well thou hast spoken truth," replied the saint, "it is finished. Take my head into your hands, for it much delighteth me to sit opposite the holy place where I used to pray, that so sitting I may call upon my Father." And thus upon the floor of his cell, singing "Glory be to the Father, and to the Son, and to the Holy Ghost," he breathed his last breath.

If we wish a death like that of St. Bede, the exemplary teaching religious, we shall have to choose also Bede's life with its mortification and sacrifice. Today, it is especially necessary that religious live a life of self-denial, self-abnegation; they alone build up in our spirits an immunity to the plague of widespread and enticing temptations which seek to destroy our vocations. Yet, a life of self-sacrifice has meaning only in death. Many in the world laugh at such a life, because of what they think of death. For them, the body simply turns to dust; that is all; there is nothing more. For all practical purposes, the worldly minded subscribe to materialism and see only earth. The saint and the aspirant-saint, the religious, see earth, but heaven too, and the road marked "self-sacrifice," which Christ has traveled, leading there. Theirs is an intense preoccupation with the supernatural; they fulfill the hope, voiced by Pope Pius XII in defining the dogma of the Assumption of the Blessed Virgin, that we "see clearly to what a lofty goal our bodies and souls are destined."

This embraces the whole vision, the true Christian outlook. The Trinity, the Holy Family, the angels, the saints, our predecessors in religious life—all make up our world and are as real as the people we actually see about us. Only for a while does life hold up a thin curtain of separation; at death we are all united for the happy eternity of heaven. Arnold Lunn writes: "The saint wears his 'muddy vesture' with a difference, and hears the harmony to which grosser ears are deaf. To the ordinary Christian, God is a belief; to the saint, a lover. The saint walks by sight where others walk by faith. He has seen the spirit of God moving on the face of the waters, and from that moment the common round has been transformed."

How marvelous is Christian death when the religious views it with the vision of the saint. How consoling to such a religious the last earthly prayer her ears will hear:

Depart, O Christian soul, out of this miserable world, in the name of God the Father Almighty, who created thee; in the name of Jesus Christ the Son of the Living God, who suffered for thee; in the name of the Holy Ghost, who sanctified thee; in the name of the glorious and holy Mother of God, the Blessed Virgin Mary; in the name of Blessed Joseph, the illustrious spouse of the Blessed Virgin; in the name of the Angels, Archangels, Thrones, Dominations, Principalities, Hosts, Cherubim and Seraphim; in the name of the patriarchs and prophets, of the holy martyrs and confessors, of the holy virgins and of all the saints of God; let thy place be this day in peace, and thy abode in holy Sion: through the same Christ our Lord. Amen.

8

Interior Trials, Their Nature and Purpose

TERMS SUCH AS DARKNESS OF MIND, ARIDITY, IN-
sensibility of heart, generally grouped together as interior trials,
are legitimate entries in any lexicon of the spiritual life. They
correspond to significant realities in the lives of souls seriously
striving after perfection. Each individual soul need not encounter
all of them, but certainly, at one time or another, the zealous
religious will experience some interior trials. Whatever their
aspects, whatever their dimension, we must expect them as our
lot.

Spiritual reading, perhaps, has not sufficiently prepared us
for these experiences. Saints' lives, which we enjoy and from
which we drink inspiration, describe the role played by interior
trials in the sanctification of their subjects. Unfortunately—in a
sense—so great were those saints, so correspondingly Promethean
their trials, we find little that resembles the prosaic difficulties of
our own lives. In the same fashion, many ascetical treatises fail
to take sufficient cognizance of the way that interior trials, at
least in our own lives, are often closely blended with our daily
tasks and our personalities. In brief, spiritual reading rarely presents these trials "cut down to our own size" and in the ordinary

perspective of the workaday world of the religious. We are left like the child who, while standing on Thirty-fourth Street in New York City, admired the vast eminence of the Empire State Building, yet later failed to realize that a table-scale model of the Empire State represented the same building. We do not realize, because of the contrastingly meager dimensions of our own aridities, that what is happening to us spiritually may be quite similar to what has happened to the saints.

Usually, there is a further complication; under the siege of a particular trial, we are seldom able to measure things with calm objectivity; our reactions easily become emotional. Precisely because of their almost overwhelming impact, trials sometimes leave us not quite ourselves. Ordinary resources of strength seem missing and accustomed self-possession impaired. This can even be physical. To bear a wearisome, painful sickness while faithfully fulfilling the regular teaching day, has measurably weakening and depressing effects. Should sickness mount to the point that we are left entirely bed-ridden, concentration, prayerfulness, sense of humor, and so forth, are almost drained from us. Thus, the prosaic and the external can culminate in interior trials when our resistance is at a low ebb.

Even hardships less drastic and less physical can inflict similar results. It could happen that a religious is dismissed from an academic post of honor and importance. Possibly no reason is given for her removal, nor is any justifying circumstance apparent. This can be a dreadful blow, just as shattering as a physical catastrophe.

An eventuality of this nature is surely rare, and in time an understandable explanation is usually provided. Going further down the scales, however, we know that appointments can occasionally be complete surprises and constitute severe crosses. Undoubtedly, we want to do what we can to accept them with good grace and to serve well in the particular capacity enjoined. But this does not erase the fierce psychological struggle churning within the soul; even fine holy people can be terribly disturbed both mentally and spiritually at the beginning of the effort of adjustment. Here again, the onset of very real interior trial can develop quite naturally, and so forcefully that our counterattack begins at a disadvantage.

Other trials, less sensational in nature and not nearly as inundating in effect, can, nonetheless, substantially disturb the person who must meet them; to the extent at least that the personality does not function as smoothly or as efficiently as it does generally. One who has been treated unkindly, even with bitter uncharity, by another religious, will find, under the duress of such treatment, that it is almost impossible to see things with complete detachment and retain a cold, disinterested objectivity. Such things are emotionally charged; flesh and blood acutely feels them. So it is when severe conflicts arise between teacher and students; a kind of undeclared war with bad feelings contaminates the air from beginning to end of class. Such happenings give rise within the soul to genuine, if not heroic, interior trials.

Very strong temptations can likewise initiate difficult trials. A little more is envisaged here than the ordinary temptations most of us experience periodically. Grave temptations constitute a veritable fifth column within us, attacking our senses, our thinking, our emotional stability. We try to combat them, but as they intensify, as figuratively the struggle finds us bloody and bowed, our calmness, our steadfastness, our mental keenness, are sorely tried. Factually, these, and many other examples which could be marshaled, induce difficult interior trials while simultaneously taking their toll of us. As we carry on the encounter, it is hard to do so as the fresh, poised, confident individual we are apart from them.

In our lives the beginnings of aridity, or intermittent periods of aridity, can arise because of routine. Routine, with its wearying and stifling consequence, can gain the upper hand. Youngsters in institutions, adults in army or factory, make plain their constant bewailment of routine. Necessarily, in the clockwork regime of the religious community there is even greater routine.

Here, too, the reaction can become, from time to time, a feeling of being weary of the same things, of having had enough of routine. Natural as is the genesis of this reaction, nonetheless, it can provide the gateway to aridity. God causes interior trials and sends them to the soul in accordance with his divine purposes. His providence utilizes all things, and may permit such simple occasions and natural reactions to develop into prolonged interior trials.

When this is his plan for a particular religious, then darkness gradually seeps into every corner of the soul; a feeling develops that life has somehow closed in upon her. The sacramental life, prayer, mortification, the exercise of virtue—all previously a routine of inspiration—appear now to lose that inspiring quality. Instead of the customary prompt, glad rising to offer another day of praise to God, she frowns at the thought of having to face the day's round of hardships. Not only does meditation fail to raise the heart on high; its moments tick slowly, aimlessly. At other times, how eagerly was the Mass awaited; now it seems almost a cold, rubrical pattern to be "gotten through." Even communion, which generally had been found so rewarding, strikes no spark from the aches shored up around the heart. So it goes; devoid of all consolation, the day limps along. As she faces the burdens and the heats, the religious asks herself: Where has my strength fled?

In community life trials can come from others and from ourselves; and both can be severe. As a rule, when people in the outside world are congenitally incompatible, they can charitably remain at arm's length. For religious, who live in the most compact of worlds, that is not possible, and the situation can be quite difficult. Even more difficult are trials that come from ourselves; they too have added intensity because of the context of a compact community world. At times things appear out of balance, because we ourselves have lost a little of our own sense of equilibrium. We are weighed down by the feeling of personal inadequacy; outside us, all is well, but things seem wrong inside.

Those who lack a buoyant disposition—the over-sensitive on the occasion of disappointment or rebuff, and similar temperaments in the face of kindred difficulties—easily fall victim.

While these difficulties may grow out of and be conditioned by the personality, again the unfathomable ways of God may permit them to lead to an arduous interior trial, that the soul may be purified. Under the pressures of such an interior trial we are inclined to contrast almost scornfully our past, ambitious, spiritual desires with accomplishments we now sadly conclude to be banal. What in the past we triumphantly regarded as our successes, now ring with a sound apparently hollow and false. This disappointment with self grows particularly keen when we dwell upon our shortcomings and upon our sins, past and present. As we reach out reassuringly to touch our virtues, they evade our grasp; a painful anxiety stirs increasingly within us; our helplessness drives a wedge, at least so we fear, between our sinful selves and an all-good God.

This serves to illustrate helpfully the manner in which such experiences can benefit us, how under God and our own perseverance, they can become a vehicle of valuable spiritual advancement. Of necessity, when undergoing such trials we are limited to the way of humility. The harsh realities of our own helplessness, so tellingly experienced, drives this home to us. The weakness and insufficiency of self forces us to place all our aspirations in the hands of God, asking his help, realizing that otherwise we cannot successfully ride out an enveloping oppressive wave. Only then can one swim out to more difficult landmarks. We are brought closer to God and we increase our dependence on him and his graces. Not only in practice is this true, but, of greater value, we gain the important conviction that it is theoretically necessary for us to ask God's aid even beyond the present moment; such dependence is the perpetual cornerstone of our spiritual efforts and our hopes for spiritual progress.

In addition to the acceptance of humility, a basic foundation of strong faith is erected in the soul. This follows quite logically from our lack of consolations, our dissatisfaction with self. Again, we accept this as more than a momentary practical need; strong faith, as we are enlightened by our experience of trial, is seen to be a staple of asceticism which cannot with impunity be taken for granted or undervalued. We resolve that we must concern ourself with the nourishment and strengthening of our faith, for that faith must leaven all future higher ascetical efforts. As a result, much of our effort is simplified, is reduced to the cardinal principle of doing God's will, of finding out what that will appears to be, and then accepting it as the over-all principle to which everything else that we do must be subordinate. This attitude, firm and universally applied, arms us with a spiritual possession utterly invaluable to us; true holiness, without full allegiance to the subjection of self to God's will, could never be begun nor advanced.

Another vestibule to interior trial, found especially in the lives of religious dedicated to teaching work, is the periodic sense of a lack of professional achievement. During this trial, it seems that we pour out both mind and heart to students who apparently cannot learn or have taken a secret oath not to. The depression and frustration attendant upon this discovery can quite easily and unobtrusively mushroom like an atomic cloud, casting a deadly pall over all our efforts, our spiritual efforts included. In his divine wisdom, God can permit a genuine trial to eventuate from these beginnings. Progressively, even our inner consciousness seems shrouded in darkness. Such becomes our state of mind that, as multiplying temptations continue to harass us, we must grope to convince ourselves we have resisted those temptations sufficiently well. We find it hard to hold on to the assurance that God has not forsaken our efforts.

Here, as in many of these interior trials, the religious does not experience all of the classic symptoms of either aridity, or insensibility of heart, or darkness of mind. Often, there is a blend. More often, the average religious experiences only relatively light beginnings, partial manifestations of such trials; in

their fullness, these are most grave purifications reserved for the
heroic soul. Be the extent great or small, however, these phenomena are quite properly categorized as interior trials, and that
despite the fact they can develop very naturally from the everyday affairs of our duties or the normal bent of our personalities.

If trials must exist we quite naturally ask, what is to be done
about them? Before all else, we must have the ability to recognize such experiences for what they are, namely, spiritual trials.
This is most important. When we acknowledge interior trials as
an integral part of our spiritual life, it is that much easier to
learn to live with them.

The consequences of a doctor's wrong diagnosis of a patient's ailment are, of course, very dire; the resultant harm is
self-evident. While not as readily observable, our failure to di-
agnose interior trials for what they are, can be just as harmful in
the spiritual order as was the doctor's error in the physical order.

It is opportune, then, to note here the importance of the
role of a spiritual director. If he is skilled and experienced, he
can be of the greatest help through his early recognition of what
is the true situation of soul. The importance is underscored, too,
of our practice of regular confession. That practice throws light
upon our trials, makes them more quickly identifiable. It immediately gives the proper context for evaluating the symptoms
and for appraising the plan of meeting these trials.

Since interior trials do not usually crop up overnight, nor
take unprecedented outlines, this liaison with spiritual director
or confessor represents a great asset to us at such times. In this
way, the trials are rather matter-of-factly assimilated into an almost expected routine and dealt with as naturally as we would
deal with any other problems.

Two courses must be strenuously avoided. First, we should
never permit these trials to be the occasion for a period of marking time spiritually. This amounts to capitulation, and is the
mark of the religious tyro. Veteran religious quietly ride out the

storm. Continuing unabated their vigorous pursuit of perfection, they steadily store up valuable spiritual gains.

How unreasonable, actually, to do otherwise. Any sincere religious has had to be conscientious about the need for, and the practice of, mortification. At different times, presumably, mortifications have been sought out. But seeking them and choosing them can be a ticklish affair requiring the greatest prudence. Yet, trials confront us with very real mortification, and as we have not sought them but rather they have sought us, there can be no question of any unconscious self-seeking nor any worry about whether or not they possess a proper aptness for our soul.

Our prayers, too, must have included the petition that, under God's grace, we would be able to move steadily along the path of spiritual progress. Do we not find in interior trials our answer to such petitions? How can our petitions be sincere, if, when the means are offered to us, instead of employing them, we sit gazing idly at them, stolidly waiting for them to disappear? We must make ourselves realize such times as ripe for vigorous action. Otherwise our desire for holiness resembles St. Augustine's petition for chastity. He asked it of God, but in his early days would subjoin the qualification, "not yet, O Lord." Interior trials call for a certain spiritual maturity and are at the same time a test of that maturity. The potency which is in the soul must be converted to act, as with quiet, confident wisdom we recognize and exploit a spiritual opportunity, which leads on to the building of yet statelier mansions in the soul.

A second mistake is to panic or tighten up under the stress of trial. If, as a teacher, you have trained public speakers, directed plays, or coached athletic teams, you can probably recall how you attempted to get your students to relax and retain their poise. You warned them that tenseness would mar the flexibility and smooth efficacy of performance. Any similar tightness of the soul under duress, likewise mars the perfection of our spiritual performance.

Panic here may be a giveaway; a confession that we lack the necessary greatness of soul to proceed further spiritually, that for us the heights will never be more than an unattainable mirage. At this point, we are face to face with the need of firmly established control over our faculties; the intellect must be in command; the will has to be a force sufficiently trained and powerful enough to carry out its proper domination over imaginings and fears which attempt to sabotage our hope of holiness. We need also a solid grasp of the roles of God and self in the ascetical life. Self follows God's graces; our weakness does not carry the day, it leans confidently and trustfully upon his strength. God's presence within us through grace becomes an increasingly adverted-to reality, both all-powerful and all-good, attracting us to him more and more; amidst darkness, he is our only light. When such faith-generated insight hardens to practical conviction, it is impossible for panic to trouble the soul.

Before continuing our discussion, a precaution should be inserted here: the phenomena described above as the material of interior trials can sometimes be due to physical ill health—for example, exhaustion or mental ill health. Sometimes, too, unfortunately, they can be due to spiritual laxity. If the mind deliberately concentrates on worldly pleasures and the will, neglectful of duty, is attached to sinful habits—that is plainly the fostered evil of tepidity.

To enable us to distinguish genuine interior trials from tepidity and laxity, ascetical writers, following St. John of the Cross, generally offer these criteria:

1) We find no comfort in the things of God, nor in created things; the tepid are drawn to earthly pleasures.

2) The memory dwells upon God in a rather anxious fashion, because we fear we are going backwards spiritually. Tepid persons lack this earnest solicitude for the things of God.

3) When God has sent dryness as a purifying preparation for contemplation, the soul experiences an inability, at least periodically, to practice discursive prayer.

We are not concerned with effects of which either laxity or ill health is the cause. Our presumption here—and, were it otherwise, everything that follows would be downright misleading—is that the soul involved in these interior trials has been devoted to duty, has vigorously practiced virtue, and has been dominated by a burning love of God. To that soul we turn our attention now.

The religious who experience genuine interior trials, should keep foremost in her consciousness one encouraging note: the realization that she can profit from them. Trials are not evil in themselves; properly handled, they make possible invaluable spiritual advancement. They effect, under God, a purgation of soul; a necessary clearing of the path which leads to greater progress. Because they ready us for lofty spirituality, such trials, in a way, should be matter for rejoicing. Some souls may always remain untroubled and undisturbed, but untroubled and undisturbed on a lower spiritual level. Should our lot embrace these interior trials, we ought to harken to the words of Jeremias: "Cease your cries of mourning, wipe the tears from your eyes. The sorrow you have shown shall have its reward, says the Lord" (Jer. 31:16).

Perhaps this same thought can be brought home by the traditional story, found in the writings of Archbishop Martinez of Mexico, about a farmer who besought God to allow the rains, the sun, and all the elements to be subject to his desires, so that there would be no storms. "God granted this to him, and the farmer said: Now I need rain, and it rained; now sun, and the sun came out resplendently. And, in the end, after a whole year in spite of those extraordinary powers that had been granted him, the harvest was lost.

" 'Lord,' the farmer then said, 'what happened?'

" 'You besought everything,' our Lord answered him, 'and everything was granted you. But you did not ask for storms, and storms are necessary that the seed may germinate and develop' "
(*Secrets of the Interior Life*, p. 105). We, too, need storms in

our spiritual life; we need them particularly when there has been previously only sunshine.

When our spiritual pilgrimage began, we marshaled our efforts energetically and we detached ourselves from created things, from the ways and pleasures of the world. When gently and sweetly God's grace drew us from these attractions, consolations bestrewed our path. Prayer and devotion held a pleasant charm. Tasks moved along effortlessly. Doubtless, this could continue right on to perfection, did God so wish. Often, however, it is quite otherwise; the pattern of divine providence decrees that the next upward step of the soul is to be marked by interior trials. St. Teresa of Spain, who knew these steps well, expressed it in this way: "Those whom he greatly loves God leads by way of trial, and the dearer they are to him the greater the trials he sends . . ." (*The Way of Perfection*, p. 85). Much of our past delight in virtue and devotion may have leaned heavily on sweetness and consolation. Now the moment has come to serve God without the props of sentiment, to become detached from self.

In the past we may have tended to attribute all progress to our personal efforts; grandiose notions of accomplishment were secretly gaining ground within us. Perhaps, subconsciously, we began to look down on others. Here was sabotage undermining our spirituality. "There are impediments to union with him which our sight is too feeble to discern and our good will powerless to remove" (Graham, *The Love of God*, p. 172). Because of our trials a more salutary perspective is instilled; the soul learns its shortcomings only too well; imperfections, once glossed over, are brought to light. Father Tanquery uses this example: "When we examine a glass of water with the naked eye, we see nothing to startle us; but if we look at the same water through the microscope, we shudder at the sight of the germs we now discover." In this state of soul, present and past sins take on a graver aspect; repentance and compunction become deep preoccupations, and humility is, we might say, forced upon us. Our inflated self-esteem dies, but it dies hard. "I will both play and make myself meaner than I have done: and I will be little in my own eyes . . ." (II Kgs. 6:22).

A fundamental requisite in practicing penance and reparation is motivation. Interior trials, which expose our faults and imperfections, supply such motivation. They show us graphically that penance and reparation is imperative for spiritual progress. By means of these trials God's goodness favors us with so privileged an insight into self that we are able to accept penance and to offer reparation.

A serviceable test of the purity of our motivation is provided in our reactions to interior trials. Should our desire for perfection be a spotted one, stemming from self-love, we betray that fact in time of interior trials. Such motivation will be uncovered in our anxieties and agitation, our troubled over-eagerness. The pursuit of perfection inspired by divine love has only the wish to do God's will, and is quite content to suffer whatever darkness or aridities he has sent. All else is rightly considered but a means; for example, consolations at one time, desolations at another. Efforts that are marked by consolations are not necessarily more pleasing to Christ. What counts is not the accidentals of our sentiments, but the essence—our effective will, determined to act in harmony with the will of God. Permitting these trials to get the better of us, succumbing to a dark melancholia, may well be the defense mechanism of transparent self-love, seeking escape from the rigors of purification.

When this all-absorbing dedication to the will of God becomes the guiding compass of our entire spiritual effort, we draw closer to Christ, our exemplar. In times of trials or joys, we need to say, as he did: "My food is to do the will of him who sent me, to accomplish his work" (John 4:34). The whole life of Christ was lived for the Father and in obedience to the Father's will—from his birth in the stable at Bethlehem in exact fulfillment of the prophecies, to his final accomplishment (he humbled himself, becoming obedient unto death) on Calvary, when life itself was expressly offered in those beautiful words, "Father, into thy hands I commend my spirit." Our acceptance of a religious vocation also says in effect, "Father, into thy hands I commend my spirit." In times of trial, above all other times, we must live that pledge loyally.

When our confidence is rooted in God and not in ourselves, we become strong, because we partake of his strength. Self, weak and unpredictable, offers no assurance. During interior trials we ought to be as little children and cast all our cares upon the Lord. Otherwise, we will be frustrated in our attempts to judge interior trials, which properly belong to the order of eternity and are subject to eternal designs. Our American temperament, traditionally go-getting and highly sensitive to results, needs to be most wary in times of interior trial. Everything, we must remind ourselves, happens between self and God; this is fundamental, all other aspects of created things are peripheral. Success or failure, consolation of desolation, plaudits or disesteem, all are but means to perfect our relationship with God. A spirit of holy abandonment, then, gives the essential answer to interior trials. How good we are, or how well we have done, is not the main concern, for the basis of our trustful abandonment rests on God; his goodness and love are eternally ready to aid us.

This trust must be reflected especially in our prayer. Although prayer may seem ineffectual, we must not lessen or abandon it. God often employs interior trials to open up new, beautiful, far-reaching vistas of contemplation. Through their purifying influence, accepted in complete resignation, we are malleable clay in the hands of the divine Potter, perfectly docile to the inspirations of his Holy Spirit. As a more intimate union with the Creator unfolds, we begin to understand that his way for us, as for his Son, is the way of crucified love. May there burn in our hearts the joyful hope of those whose interior trials were not nearly as great as their sanctity:

> Having no light nor guide
> Excepting that which burned within my heart,

Which lit my way
More safely than the glare of noon-day sun
To where, expectant,
He waited for me who doth know me well,
Where none appeared but he.

(St. John of the Cross)

9

Poverty, from
Creature to Creator

SEEKING TO ACQUIRE A MASTERY OF LOGIC IN
the philosophy course, college students become familiar with
many modes of argumentation, and find among them one called
the *argumentum ad absurdum*. This particular argument endeavors to demonstrate the truth of a position by attacking the
opposite position and showing its absurdities. This approach
may be a good way to begin any discussion of poverty; namely,
to demonstrate on the level of common sense, through the
argumentum ad absurdum, how pitiful and confusing a place
the religious community would be, were it minus its vow of
poverty.

One member of a community may revel in wearing a habit
of silk, while another slinks about in one of sackcloth. A third
may require a battery of morning papers to scan business reactions and plot the buying and selling of valuable stock holdings.
The sister whose slender means affords only the subway, may
find it quite difficult to secure a traveling companion; the proud
possessor of a shining red Cadillac may find it too easy. Dinner
may find the ecstatic features of one devouring steak next to the
morose grimaces of one who could obtain only hash. Lazarus,

122

rooming next to Dives, may have to beseech crumbs from that opulence. Take away poverty and you will find a strange situation, that of a community doomed to become an economic Tower of Babel. Surely, peace and harmony and happiness would be strangers to such a motley group.

On the other hand, the vow of poverty, genuinely loved and reverenced, offers the means of a wonderful life together. A life that holds all things in common is a gracious life, one that is literally grace-giving. The past history of the world bears sad witness of how emphasis on "mine" separates people into strife; nothing unites as does the pronoun "ours." Having all things in common truly makes a place home, really enfolds us in a family. In the religious community which has become both family and home to its members, we discover that possession in common is a powerful means of fostering authentic, helpful affection.

In offering a way of life that is truly gracious in the best sense, the religious community exposes a number of fallacious notions widely propagated by current "snob" advertising. Gracious living has become equated with costly silver plate, sensualized gourmand appetites, expensive clothing, and flashing jewelry. Such frills, mere externals, have received constant stress; stress of a sort that has been generally inimical to the ideal of poverty. Wise allegiance to poverty is quite compatible with the inner spirit, and constitutes genuine gracious living. Authentic good manners—in contrast to those artificialities, the by-product of an awkward, self-conscious snobbery—flow naturally and effortlessly from kindliness and unselfishness generated by a true devotion to poverty.

Sound community spirit can boast an admirable *savoir-faire*, one prompted by a Christlike sensitivity to the tastes and desires of others; and from it there follows a *noblesse oblige* of the highest caliber. It recognizes the other person, any other person, to be a sister of Christ, our Brother, and the invaluable object of his redemptive blood. Those who understand fully the firm and beautiful bond of religious sisterhood live their lives in conformity with the best Christian graciousness. The ascetical milieu of the religious community leads to consummate graciousness—the spiritual perfection of personality and activity—inevitably the goal of those *ex professo* seeking union with God.

Such lofty concepts, however, do not obligate the religious to any blind obtuseness or blithe belief that everything on the horizon is always and in every way ideal. Quite realistically, there is room for a sisterly awareness of each other's faults, with an accompanying awareness of one's own. Rather than being a harbinger of carping criticism or bland uncharity, such an awareness can shield sore spots in the make-up of others and bring about a delicate buoying up of those who may otherwise grow disheartened and founder. Gracious living quietly passes over the inconsequential gaffes and bears patiently the irritations of light faults, both of which inevitably are met within any congress of human beings. Humility and charity gracefully combine to realize that all of the sisters occupy a common testing ground and face the same spiritual struggle; the exigencies of poverty remind us of this. Sharing the same difficulties of poverty makes it easier for each one to sense the trials of other sisters and sympathize with them.

Life together with the give and take of possessions in common, inherently contains a wonderful training—like that which is part and parcel of family life when a number of children must make a little go a long way. Members of such a family, if for no other reason than self-preservation, are forced to be considerate of each other. Should charitable courteousness be missing, strife remains the only alternative. When one member yields to flagrant selfishness, the group is aware of it; this makes life seem a continuing court-martial to the guilty imagination of the offender. Sad experience teaches, should no other way prevail, that unselfishness has to be accepted simply as a necessary virtue.

Merely to live in an honest and friendly community rubs off

the edges of too high-grained a sensitivity. Only egotism born of terribly stubborn obtuseness survives. Trials undergone in common by a spiritually healthy community promote a life of good-natured repartee; since everyone belongs equally, everyone is greatly concerned about everyone else, about all that happens, and about the aggregate welfare. There is born, as time goes on, an over-all spirit of fun and joy, the only serviceable lubricant for the whole process of family life, including religious family life.

Individual possessions too often create a combativeness nurtured in competition. Possessions which are mine can gradually become an extension of the ego; consciously or subconsciously, I am closely associated with them. Protective, defensive attitudes are generated; such possessions repeatedly interfere with the free flow of personal relations. I begin to see not only thou, but thine; then, to institute comparisons between thine and mine, and taste triumph or envy. Individual possessions thus become fences separating human beings, while those held in common draw people together.

How easy to relax among those we trust. We feel no need for caginess of speech, no need to adopt any artificial pose, no need for any allaying armor of suspicious self-protection. Quietly and contentedly one can be one's self with others who are truly what they seem. How helpful, consequently, is the observance of poverty to those who genuinely desire to be true sisters to each other. The burdens of life grow lighter because many joined shoulders support them. Problems are never insoluble when they flow from understood and appreciated common concerns. Sincere sympathy abounds because each in turn comes to understand the difficulties which others experience. A combined strength vanquishes that which may destroy an isolated weakness.

Community joy and fun can be the best joy and fun precisely because it is in common; those outside this circle cannot possibly find joy, for only those who belong to the household and share common hardships earn the right and the ability to appreciate the joys of a religious community. Much of this happiness has a real relationship to the vow of poverty.

Many legions of people living in the world, were the truth known, would admit feelings of weary futility in their apparently never-ceasing daily strife for possessions. Strife for increased possessions has pitted them against their fellows with whom they have no real quarrel. Probably they would prefer to say plainly to each other, "Let us forget the possessions, rather let us live in peace and friendship."

And saddest of all, when the total earthly score is finally added up, what disappointments and dissatisfactions. In the ultimate summing up, what does it all mean, what has been accomplished? Overconcern with possessions has shut out the more valuable things in life; the loss of higher values has been much greater than the possessions which have usurped their place. How disillusioning the realization, "You can't take it with you," when an open grave threatens; and because of what you cannot take, many things that are necessary are missing.

Equality as effected by the vow of poverty seems to be an indispensable condition of kinship. Even modern writers who write on friendship still recall Cicero's *De Amicitia*, and they continue to honor as true his dictum that friendship either finds, or makes, equals. In no other way can each member of the community enjoy the happy conviction and pleasant feeling of completely "belonging." Those living in a community are not in a position to appreciate the awful, aching loneliness to be found in the world; the bleak despair of a surprising number of people, quite successful people included, who feel that they have no group, no place to which they truly belong. Loneliness of this sort can be a gnawing interior cancer. We should treasure that common life of which poverty is the architect, for poverty can build into our community a true *esprit de corps*.

How often does one hear in conversations and read in books and magazines utterly false notions about poverty; indeed many people proclaim poverty the worst of evils. A percentage of the population believes that they would be happy simply in the ownership of vast possessions. This is far from the truth. Certainly, the possession of evil things does not bring happiness, nor does happiness consist solely in the good and pleasant possessions of this earth. In the economic warfare which marks life, the fear and possibility of losing such possessions lurks always near.

When a man's possessions have been ill-gotten, they can never bring true peace and happiness, for he will find conscience an ever-gnawing worm. If the fraud which gained them becomes known, he is conscious or suspicious of the bitterness of others toward him. Even if the fraud be unknown, fear that his secret will out, weighs him down with pangs of remorse; he is haunted by the phantasm of his chicanery about to be discovered, his true self exposed, his dreadful disgrace before all, even those who had been called friends—friends, but upon what false pretenses.

So deep-rooted and far-reaching are such fears, all of life grows into a pretense, a game of acting out a deceitful part in a play that is known to be untrue. Should he succeed in carrying out the masquerade, it brings little satisfaction. Yet detection, the other horn of the dilemma, is too shameful to contemplate.

Even an abundance of possessions honorably come by, do not offer an unfailing guarantee of true happiness. This very realization, certainly for most of the members of a religious community, constitutes a contributory motive leading to the religious life. Such a realization may not have been fully spelled out, but there lurked in our hearts at least a latent awareness that life comprises more than luxuries, houses, cars, and all the other things that money makes possible. The religious vocation is often preceded by some taste of these things—at times even a cloying superabundance—then, one feels that something more is needed for happiness.

Our novitiate with its intense spiritual training gave us, as it were, the words for these previous feelings; the reasonings and the faith behind what had already seemed to us to be true. We saw with surety that the goods of this world could never of themselves satisfy, and for a quite fundamental reason: the very nature of the human being as created by the hand of God. What the soul craves is an absolute good, a good without any drawbacks, limitations, or imperfections. Such requisites, of course, can never be verified in any of the possessions of this earth. Always, something is lacking, some corner in the human heart ever remains unfilled. In St. Augustine's warm, human terms: "Thou hast made us for thyself, O Lord, and our hearts are restless until they rest in thee." Or, reduced to strict scholasticism: created in the image and likeness of God, our immortal soul possesses as its highest faculties intellect and will whose objects are truth and goodness; perfect surcease is found only in God, who alone is all Truth and Goodness itself. Our happiness, or anyone else's definitive happiness—to state it succinctly—can consist only in knowing and loving God.

How consoling all this should be. It means that by virtue of our state of life we are already oriented to complete happiness; this is the basis for seeking to develop the religious vocation. Knowing God and loving him rises above any ownership of possessions; it does not require affluence. Under the influence of grace, our religious life deepens this conviction, and reveals very clearly that before our own reasonings had concluded to it, the gospels had already taught it. Christ himself, warned us that God may say, when worldly possessions are piled up; "Thou fool, this night do they require thy soul of thee." We have wisely chosen to place our treasure where our heart is, namely, in the pursuit of spiritual riches. These riches will suffer no rust; here no moth can consume.

Having adopted a true spirit of detachment, the soul devoted to poverty seeks to see creatures as reflections of the goodness of God. Such a beautiful and sustained vision awaits the reader of Cardinal Bellarmine's treatise, *The Ascent of the Mind to God*. He writes in a tradition that is saintly and in express imitation of St. Bonaventure. Following that tradition he tells us that in his pages he has "essayed from the contemplation of creatures, to make a ladder by the which we may in some sort ascend unto God" (Preface).

Since the garden of God's creatures, this earth, was home to the Son of God, creatures received a new dimension, a relationship to Christ. He looked upon them, touched them, used them; our own use of them was thus sanctified. Through the purification of poverty we can view them with the vision of the saint; through the faith of holiness we can discern the Savior mirrored therein.

> I see his blood upon the rose
> And in the stars the glory of his eyes,
> His body gleams amid eternal snows,
> His tears fall from the skies.
> (PLUNKETT, *I See His Blood Upon the Rose*)

True happiness, St. Augustine explains in his *De Beata Vita*, consists in desiring only what conforms to virtuous duty or divine wisdom. When our happiness consists in doing God's will, we live superior to the changings of this world, independent of the vagaries of Fortune's wheel. Those who possess God are truly happy; here lies the precise function of the virtue of poverty—it helps us to possess God.

To go to God as surely and as quickly as possible, burns as a constant desire in the heart of every devout religious, and the virtue of poverty works to remove any obstacles which may prevent the fulfillment of that desire. Riches, vast possessions of material things, can erect sizeable obstacles. Affluence gives birth to attachments, and attachments make it very difficult to give one's whole heart to Christ; affluence breeds anxieties and distractions, which in turn dissipate much time and stir up much trouble; many possessions subtly engender pride and vanity. How easy for a person to become self-sufficient and superior toward others. Too many biographies repeat the trite story of men whose obsession for riches drove them to betray friends and soil their own honor.

Why do people want riches? Actually, not for the riches themselves so much as for the things riches bring. Riches mean ease, riches mean honors, riches mean power; but these things are not the goals of the religious ascetic. Ease, honors, power become spiritual boobytraps as they compete with God for our affection. Hence, the wisdom behind the vow of poverty; poverty desires to bring us close to Christ by the removal of attachments which may sidetrack us; poverty seeks to speed our progress, to help us win the spiritual race.

An old story in the *Gesta Romanorum* tells of a princess famous for her fleetness as a runner; no one in the kingdom could match her speed. According to the story, however, a wily old man challenged the maiden, and he won his race. To accomplish this feat, before the race he stuffed his cloak with all sorts of trinkets and baubles. Then, in the course of the race, he tossed them out along the roadside. Attracted by their shining colors, the damsel would stop to pick them up and admire them, and each time she came abreast, he repeated this. As a result the old man crossed the finish line while she was still admiring the trinkets. In the spiritual race we run, the world tosses out many baubles and trinkets to catch our attention, to divert us from the race. Poverty puts beyond our sight and reach the things of the world which may make us forget our pledged goal of going surely and quickly to Christ.

While without much effort we are able to admit this to be theoretically true, alas, at times the eyes of the spirit as they behold the here and now grow rather weary; Christ seems a long way distant, while the unceasing allure of the world's baubles and trinkets lies bewitchingly near. Poverty, make no mistake about it, is a hard practice; yet while we know it is hard for us, we also know it is good for us. As a sort of cathartic for the soul, a salutary spiritual medicine, we ought to welcome the practice of the virtue of poverty. When its hardships are cheerfully accepted, when despite all obstacles the virtue is diligently plied, we offer Christ a most pleasing sacrifice.

To do without things when our first inclination feels that to have them would make life so much easier, means a continual and effective mortification of the will. We do not find it easy to request the things we need or to accept periodic refusals, yet this is a good proving ground for the sincerity of our humility and the strength of our obedience. Strong religious training is effected, over the years, through discipline. Poverty serves as a sound check to excessive self-assertion, as a curt rein upon the ego, and it can produce a beautiful, unselfish charity. We must expect that, in following the crucified Master, sacrifice must water the plant of virtue. St. Francis de Sales reminds us: "To desire to be poor and not to feel any of the inconveniences of poverty, is to wish for the honor of poverty and the advantages of riches."

Window shopping undoubtedly offers a pleasant recreation when we have the opportunity for a refreshing and relaxing walk, but alas, we then feel somewhat the sting of our vow of poverty. To look at all the nice things, always so attractively displayed, perhaps to long for them subconsciously, and then to be wrenched back from pleasant daydreams to the reality of our condition of poverty, can indeed be hard.

Shopkeepers, too, sometimes sense our weakness. It is related that on one occasion one of them sought to persuade some religious to buy a certain product by stressing that it was clearly the very best. A lesson can be found in their simple, definitive reply, "But we don't use the best." It is true; we do not, and therein lies the day to day expression of poverty—being content with things that are not the best, be it clothing, food, furniture, school bags, watches, transportation, and so forth.

Privation remains constantly with us, turn which way we will in the daily routine. Our basic attitude toward poverty either becomes a nagging nuisance we would like to be rid of, or it is willingly accepted as a salutary spiritual discipline. This acceptance, of course, does not rule out moments of irritation when a particular aspect of poverty nettles us—unless, happily, we have reached an enviable degree of holiness.

There is a danger of worldliness seeping into this area of asceticism. It takes the shape of an attitude of contempt or cynicism toward those little economies which, necessarily, must be part and parcel of the practice of the vow. Here, the urbanity of the world is not helpful; we are helped instead by kinship with the humility and simplicity of the peasant. When we adopt a demanding attitude according to the standards of the world, what people would be entitled to because of their education or family background, we simply fail to live up to the higher values of the spiritual order. We should resolve the conflict by choosing to follow Christ's example.

Yet, we also must beware of the other extreme, any miserliness or meanness. This makes senseless and harsh economies an end in themselves, and can grow into a real obsession to save and hoard every possible penny. Such an approach achieves no virtue; rather it coarsens and cheapens; it brings the vow into disrepute. There can result a rather grim competition among the community members who, in resentment, vie to grab as much as possible of what commodities are available. Detachment is not fostered; rather, it is discouraged. One can apply justly the old nursery rhyme to Lady Poverty: "When she was good, she was very very good, but when she was bad, she was horrid."

A sound Christian attitude toward poverty postulates a healthful prudence and a certain generous large-mindedness. Legitimate and reasonably necessary objects ought to be granted in a matter-of-fact fashion. Surely a lofty spiritual charity should not lag behind the worldly finesse of a human-relations-minded age. And there ought to be room, too, for a happy and "heavenly" epikia. As St. Theresa of Avila remarked with inspiration to a censoriously-minded young sister: "There is also a time to eat partridges."

In a community where love of poverty reigns, a readiness and willingness to give up things, to resign them for the use of the group or the individual, will be found. Ready willingness to sacrifice is the touchstone of lofty virtue, which is neither easily achieved nor easily maintained; for whenever material things and human nature meet danger of attachment is born. Adults struggle with each other over money, small children over toys; attachments mark the seven ages of man, as the years move along from the first cry of the infant to the final silence of the grave. We can conceive attachments for the valuable things in the community, or the insignificant, small things; it is not the size that counts, the attachment reveals the deordination. Do not be tricked in this regard; beware of pledging allegiance to poverty in a general way while withholding particular exceptions, for exceptions keep outside the scope of the virtue those very attachments which have caused our faithfulness to poverty.

Somewhere in his works, St. John Chrysostom recounts that St. Sebastian on one occasion promised the Prefect of Rome, Cromatius, he would be cured if he broke all his idols. Cromatius broke all except two, his favorites. Not until those two also were broken was he cured. We ought to search our own hearts, lest idols be hidden away there which we have refused to break for the sake of poverty. Constitutions and rules of communities vary, as you know, in the specific practices of the vow. However, our sound and honest application of those particular regulations to which we are subject will guide the practice of the vow aright, welcoming whatever concessions are legitimate, accepting whatever limitations are imposed.

Nothing so arouses the suspicion and distrust of the people to whom the religious institution must minister as does the disloyalty of a community to the spirit of poverty. Great freedom of the spirit has been imparted to the representatives of Christ through their fidelity to poverty, and when, in allegiance to that poverty, they labor without self-interest their mission grows fruitful. Poverty links them to the people, especially the poor, and the people receive them in a spirit of trust, welcoming them with open, willing hearts.

God will not be less cooperative than his people. Because, through poverty, the religious community has rejected materialistic, purely natural formulae for success, God has agreed, in return, to grant supernatural success through supernatural means. Poverty proves that we have consigned our efforts to the providence of God; God will not be found wanting. When St. Francis stripped himself of this world's goods, he spoke the words: "Now can I truly say, 'Our Father who art in heaven!' " Similarly, the poverty-loving religious community, trusting in the Heavenly Father, has learned the first law of supernatural success: "Only God giveth the increase."

In our present day, with the idolatry of material goods so widespread, poverty constitutes a steadfast defense of monotheism. Not idols of clay, no matter how costly or attractive, but God alone, who is pure Spirit, must be the proper object of man's adoration. Thus has Cardinal Suhard repeatedly and beautifully reminded the French people; the whole modern world may well join in his prayer that out of the *Weltschmerz,* resultant upon man's materialistic rejection of spiritual values, there will perhaps come to the twentieth century a greater insight into the importance of the virtue of poverty.

God himself, when he dwelt on this earth, made poverty his own. Worldly calculation may have anticipated that Christ would utilize a plenitude of this world's goods to advance his kingdom. Quite plainly, that was not the view of divine Wisdom. Christ chose the hardships of the stable, the cold of the manger. The bulk of his life was spent toiling as a poor carpenter amid the surroundings of an average poor home. He made his poverty clear to his followers, before accepting their comradeship: "The foxes have holes, the birds of the air nests, but the Son of Man hath not whereon to lay his head"; their following of Christ plighted their kindred willingness to embrace that same poverty. Our own zeal and zest for poverty were wholehearted upon our entrance into religion; to permit that love of poverty to flag with the years would be a tragic mistake. That love should deepen and develop as we realize, with increasing understanding, that the external practice of the virtue has value only in the proportion that its motivating force becomes the love of God. Detachment from creatures which poverty fosters is not enough; detachment must be accompanied by a strong, positive attachment to the greatest ultimate reality, Christ himself. Poverty offers but the means, Christ is the end. When this concept of poverty dominates our thinking, our whole life joins itself more closely to Christ and flows more directly from God; God becomes the center and source of all our activity. To conclude our discussion of poverty, it is fitting to repeat the immortal tribute, our holy legacy, from the little poor man of Assisi:

> Yea! Celestial is poverty whereby all earthly and transitory things are trodden underfoot and whereby every hindrance is removed from the soul that she may be freely conjoined with the eternal God. Holy poverty maketh the soul, while yet on earth, have communion with the angels in heaven; holy poverty companioned Christ on the cross, with Christ was buried, with Christ rose again, and with Christ ascended into heaven. Holy poverty easeth the flight into heaven of those souls that love it; for it guards the armour of true humility and charity. Therefore, let us pray unto the most holy apostles of Christ, who were perfect lovers of this pearl evangelical, to obtain for us this grace from our Lord Jesus Christ, that he in his holy mercy may vouchsafe to us to grow worthy to be true lovers and followers and humble disciples of the most precious and most lovable gospel, poverty.
>
> (*Fioretti*, p. 24)

10

Temptations, Fire
for Virtue's Gold*

RICHARD II AND MACBETH, AS WELL AS OTHER
plays molded by Shakespeare's genius, picture most graphically
and dramatically how evil tendencies, if unchecked, lead straight
to vice and ultimately to human ruin. Great tragedy at times has
very small beginnings; little seeds of destruction within the human soul can slowly but surely bring forth a monstrous yield of
the cockle of evil. Especially dreadful are the consequences of
a fundamental weakness of character. This "tragic flaw," as it is
wont to be designated in the literature of dramatic criticism, or
"ruling passion" or "dominant fault," as it is termed in ascetical
writings, has spelled the undoing of even the greatest human
personages.

The Catholic Church in its timeless vision has witnessed the
processions of the mighty through history, life's greatest heroes
and life's greatest villains. Divine as it is, the Catholic Church
guides human conduct with lofty heavenly wisdom, yet in that
very heavenly wisdom, knows all too well that human kind can

---

* Before beginning, it is necessary to state that temptations against
the sixth commandment are not included among those for which certain
remedial procedures are suggested in the body of this chapter.

be, like the earth, earthy. While seeking with might and main to raise up sons and daughters of predeliction—those bound to her special service by a life of the evangelical counsels—to the highest spirituality, the closest, most intimate union with Christ, the Church, wise with the experience of centuries—sometimes very unhappy experience—also includes in her legislation a sad, grave tract: dismissal from religious life.

Just as a brilliant Lucifer fell like lightning from the heavens, so too it has happened that some among the chosen ones have fallen; religious have been dismissed in shame from the cloister and clerics have been committed to the awesome rite of degradation. Sons of Adam and daughters of Eve have relived that terrible moment when the Angels' burning brand drove their first parents from Paradise:

> They, looking back, all the eastern side beheld
> Of Paradise, so late their happy seat,
> Waved over by that flaming brand; the gate
> With dreadful faces thronged and fiery arms.
> Some natural tears they dropped, but wiped them soon;
> The world was all before them, where to choose
> Their place of rest, and Providence their guide.
> They, hand in hand, with wandering steps and slow,
> Through Eden took their solitary way.
>   (*Paradise Lost*, XII, 641 ff.)

Unfortunately, lapses are not merely the imaginative stuff of dreams, but rather the subject matter of unfeeling scientific history, which is no respecter of persons—even consecrated religious. With solid fact and authentic documentation, history matter-of-factly relates that in certain places at certain times those who had willingly accepted the veil of the Bride of Christ departed from him; that in the Papal Curia itself, clerics have stooped to serve Satan. Proportion, however, must be wisely observed here. On the whole, wonderful miracles of grace have been haloed by the searchlight of research. The fact that the pages of history do not show a large percentage of religious failures, is in itself

an invaluable testimony to God's unusual goodness and special
providence toward those seeking to follow closely the Lamb of
God.

Nonetheless, it is a sobering experience to read over the
Canon Law delineating the dismissal of a religious. Such a task
need not be prompted by morbid curiosity; a salutary realism
forces us to confess the words of St. Francis:

> Truly I understand and believe that, if God had done to
> a highway man, or to the greatest of all sinners, the mercies and
> favors that he has done to me, he would be a much better man
> than I am, and more grateful than I. And on the other hand I
> understand and believe that, if God withdrew his hand from
> me and did not hold me up, I should commit greater sins than
> all the rest of mankind and be the worst of them.

It is shocking to realize, as did some of our predecessors, that we
too can fall. It can happen and a healthful fear admits it. Fear,
the Scriptures plainly say, can mark the beginning of great wisdom.

Wholesome fear took no part in the pride of Lucifer as his
arrogant outburst, "I will not serve," shattered the skies. Not fear,
but dalliance conditioned Eve's reaction to the fateful suggestion
that she take of the fruit and eat; in Eve, curiosity and vanity
flirted with temptation. Such fear was absent from the youth
of King Richard II, and he himself became the architect of his
own disaster. Lady Macbeth felt the terrified fear of those on
the brink of insanity when, unsuccessfully, she strove to wash
from her hands the blood of guilt; before her evil deed she had
scoffed at fear. Thus, sad to say, there is usually a lack of wholesome and salutary fear of the Lord in the early consciousness of
an unfortunate dismissed religious.

Great falls generally do not happen overnight; total moral
surrender does not suddenly come from outer space. The phi-
losopher's axiom says, *natura non agit per saltem*—nature does
not function by leaps and bounds. A corrupt character, like a
fine character, is built by repetition. Step by step the mountain

of sin is climbed; falling over the cliff is but the final step. Lucifer secretly hoarded up his pride; longingly, Eve eyed the forbidden fruit; the black desires of Lady Macbeth simply awaited their opportunity; faced with his dreadful climax, Richard II moaned, "Must I ravel out my weaved-up folly." The case history of a dismissed religious generally contains a long clinical analysis dating back over a period of years.

Only after a considerable time has passed and prolonged training has been submitted to, does the Church permit those desirous of pursuing the evangelical counsels, in the helpful context of community life, to become religious. Preparation embraces a demanding, disciplined routine, arduous tasks to be performed meticulously, detailed instruction in prayer, mortification, and the general principles of the spiritual life. At the time of full acceptance by the community—after those in authority have given approval to this completed apprenticeship—it is factually true that the religious is living an exemplary life, is endowed with the requisite virtues, and—as far as it can be humanly ascertained—has overcome any contrary tendencies to vice.

Alas, how great a change has intervened, since those propitious days, in the case of a dismissed religious; what a strange about-face. As the end closes in upon a life in religion, the change becomes plainly visible; the contrast with former days is very marked. Dismissal, however, is most rare; having highlighted its possibility where there is spiritual carelessness and rashness, having properly sounded its necessary note of warning, we need not make it our further concern. Leaving the extreme case, let us now turn our attention to lesser changes, but changes involving real problems.

The religious who is a proud person, the religious known for want of charity, the religious avoided because of angry tantrums and bitter tongue, all such religious at one time—the time of profession or ordination—were quite different. Then, they were not victims of pride, of anger, or of uncharity. What has happened? The answer is painfully simple. Temptations attacked;

a small battle was somewhere lost, then a series of small battles, at length some big ones, and finally the will to fight was abandoned. The small beginnings of anger, uncharity, pride—or of any other vice—were not resisted.

Small beginnings can teach big lessons; most basically, the lesson that temptations must be resisted *at the very outset*. A wise observer of human foibles, Alexander Pope, witnessed many falls from virtue in the society of his day, and rightly concluded:

> Vice is a monster of so frightful mien
> As to be hated needs but to be seen:
> Yet seen too oft, familiar with her face,
> We first endure, then pity, then embrace.

Vigor and stern determination should mark our resistance. When dalliance obtains a foothold, decisive, clear-cut victory eludes us. A halfhearted victory loses the opportunity for a confident "follow-through" pressing home its spiritual gains.

Unless our initial resistance is what it should be, what happens? Take the example of anger. In class a delinquent child may require stern discipline; on certain occasions discipline can be effective through the shrewd use of controlled anger. However, controlled anger is not the only anger classrooms witness. What happens when anger lacks justification or, if warranted, is excessive and uncontrolled? Wrongful anger is either instantly checked or it quickly goes out of control. Like fire, it grows hotter, accelerates its speed, becomes more destructive, and culminates in chaos. Later, in calmer moments, with the incident put safely behind her, the no-longer-angry teacher feels amazement at what self said or did; is almost inclined to laugh, it all seems so absurd in retrospect; except that it is also very sad.

Take the temptation to vanity; a person with any pronounced amount of sensitivity finds this a recurrent temptation in teaching work. Vanity, possessed of perpetual motion, seems ubiquitous; so many occasions occur during the course of a single day, when, in a quite human fashion, we like to put ourselves in a good light. Vanity proposes a perennial dilemma in the class-room—either students ask questions we cannot answer or, what is worse, they never ask anything because we have not sufficiently stimulated their minds. At moments of questioning, a great desire to appear learned wells up within us. If we happen to be learned, and can therefore quite legitimately appear learned, fine. Successful bluffs, just to assuage our vanity, however, generally prove Pyrrhic victories; they often catch up with us in the class of another teacher; our reputation has not gained, only our vanity has increased.

There is always a split second when we realize, albeit vaguely, that we are yielding to vanity. The same is true in conversations of ours when vanity scores; momentarily we realized the temptation, but action surrenders to vanity. There is a moment when we could have, and should have, resisted. Next time resistance is that much harder. And after many next times—?

When we resist efforts to dislodge us from the secure possession of virtue, we perform a valuable achievement, but it is not enough; we must not stop there. A skillful general, after winning a particular battle, does not remain content merely to celebrate victory, he wisely examines the strategy of the enemy's attack. Why was it launched at a special time? Why in a certain direction? Why at a particular flank?

Temptations, even the elementary catechism teaches, arise from the world, the flesh, and the devil. The devil must be considered a real factor in human life; to discount his activities means to borrow trouble. Ultra moderns, boasting more sophistication than sense and caring little for religion, deride the devil as a fanciful creation of archaic biblical myth. Denying the devil, they themselves live in a make-believe world; too late, some of them will find their eternal neighbor very real indeed. A percentage of our temptations may be traced to diabolic influence; they are formidable and dangerous. Possessing an intellect vastly superior to ours, the devil calculates well our personal weaknesses, our times of vulnerability. It will pay us to analyze the approaches

of such temptations; self-knowledge of weaknesses make us better
prepared against future assaults. Even when temptations derive
not from the devil but from ourselves or the world, they reveal
what tendencies of our character must be checked, where our
defenses need strengthening. In illustration of the foregoing, we
can examine our efforts to practice any of the virtues. However,
let us select charity—our attempts to be charitable in speech,
thought, and in every deed. Obviously, we find a wide field here;
charity, or its lack, affects practically everything in which we
play even a small part. Concerning the tongue, St. James writes:
"If any man offend not in word, the same is a perfect man."
What are our personal weaknesses as far as charity is concerned?
When do we find ourselves acting uncharitably? What conditions seem to provoke us to slight slips or resounding falls?

An interesting case in this regard is a factual one involving
a very successful businessman who had many responsibilities and
wielded considerable economic power in a limited area of industry. During most of the week the gentleman in question observed
a better than average charity; his associates and subordinates
were accustomed to pleasant and kindly usage at his hands. Yet,
on Friday afternoon he became often quite intolerable; subordinates received brusque, unreasonable assignments; secretaries
came close to tears; even his associates were cut down by a sharp
tongue. Being conscientious, he took note, after a while, of these
facts. He analyzed the situation carefully and finally concluded
—quite correctly—that his lapses from charity were due to the
accumulated tensions of his high-powered work-week plus the
fact that he could not have his usual heavy meat lunch on Friday.
Having once stripped the temptation, he was afterwards successful in guarding charity on Friday afternoons.

Conducting a similar examination of our own failings in
charity may likewise discover hidden roots of our troubles. Perhaps we find we are uncharitable in conversation because a particular sister takes part who leads us on by her clever but un-

charitable conversational gifts. It may happen, on the contrary, that another sister kindles a spirit of contradiction; we so like to deflate her remarks, we do so even if it means violating charity. Our lack of charity may be caused by bitterness or disgruntlement when occasions arise to perform certain duties we intensely dislike. In the midst of such duties thoughts become quite dark, and, in our own mind, we paint some of our associates in very uncharitable terms. Sometimes, duties are shared with others; instead of softening and sweetening the tasks for our associates, we create additional hardships by acting and speaking uncharitably toward the group. An examination of our charity could be greatly prolonged; on an individual basis we should go more deeply into it. Its importance for community life cannot be overstressed; "To love one's neighbor as oneself is a greater thing than all holocausts and sacrifices" (Mark 12:33).

Although the above has been an examination of failings against the virtue of charity, the same process, with the same results, could be applied to any or all of the virtues. Insights into the whys and wherefores of our failings achieve a major step on the road to the elimination of those failings. When the future re-creates situations, which previously had spelled disaster for us, our acquired foreknowledge enables us to enter such situations forearmed. We grow strong, as a consequence, in prayerful resolution, become keenly alert for the beginnings of attack, and are well-prepared with a quick, energetic counterattack; in defense of virtue our human skill has become a willing handmaiden of God's grace.

More must be done, however, than to plan successful resistance to temptations against the virtues. Zeal for virtue must go a step further; victories must be followed up; only then will success reach its full fruition. "All quiet along the Potomac," was a Civil War phrase which designated times when there was no actual fighting. Applied to General McClellan, it emphasized his failure to follow up victories which had routed the enemy.

His policy, some historians feel, delayed the Southern surrender two years. In spiritual warfare one makes the same mistake if no effort is made to capitalize upon the victories of the soul.

We follow up our victories by learning well and remembering well the tactics of the defeated temptations which have attacked a particular virtue. Placed again in the same situations quickly we utilize that "know-how" to win again and again increasingly overwhelming victories. Victory thus passes from the single good act to a habit, which, as we know, constitutes the essential definition of a virtue. This process resembles the prescriptions of psychiatry to overcome certain trivial phobias; it draws upon similar psychological factors. A child afraid of the dark, for example, can increase his victories over that fear until he has completely vanquished all forms and conditions of darkness and the phobia has disappeared. Returning to the previous examples of anger and vanity, we can illustrate this procedure in concrete terms.

After we have defeated the temptation to wrongful anger in the classroom, we can, having carefully prepared ourselves, repeat our restraint more easily. Each time this is done, our adjusted reflexes find it easier; the reaction grows to be habitual, until gradually the temptation becomes ineffective. Against vanity, too, we can press victories. Strengthening ourselves bit by bit, we finally become able to impart knowledge we possess in a humble fashion; graciously, we can even underplay the achievement its possession represents. We can school ourselves, under certain circumtances, to make frank admissions of ignorance. Generally, as vanity disappears, our sense of humor becomes more pronounced. In time, we are able to regard our vanity with amusement; ridicule kills vanity.

One of the greatest means of overcoming temptations is to build a past history of faithful self-denial and mortification in order to establish strong dominion over the waywardness of our fallen human nature. We may have listened to numerous sermons which pleaded with us to recognize the importance of

mortification for advancement in the spiritual life, or we may
have read books stressing the same theme, but in all probability,
no argument for the need of mortification is quite as convincing
as the personally experienced lesson of our struggle against temptation. Temptation prods us to be faithful to mortification. It
resembles the awareness of a penitent who is soon going to confession, and vigorously resists sin to make his Saturday evening
recital less onerous. Temptations emphasize weaknesses; weaknesses emphasize the need of mortification.

The sophistry of worldly sophistication considers mortification archaic. Mature analysis of our temptations forces from us
the conclusion that our yielding was often directly traceable to
a lack of mortification. Mortification, in isolated instances, is
hard to glorify; but when mortification is the essential background
of spiritual triumph over severe temptation, its justification is
easily argued and the wisdom of our loyalty to it gains commendation.

Refusing a second piece of pie, eating dinner without salt
on some items, drinking coffee instead of tea, or foregoing sugar
and cream—admittedly small things, by themselves probably of
no great spiritual worth—involves some degree of deprivation.
Their importance lies in the fact that they represent an awareness
of the need of detachment and an actual implementation of the
control of the will in the area of sense pleasure. The character of
such a mortified person is well prepared to joust with temptations.

Other mortifications could be similarly commented upon and
related to the vanquishing of temptation. Essentially, however,
the cumulative picture points to one conclusion: sound and
thorough mortification contributes to a well-integrated, spiritually
orientated personality. Such a personality is the strongest bulwark
against all temptations. A noble character, apart from any consideration of temptations, reveals lasting moral beauty, the triumph of rational creation, and, as it subsumes sanctity, deserves
to be acknowledged the pinnacle of the Christian universe.

Temptations succeed because of flaws in our human mechanism; because emotions, some or one of them, are not properly controlled; because the intellect is not properly alerted to survey clearly, to penetrate thoroughly; because the body, in nerves or tone, is out of kilter; because of a will, unskilled and unstrung. On the other hand, the ordered, efficient meshing of the faculties in an individual is beautiful to behold, and additionally resplendent as holiness dawns. Just as one admires an athlete's triumph of prowess, or a dancer's virtuoso performance, one also, in the spiritual order, admires the grace and marvelous quality in the soul's holy devastation of temptation. But small, constant, behind-the-scenes mortification made possible the visible flawless victory.

Resistance to temptation and their defeat show only the negative side of the coin. A soul morally strong, through mortification of self and conquest of temptation, has a predominately positive attractiveness. A sense of responsibility, a reliability in the accomplishment of any assigned tasks, a general fidelity to duty—all are assuredly present. The community can always depend on this type of religious, no matter what the need may be; even in inactivity such a person generates pleasantness, tranquillity, helpfulness; she is a joy and a tower of strength to all.

Although the tasks facing a religious community are often numerous and onerous, they are not usually esoteric in nature; sheer, lofty genius is seldom required. What is required is zeal, the command over self, the wise allotment of time, and the willingness to do faithfully and well that which we are quite able to do. In other words, there is need for the ability to resist temptations which would hinder, to confront them with self-discipline which assures their defeat.

Whatever we do should, of course, be done prayerfully. For the effort to be successful, however, a basic requirement insists that one's fundamental self be an apt receptacle for prayer. As the philosophical axiom says, *quidquid recipitur in modo recipientis recipitur*. Well-executed prayer, under God's grace, occurs when temptations to distraction, to curtailment, to ease and remissness of body or mind, have been firmly rebuffed. Victory over these temptations can be a decisive element in achieving well-controlled faculties, faculties which are thus turned to God, kept so directed, and, should the Holy Ghost so beckon, faculties which may enjoy the intimate union of contemplative prayer.

A recurrent serious temptation to which those in religious life are subject is that of giving way to improper responses, or an over-all unwholesome attitude toward authority. Since our whole life unfolds under authority, this is a very important consideration; further, this obligation derives from our voluntary assumption of the vow of obedience.

Serious troubles with duly constituted authority generally betoken an undisciplined spirit; undisciplined, because it has not properly resisted a variety of temptations. The will is not a finely trained instrument which masters annoyance or resentment at legitimate commands. The intellect often becomes proud by yielding to temptations of vanity or self-esteem. Although resistance to temptation is very light on one side of the scales, self-sufficiency, hauteur, a lack of humility, and so forth, weigh heavily on the other side. Repeated surrenders to temptation gradually sap spiritual strength; the mind grows clouded, the will weakened. Then our striving to accept duty and properly to control self for the accomplishment of obedience come hard indeed.

A vicious circle results. Disregard of authority generates an undisciplined condition, an over-all discontent, and a lack of generosity and dedication; all of which make us vulnerable to further temptations. Just as a person physically debilitated makes the easiest target for the attacks of many varieties of bacteria, so also the debilitated soul, if we may employ the term, becomes increasingly vulnerable to temptations, the bacteria of the spiritual order.

Through the directives and assignments given to us by legitimate authority, we are permitted helpful insights into ourselves. Temptations often triumph precisely because we are not well enough acquainted with our own inner selves. We are unaware of dangerous tendencies, and we lack an exact notion of our degree of strength or weakness in certain areas; our changing moods, our increased vulnerability at particular times or in particular places or circumstances, are concealed from us. The onslaughts of temptation take effective advantage of such ignorance. Temptations want to be accepted; they strike when and where this absence of forewarned self-knowledge has failed to erect defenses.

It is an old and tried saying that no one should be the judge in his own case. Self lacks the proper objectivity and disinterest to draw a full, accurate picture. Authority sees from the outside; it is a true reflection of the estimate others have of us. Paying it attention, makes additional elements of self-knowledge available. Thus, the varying tasks allotted to us from time to time, the advice and direction specifically given, and especially the continuing corrections merited over the years, provide invaluable insights. This is especially true, although we may be reluctant to admit it, of corrections. Obviously, admonitions come our way because we have yielded to certain temptations; defeats make corrections necessary. What they must also do, if we possess spiritual wisdom, is show us where temptations are likely to strike again; where, in our character, renovation or refurbishing is called for to render future assaults futile.

The true friendships we enjoy with other members of the community can serve the same purpose. Friends have the ability to see us in a somewhat different light than we see ourselves. While ascetical theology warns us of the dangers attendant upon particular friendships, nonetheless, it praises true spiritual friendship. When this exists, one of its necessary components is a charitable honesty warning of faults and flaws. It thus helps offset any capitulation to temptation. On our own part, we should equally fulfill this role when it is needful; above all, in a spirit of fairness, we ought to credit the good will and charity of our friends, who try to help us. Their efforts represent an outside observation made at first hand and motivated by a sincere concern for our spiritual well-being. A humble, determined attempt on our part to profit by their counsel can help a great deal against temptations and can facilitate spiritual advances.

What a folly to react adversely to these opportunities presented by authority or personal friends. To react adversely condemns us to a policy of making excuses for self and of attempting to explain away facts; it bares an inability to live by truth. How much more intelligent it is to acknowledge humbly that certain temptations are particularly troublesome to us, and to admit that if we do not squarely face up to a certain situation and take salutary action, we will continue to be tempted; tempted often, and often fail.

The religious engaged in teaching ought to be very severe with self in these matters. She needs to be always mindful that in her workaday environment she is often the object of full and constant youthful admiration; she is the personification of holiness, authority, and learning among those who are believing Catholics, subordinates, and pupils. This eminence of position does not aid a humble estimate of self or a pronounced receptivity to warnings about faults and imperfections. One will not be eager to confess beforehand any inferiority of soul *vis-à-vis* temptations.

A wrong attitude, when we adopt it here, can be contageous and may influence others in the community who are likewise cast in the all-important religious-teacher role. Should this occur, one can readily foresee a rather bad situation in the making. When corporate and individual blindness to temptation is widespread, the spiritual attire of the teaching religious displays many shabby spots before the daily classroom audience. The future Catholic leaders of our country are going to be that less inspired; they will not be as strong a force for good as we might have made them.

Let us probe even deeper into temptations. Is it possible to discover a mainspring, some fundamental source, of all the difficulties? Can one root-cause be isolated? Most certainly! We are not indifferent to created things; that is the root cause. We are victims of our own attachments. What is the greatest attachment? Self. We are—let us face the fact squarely—self-centered. Words, persons and events must bow to a preconceived pattern of relationship to self. Self expects and demands thoughtful people, success, words of praise; our reaction is neither neutral nor controlled; self lashes back in anger or uncharity. We act proudly, disobediently, willfully, because we are inordinately attached to our own ways, our own opinions, our own self-will. At times, in fear of certain situations or certain tasks, we may lack fortitude; again, because self, overattached to security or reputation, cannot face possible failure. There is too little disinterest, too much self-interest. Holy indifference to all creatures is the only soil in which virture can thrive; as attachment to created things decreases, virtue increases. Saints are so wrapped up in God, they become forgetful of self. One of them, St. John the Baptist, provides us with a slogan: "He must increase, I must decrease."

With these thoughts in mind we are ready to approach the very pinnacle of the practice of perfect virtue. We are prepared to enter the graduate school of perfection; namely, that mastery of self which enables us to fashion thoughts, words, and deeds directly opposed to our natural, human inclinations. If we tend to be vain, we now deliberately seek out persons, places, and situations where the expected outcome will be painful wounds to vanity. Do we have a natural bent to burst forth in wrongful anger? With holy calculation we practice the thoughts, words, and deeds of meekness. Are there some who naturally annoy us? We speak of them with great kindness; we speak but favorably of their good aspects and we keep a discreet silence about their failings.

Theresa of Lisieux forced her supernatural charity to conquer her natural abhorrence. An elderly and sickly sister of the community had grown very crochety and it became almost impossible to please her. Through trial and error, all the sisters had accumulated ample evidence for that conclusion. So had St. Theresa; but the saint said to herself, if, despite the heavy difficulties, I can consistently practice kindness in dealing with this sister, it will assure my future charity. Setting herself determinedly to the task, Theresa helped the ailing sister in every way. Never did she allow herself to be drawn into unpleasantness; she was always the smiling, willing slave. What a triumph of charity was hers when one fine day the problem sister turned to Theresa and asked, "Tell me Sister Theresa, what is there about me which you find so attractive?" Although the saint did not do so, she could have replied, "It is because you are my most valuable friend; you bring me very close to God." What nature points out to us as great trials, grace points out as wonderful opportunities.

Such acts should not content themselves with rebuffing internal weakness or external temptations, although that may well be their starting point. Acts contrary to the natural tendencies of fallen human nature should also be performed in harmless, pleasant, or perfectly legitimate situations, for in this way added strength of mind, will, and character is gained. Some particular action which we would like to place, may be quite all right—a diversion or enjoyment we are entirely entitled to. We forego the pleasure or diversion because the act of foregoing reduces the mind's attachment to these things and the will is more free to choose. Increasingly, we become the master of our soul and more powerful in character; this is especially shown, later, when situations arise which pose a threat to virtue. Such choices should be made frequently; they are a matter of training; the more often they are placed, the greater grows the potential of virtue. When only infrequent, isolated, haphazard, their effect is correspondingly weakened; the virtuous character is not as strong as it could be.

Here is our blueprint for the temple of virtue in which God will gladly dwell. It is not new, it is not strange, it is the traditional ascetical wisdom amassed over the centuries by Catholic spiritual writers. We may even say that it is easy to find the blueprint. Going a step further, we can claim that most religious have found it. We pray, however, that religious remember our conclusion—the saints have used it.

11

Human Misery,
Catalyst of Perfection

"THIS IS NOT THE BEST OF ALL POSSIBLE WORLDS."
We know that we live in a sinful world which contains much
human misery, the ineluctable consequence of sin. When we
look upon that world, often we do so through tear-stained eyes.
Such are the hard facts of life, and they must be faced by the
woman in the cloister as well as by the man in the street.

The worldling does not actually face them, he simply says,
"Oh, well!" and in presumptuous rashness makes sin a component of his routine, with its ephemeral thrills and no contrition.
Nor does the irreligious face them when he follows out the blank
despair of Job's counsellors, "Curse God and die." Neither extreme will trap the devout Catholic living in the world or in
the cloister, although some danger always lurks.

How difficult, too, after all our efforts to mold a Christlike
world, to look at, and listen to, the world-picture presented by
the mass communication media, newspapers, radio, and television.
Those avenues of information leave no doubt that, despite our
own community and all the other religious communities, im-
morality still continues to flourish and worldliness remains something at which relatively few people are taking umbrage. Such

things seem to be routinely accepted by the world surrounding us, and accepted apparently with little sorrow or shame that they are as they are. The ideals close to our hearts are simply regarded with bored disinterest or casual curiosity. The attitude of a portion of the world toward religious communities can be expressed itself in these words: "Fine, if that's the way of life they fancy, let them have it; but let them go their way and we go ours. It seems strange to us, yet they do work that helps people and, therefore, let them be. They're somewhat benighted perhaps, but that's their business; it takes all sorts to make a world."

A hard and cynical modern society is far removed from "the good old days," when everyone who became a sister was looked upon as a heroine. Universal greetings of respect, alertness to offer any possible kindness to the community and its members, which characterized former days, have ceased to be widespread. The "old parishes," those enclaves of proud, active Catholicism, of which the sisters were so honored a part, found no inconvenience too great to render any little service in gratitude to the nuns.

Today an avant-garde, naturalistic psychology voices varying suspicions about the motivations of those who dedicate themselves to such a way of life. Among the moderns who have elevated educational-sociological courses to a religion, there is also voiced considerable skepticism about the accomplishments of the religious community. At times these critics go further and maintain that the activity of the religious community could be better carried out by people they consider "professionally trained" and whose lives are lived more "normally." These are some current reactions which, humanly speaking, constitute a cross for religious to bear as they go about the unselfish fulfillment of their dedicated lives. These opinions are but a facet of the misery of a world which lacks the fullness of the appreciation of faith, a world weighed down in its viewpoints by an accumulation of sin.

The world's views, however, should not cause us to throw up our hands in despair and abandon any aspirations to high holiness. Our spiritual grounding should be made of much sterner stuff than that. Further, the spirituality which attracts us, to be genuinely worthy of our efforts, is sufficiently adequate and more than rich enough to be able to absorb such difficulties and decisively triumph over them. We need not be apprehensive about this. Surely, the axiom, "If God is with us, who can be against us," can be rightly counted on here.

Counting their blessings is something that, unfortunately, the members of religious communities do much too infrequently. One such blessing rarely adverted to, is the pure simple joy of a good conscience. Naturally speaking, we have probably no greater blessing in this life. Without it, nothing in the world can give happiness; utterly basic, it admits of no substitutes. Many people with much power in the world lack the peace and tranquillity which a good conscience affords. Some with an abundance of money lament the unsatisfying patterns of their lives; they feel uneasy, insecure, and are ridden with doubts and fears, because even though they possess a great deal, they have not good consciences. They realize, in moments of honest self-examination, that money cannot, of itself, purchase peace and contentment. Lacking a good conscience they are doomed to continue in restlessness, turmoil, and distress of soul.

Perhaps these considerations will serve to remind us how casually we take for granted a good conscience and being at peace with God and with the world. How reassuring it is to be able to look life, with all its persons, places, and situations, squarely in the eye, even if some of its vistas are somber and foreboding. How precious a boon never to have to flinch, even when trapped by severe predicaments and hemmed in by the sin and misery of the world. Despite tragedy, we remain at peace with ourselves and our hearts savor its deep calm. We may make mistakes, we may not do as well as we wish, we may even be disappointed in

some of our efforts to advance the cause of religion, and disheartened at our slow rate of spiritual progress; but none of
these things can rob us of the joy of a good conscience.

Along with acquiring inner peace of soul, we ought also
to stir up a sense of the supernatural character of our life and
rightly thank God for the sanctifying grace which his goodness
has given us. What a marvelous privilege to possess sanctifying
grace, the greatest gift God gives to man on this earth. How
thoughtless of us to forget those priceless pages of the penny
catechism which detail the divinizing effects of sanctifying grace
in the soul. Would that we might fully realize that through this
grace God himself, creator of heaven and earth and all things,
dwells within our lowly selves. Would that we might penetrate
deeply the awesome truth that God becomes our guest in a
very special way, that we are ennobled to the extent of being
accurately referred to as "temples of the Holy Ghost." Silently,
even when we are concerned with other things, this divine presence works within us, continually carrying on the process of our
sanctification.

Through this indwelling, our relationship with God becomes
such that we are truly his adopted children over whom he watches
with greatest solicitude, and on whom he lavishes infinite love
and precious graces. What majestic happiness awaits us in the
security of our title, "heirs of heaven"—a divine and eternal
beatitude in our rightful home and everlasting resting-place.
Only the thin curtain of life separates us from this complete bliss.

All difficulties and trials melt before the happy heat of the
magnificent status which is ours. They fade like incidents seen
casually and with little attention from a speeding train, all warmth
and light and happiness within, secure in its journey to the best
of destinies.

Another common oversight of which we are guilty is our
failure to remember that, no matter how unprepossessing the current milieu of our life, we are able to, and in fact actually are,

gaining merit for our souls every moment of the day. During the Lenten office we recite the constant refrain, *Non sit vobis vanum mane surgere ante lucem, quia promisit Dominus coronam vigilantibus.* This theme needs to be in our thoughts the year around —that our efforts to serve God are not in vain. A good and just God has our crown awaiting us precisely because of all these unspectacular, routine efforts. We obtain this crown through those merits which are gained day by day and year by year. Actually, the whole purpose of being created and living out our span of time on this earth is to gain merit. So much so, that it must dominate our attitude toward all things: ourselves, others, situations, problems, triumphs, and so forth. Our undeviating purpose must be to use all creatures as the means of gaining the highest possible position in heaven. Under the will of God and the largesse of his grace, the dignity of place awarded us depends on the merit we have succeeded in acquiring by loyal service to God. Not only does gaining merit constitute the quintessence of life, particularly and a fortiori, it also constitutes the quintessence of the religious vocation. In fact, becoming a religious amounts to a public statement that this is our conviction; our conviction to such an extent that we have left all other cares and values to carry out this one exclusively.

This fundamental of our religious life transforms any consequences of the sin and misery of the world. They cease to be only hard and difficult trials, they become possible opportunities to gain merit; sometimes they offer the opportunities of the greatest merit. Because they are of this nature, our triumph over them represents real achievement; the greater the labor, the more merit gained. Again, is not our vocation an admission that this is what we are after—the narrow way of real sacrifice and self-oblation? Have we not looked for, and should we not consequently welcome, such opportunities?

Further, although intelligence compels us to be aware of the streaks etched in our own lives by the sin and misery of the world, are we not sometimes guilty of exaggeration and self-pity in surveying our own little acre? The life of St. Rita of Cascia offers a particularly apt example. It demonstrates, albeit in rather bizarre fashion, some of the trials which have been endured outside the cloister by women in the single state, in marriage, and in widowhood. Sometimes our proximity to the difficulties which face us in the religious state tends to make us exaggerate them a bit; unconsciously, we begin to presume that our sisters in the world enjoy comparative freedom from trials. In reality, however, and according to the external appearances of particular cases, at times trials in the world are much greater. With this in mind, let us recall the life of St. Rita who ultimately became a religious and died in the odor of sanctity.

As a young girl, Rita experienced the intense grief, which surely those who have enjoyed the opportunity of entering the convent can poignantly understand, of being denied entrance into religious life, even though she felt called to the cloister, desired it with inexpressible ardor, and possessed more than requisite virtue. This fondest desire, the cornerstone of her human hope, had to be put aside to care for her aged and indigent parents. They pleaded their convincing necessity to her, and out of filial love and a sense of duty she consented to forego her heart's desire.

Her life as a married woman highlights also, some of the troubles that can afflict women called to that state. The choice of husband her parents had made proved most unfortunate; he was highly impulsive, constantly irascible; in almost every conceivable way a sad trial for the poor girl. Although in Rita's blameless fulfillment of all wifely duties, he had cause only for the greatest praise, he showered reproaches upon her. Repeated harsh threats rewarded her unfailing obedience, kindness, zeal, and love. Rita was subjected even to blows, yet she suffered every injustice in all patience and forgiveness. Trials and sufferings occasionally mar the married state, and certainly they dwarf those difficulties which periodically plague life in the cloister.

Because of the type of man he was and because he associated

with his own kind, Rita's husband was brutally murdered. Rita bore this tragic family episode and continued to serve God with no less trust in his goodness. The two sons of her marriage also provided bitter moments for a loving mother. Not unexpectedly, but sadly, they were much like their father; true heirs to his faults. To the alarm of their mother, they plotted revenge upon the murderers of their father. For Rita, who understood how unchristian was such an objective, this was another painful way of the cross. However, both of them died quite young and before they were able to carry out their plan of revenge. While their deaths were cruel sorrows, as is the death of any son to a true mother, Rita, nevertheless, sensed a certain kindness on the part of divine providence which had thus prevented them from staining their souls with foul murder. Nevertheless, these tragedies in the life of St. Rita, as a single girl, as wife, mother, and widow, certainly show that at times God imposes on women in the world, very heavy crosses to be accepted as his holy will.

The desire to love God with a whole heart can be accelerated and broadened by human misery. Those who have wooed the things of earth and found them, in frustration, dull, flat, and unprofitable, realize the wealth of grace; those who have experienced the harshness of fallen humanity appreciate the goodness of God; those who have felt worldly pleasures turn to ashes in their eager hands, more prayerfully stretch forth those hands for the lasting joys of heaven. When we admit, as our faith constantly reminds us, that we are sinful members of a fallen race, we are ready to practice renunciation, reparation, compunction. These sentiments are greatly needed by spiritual beginners, but are never absent in those who are close to perfection.

As we strive to stir up compunction in our own hearts, as we plead for divine forgiveness and mercy, we ourselves must extend sweet compassion and generous mercy to others. There should be in us no hardness of heart. Whether we like it or not, whether or not it is true, it is a fact that the ecclesiastic or religious is at times pictured as lacking in mercy. Such a picture has been drawn in some novels and in an occasional movie. There the religious or ecclesiastic is sometimes presented as very strait-laced, self-righteous, coldly just to a frightening degree, lacking mellowness, unsympathetic to human foibles, and harsh toward moral failures. Those who saw the movie *Joan of Arc* will not soon forget the austere, haughty faces of the masters and doctors who sat in judgment on the saint; faces utterly devoid of pity. That scene is a prime example; it was an unusually vitriolic treatment of the clergy. Other examples are discernible in some of the clerical characters of Canon Sheehan, A. J. Cronin, Kate O'Brien, and Somerset Maugham. Of course, this is often done in an exaggerated fashion for dramatic contrast: the ne'er-do-well with the heart of gold versus the righteous with heart of steel.

The wise can benefit from the thinking of others even when that thinking miscarries. Religious vocations in general are drawn from families whose conduct is highly moral. The training of those serving in the army or the Church is an arduous one; it calls for rigorous self-discipline, it demands high standards, it is a life ruled by law. This may make it difficult to appreciate the softness, the lack of law and self-discipline in those who live on the other side, morally speaking, of the tracks.

Consequently, it may be difficult at times to comprehend the conduct of those whom we teach. Some of them come from quite different, and at times quite lamentable, backgrounds. There are moments when the norms of conduct of this latter group, their codes, their *mores*, are utterly startling. Undoubtedly, it has been the experience of the veteran teacher to encounter conduct deserving of indignation; then, in amazement, to discover that the culprit had not the slightest idea the action was in any way wrong. These thoughts are a salutary meditation too, when we have the privilege of extricating those of our graduates who have enmeshed themselves in unbelievable varieties of moral failure. It would be sad indeed if here that most subtle worldliness, school vanity, triumphed over the teachings of Christ.

Hence, our need to be persons of forgiveness. All applaud forgiveness. The schoolboy who may remember little else, is touched by the scene at Appomatox Court House where Grant gave back his sword to General Lee. There is no better key to the human heart than forgiveness. Forgiveness is a beautiful quality of the human personality. Those who have dealt closely with the intimate workings of souls and have seen in them the effect of sin, testify that other vices, bad as they are, do not so wither and shrivel the human heart as does unforgiveness. Some vices are punished only in hell, but unforgiveness carries its own punishment in this life; unforgiveness corrupts every waking moment and covers all the beauty of life with a dark pall.

The explanations which Christ gave on the subject of forgiveness to his first followers also must be mastered by those who are his twentieth-century disciples. Christ explained to the chief of the apostles, St. Peter, the first Pope, that forgiveness must be seventy times seven; in other words, it must be boundless. He cautioned his beloved John and James that calling down thunder upon an erring city was not to be the way of his followers. He taught them only one prayer, the "Our Father," and in it are these words: "Forgive us our trespasses, as we forgive those who trespass against us." We say those words each morning at Mass. Our Mass is not fully fruitful if those words are not lived.

These words, this sentiment of Christ, of God, have always found echo in the breast of mankind. Shakespeare's oft-repeated quotation is oft-repeated because responsive audiences, over the centuries, have felt the truth of the poet's words:

> The quality of mercy is not strain'd:
> It droppeth as the gentle rain from heaven
> Upon the place beneath; it is twice bless'd;
> It blesseth him that gives, and him that takes:
> 'Tis mightiest in the mightiest;
>
> It is an attribute to God himself
> And earthly power doth then show likest God's,
> When mercy seasons justice. . . .

Consider this,—
That in the course of justice none of us
Should see salvation: we do pray for mercy,
And that same prayer doth teach us all to render
The deeds of mercy.

Another consequence of sin and misery in the world is the curse of evil ambition. Alas, what havoc it wreaks upon the world at large, upon families, upon friendships, upon individuals. Prescinding from its rightness or wrongness, it is a deeply rooted tendency in human nature. Ambition does not boycott the religious community; as an integral part of our religious training, the quite natural drive of ambition has to be controlled. In religious life there is literally "no room at the top." Religious life is lived "at the bottom" by the overwhelming majority of those who have freely chosen that vocation. And this is simply in the nature of things; it could not be otherwise.

What makes this necessary arrangement hard to bear for some of us is our thoughtless penchant for reading a false theory into it—that we are not appreciated, that our talents have been overlooked and disregarded. Such an interpretation is utterly untrue. Christ, whom we serve primarily and exclusively, and through whom we serve others, knows and appreciates all that we are and all that we do. Even apart from this major consideration, which must always be kept before our eyes, our superiors also appreciate us.

Many religious of excellent abilities, with flawless records of valuable service, remain in subordinate positions. This statement is verified in the lives of religious we have observed in such positions. The distribution of positions of authority often depends upon extrinsic things: the force of circumstances, little accidental happenings. No one realizes this better than honest superiors, although naturally it cannot be unduly publicized and spelled out in specific detail. Often, indeed, only those who look from the vantage point of superiors are able fully to understand the great importance of many subordinate positions. In fact, it frequently happens that precisely because of the appreciation of personal talents and contributions, religious are maintained in certain subordinate positions. In many ways these positions defend more vital beachheads for the cause than a number of others which may be technically more high ranking. One need not be cynical to observe that people are periodically placed in authority to solve problems at the other end. At times this can salvage the well-being of a religious or serve as an apt means to develop their potential.

We should, however, apply an ointment more vitally spiritual to this wound. God said: "I am a jealous God"; these are significant words. Advance in the spiritual life, progress toward union in prayer, cannot be achieved without detachment. We have to be able to say in practice, "My God and my all." To do so requires the mortification of this last-ditch attachment—the attachment to our own selves revealed in a deep-seated spirit of ambition. We must have the conviction, and then live that conviction, thus expressed by Father Lallemant:

> O blessed interior life, which causes God alone to live in hearts, and hearts to live but for God alone, and to take no pleasure save in him! Blessed the life of that heart wherein God reigns, and which he possessed fully! A life separated from the world, and hidden in God, a life of love and holy liberty; a life which causes the heart to find in the kingdom of God its joys, its peace, true pleasures, glory, solid greatness, goods, and riches, which the world can neither give nor take away (*Spiritual Doctrine*, p. 31).

That orientation not only supplies the antidote to inordinate ambition, it is also the antidote to anything which would serve to withdraw us from God. Certainly there is no more effective answer to trials and troubles generated in the sin and misery of the world. On our part there should be no slackening, since God alone provides our whole incentive. If other things have interest for us, it is only because they are related to him. How can the world possibly overcome us when we have God; we want nothing else. Whatever harm misery and sin can effect lies outside that impregnable circle of our relationship with him. And no man has penetrated this truth more deeply nor expressed it more tellingly than St. Paul:

> Who shall separate us from the love of Christ? Shall tribulation, or distress, or persecution, or hunger, or nakedness, or danger, or the sword? Even as it is written: "For thy sake we are put to death all the day long. We are accounted as sheep for the slaughter. But in all these things we overcome, because of him who has loved us. For I am sure that neither death, nor life, nor angels, nor principalities, nor things present, nor things to come, nor powers, nor height, nor depth, nor any other creature will be able to separate us from the love of God, which is in Christ Jesus our Lord (Rom. 8:35–39).

With this faith-inspired charity, there should be no lessening of our effort to achieve our spiritual goal, no matter how oppressive may be the sin and misery of the world. In the work allotted we do our best; in community effort we play our proper part; in our own souls we accept the raw material, and labor to shape it well; the best we can give is offered to the world, our community, and our interior life. Whatever there may be of hostility in the world, of disappointment in the community, of chagrin with self, we shall always recognize that nothing can happen without God's knowledge and permissive will. Let there be no turning back regardless of the mask of evil life may wear. In our course set for perfection it must always be full speed ahead. Truly, to those who love God, all things work together unto good.

12

Prayers for
Sinners Ricochet

TODAY WE HEAR MUCH ABOUT JUVENILE DELIN-
quency, a topic apparently never failing to supply its exponents
with an abundance of subject matter. Less is said about adult
delinquency; yet, were a sort of comptometer devised to tally
adult delinquency, the results would probably prove surprising.
When, on occasion, we are confronted in a personal fashion with
delinquents, be they adult or juvenile, it often seems that a
percentage of them, as far as our limited human insight can see,
are "not bad at heart," a factor for ourselves and society to take
into consideration.

Although our lives are now cloistered lives, there was a time
when they were not, a time when our gaze fell upon some of
the world's evil. Now the world's sin lies hidden far from our
gaze—beyond convent walls. This is a most desirable arrangement, but it could generate the dangerous inclination to turn
our backs on the world, to wash our hands of it. We cannot do
this, however, because our fellow-human beings, our brothers and
sisters for whom Christ's redemptive blood was shed, are involved
in this evil as its victims, and we have an obligation toward them.

Surely the doctrine of the Mystical Body offers invaluable

aid and comfort for undertaking the obligation. In our era it has received increasing attention and has been warmly welcomed as an antidote to that lamentable individualism which was an aftermath of much eighteenth and nineteenth-century philosophy. Excessive individualism has adversely affected religion and has led to instances of piety reflective of an ivory-tower Christianity —personal exercises and devotions highly developed, but entirely apart from charity toward neighbor and a concern for the needs of the commonweal.

The religious community must eschew this type of "piety," for a love of the Mystical Body should characterize the community's spirituality. Since the doctrine to be followed postulates a spirit of firm faith and a fervent attitude of charity, devotion to it should reach the highest level in religious life. Actually, when Pope Pius XII gave us his full and beautiful treatise on the Mystical Body, he stated expressly that among religious there ought to be an ever-present consciousness of this doctrine and an eager desire to work for the growth of this Body.

Our vocation constitutes a special commitment in this direction; love of the Mystical Body is an integral part of it. Otherwise, we give plausibility to the recurrent charge that people enter convents to escape the world and turn their backs on its problems. To love the Mystical Body means not only to love Christ, its Head, but to love also his members. Indeed, no religious can exist without love of Christ, but neither should she forget that to love Christ means to love the whole Christ, Christ in his members. This love includes those who are weak and unloveable, and it must extend even to loving sinners, the lapsed or potential members. Did not Christ give us the example during his life upon earth? We have also our Blessed Mother as our patroness, for the encyclical of Pius XII reminds us that Mary, corporally the mother of the Head, is spiritually mother of its members.

Our calling binds us not only to save our own souls, but to save the souls of others as well. Hence, just because the evil of the world menaces, we cannot run and hide ourselves in secure, disinterested retirement, as did Boccaccio's aristocrats from attacks of the plague. While we are not expected to seek out this evil and move about in it—that would be worse than foolhardy— we are expected to come to grips with it in prayer. Our prayer must intercede for the progress upon this earth of Christ's grace-laden Kingdom, until all the highways and byways are reached, not excepting the most sordid hovels and the strongest citadels of sin. For fifty years a certain priest used in the Mass a chalice bearing the inscription, "Jesus, merciful Savior, cleanse in the laver of thy most precious blood all the sinners of the world." Our vocation should bear the same inscription.

Prayer ought to be offered to the Mother of God. Close association with the young, by virtue of our teaching position, has provided examples of the all-important role of mother. Yet, alas, earthly mothers are sometimes sadly unfitted for these lofty tasks. Often in delinquency cases, children fail society because mothers fail their children. How consoling in such cases to remember another mother, Mary, the mother of us all who never has failed nor ever will fail her children. No matter how deeply into the mire prodigals may fall, Mary remains their true mother, ever awaiting with open arms their return to grace. "I am the Mother . . . of Holy Hope" (Ecclus. 24:14, Douay version).

How badly the delinquents of today need the care of the Mother of God; nor have adult delinquents any less need. While modern parlance employs the word, delinquency, theological parlance still retains the term, sin. So closely allied to fallen human nature is the evil of delinquency or sin, that society must use more effort in rehabilitation than in community planning, sociology, and education—although undeniably all those things are helpful. With a basically theological problem the corrective to be applied posits the assistance of supernatural help. Specifically, a great need today, already pointed out, is prayer to the Heavenly Mother of the fallen, our Mother of Grace: "Remember O most gracious Virgin Mary, that never was it known that anyone who fled to thy protection, implored thy help, and sought thy intercession, was left unaided."

But to pray for help the sinner must first acknowledge his need of help. On the part of the world, and particularly on the part of sinners, wrong attitudes toward sin have become widespread. Many, indeed, fail to recognize the reality of sin. Since it is in the milieu of the world that the religious community's work must be carried out, we cannot discount the possibility that some erosion may have taken place in our own thinking about sin.

Humanly and naturally, sensitivity to sin's malice does not come easily; it requires assiduous cultivation. Prayer for sinners will secure this saintly sensitivity.

When we are devoted to sinners, there is an awareness of their plight, a desire to aid them, a willingness to spend self for them. All of this imprints on our own consciousness keen alertness when anything savors of sin. We are antagonistic to sin's myriad temptations, and ruthlessly reject sin in our daily lives. It would be an incredible inconsistency for us to be generously interested in separating the sinner from his sin, while admitting and welcoming it in our own lives.

Prayerful concern for sinners can furnish a certain *élan* to our spiritual routine. Left to itself, even a routine of so lofty a nature as that found in religious life, may grow monotonous and mechanical; activities, while very worthwhile, may lose their inspiration. A conscious dedication, a specific offering, is needed to keep that regime really voluntary and adequately motivated. When our day, or various parts of it, are offered for sinners, especially for specific cases we are familiar with, our religious exercises and our good deeds take on a crusading aspect. Thus, the soul is invigorated and keeps high its interest in these staples of asceticism; they are performed eagerly, with care and unction. An arrangement mutually advantageous to self and sinner is established.

Efforts in behalf of sinners spur on our quest for perfection in a very important area, that of avoiding venial sin. Unless in some concerted way the evil of venial sin is kept before our minds, we will grow lax. Prayers for sinners naturally impart a detestation for sin as we realize the havoc it has wreaked in the souls of individuals. Salutary truths about venial sin are recalled: it inevitably weakens the whole fiber of our moral person, hampers all the good we attempt, takes the edge off our virtue, blunts the impact of the good done, and hinders unnecessarily the forward motion of our asceticism.

Laxity toward venial sin predisposes us to sin. Attachment to it, when temptation strikes, makes capitulation that much easier. Sin has become a familiar thing; something that does not startle and scare us as fully as it should. Concern for sinners reinforces our conviction that, after mortal sin, venial sin is the greatest of evils, and, despite any palliatives or excuses, it stands forth clearly as a transgression of the just law of an all-powerful and an all-good God. Venial sin can consign us to Purgatory, there to suffer unspeakable torments, a process of purification, before entering into heaven.

If such is the lot even of lay people careless about venial sin, lay people who have had less schooling in, and fewer aids to holiness, how much more accountable will be the religious who compromises with venial sin. It would be well, occasionally, to make venial sin the topic of our meditation; our considerations can include an examination of the care we have had for sinners. Horror for sin makes us zealous to aid sinners; our prayers for them may effectively help us to avoid moral deviation.

Those needing this prayer often will not offer it to Mary; sin dims the brighter vision; as unrestrained passion flames, faith cools. Although everyone finds prayer difficult, prolonged vice renders the effort to raise mind and heart to God almost unattainable; unfortunately, those who need this spiritual help most will generally not do the necessary praying. Who then will offer this prayer to Our Lady? Strangely enough, were you to direct this query to these sinners themselves, they would supply you a good answer. Many of them would reply that praying to the Mother of God for sinners should be done by the sisters in the convent.

Their reason for saying so rests upon the realization of a great truth, one which we ourselves must never lose sight of: Mary, in a very special way, serves as mother to those who have dedicated life itself to her service; consequently, the prayers of her daughters in religion receive a special hearing. By embracing the common life of the convent and the apostolic work symbolized by the convent, devout religious draw close to the Mother of God. In this closeness, religious can petition successfully for the erring. As spiritual conveyors, their prayers to Mary bring bewitched hearts to her maternal heart. Mary's solicitude for her wayward children, although their lives may have accepted deep, pervasive compromises with sin, does not lag or falter. Great indeed is her joy when, through our prayers, they turn again toward their mother.

In our prayerful remembrance of the unfortunate we follow that noble, scriptural tradition of the Valiant Woman, who "hath opened her hand to the needy, and stretched out her hands to the poor." None are poorer than the sinner, none more needy. Never more nobly is the "law of clemency on her tongue" than when the consecrated religious prays for prodigals—despaired of and despairing. Here before us lies the example of Esther and Judith, Old Testament heroines, prototypes of our Heavenly Mother, who dedicated themselves heroically to the welfare of their people. So, too, sinners, lost sheep who have wandered from the true fold, are our people; we want to bring them home to the court of Mary, where they will find her divine Son.

As did Esther at the oriental court, the prayerful religious has special privileges at the court of the Queen of Heaven. Although part of the etiquette of Esther's time prevented anyone from entering the royal court unbidden, she was permitted to do so and, once inside, pleaded effectively for her people. You must be the Esthers of your people at the court of the Queen of

Heaven, for there your prayers enter and find favor. Your pleas save sinners, sinners who are menaced, not by transient bodily death, but by the eternal death of the soul. Then will the praises awarded Judith from the hearts of a grateful people be yours also: "They all blessed her with one voice, saying: 'Thou art the glory of Jerusalem, thou art the joy of Israel, thou art the honor of our people' " (Jth. 15:10).

Surely it has often been your experience to receive the petition, "Mother, say a prayer for me," or "Sister, please remember a special intention of mine." Such requests are not limited to good people, for even sinful people, when they come in contact with religious, rarely fail to ask somewhere in the conversation, "Say a prayer for me." Perhaps they do it unthinkingly, perhaps they cannot think of anything else to say, or they may feel that it is expected, as one says hello to other people. But they do ask it. In some lives, it may be the last glimmer of a dying faith. Whatever the reason, we should not turn it aside.

On one occasion a group of priests were startled when a day laborer, who had never the opportunity for much formal education, was telling of the prayerfulness that he felt marked Mary's consecrated religious. To illustrate his belief he quoted accurately and with considerable feeling the following lines:

> Come, pensive nun, devout and pure,
> Sober, steadfast, and demure,
> All in a robe of darkest grain,
> Flowing with majestic train,
> And sable stole of cypress lawn
> Over thy decent shoulders drawn
> Come; but keep thy wonted state,
> With even step and musing gait
> And looks commercing with the skies,
> Thy wrapt soul sitting in thy eyes.
> There, held in holy passion still
> Forget thyself to marble . . .

He remembered those lines he had memorized in school because he felt their poetry beautifully imaged the prayerful nun; the prayerful nun who kept him and all others close to Mary's care. Even sinners share that faith in our prayerfulness; indeed how sad it would be were we ever to "let them down." That is the way the people picture us; that is the way the people want us. Such a splendid, enviable reputation cannot afford a demeaning of our prayer-life by shoddy eclecticism, which would be mindful only of the spiritually elite.

Once established, the extension of prayerful concern to sinners leads us on to a rather fundamental question: Why has an individual sister been given the grace of vocation? Here, of course, we must move with great caution, remembering the words of the Epistle to the Romans: "O the depth of the riches of the wisdom and of the knowledge of God! How incomprehensible are his judgments and how unsearchable his ways. For who has known the mind of the Lord, or who has been his counsellor?" (Rom. 11:33-34). Why the favor of God—perhaps at Mary's intercession—has chosen us, we simply do not know. Without effort we remember well that in schooldays there were associates of ours with equally commendable qualities; yet they were not chosen. Why they were not and why we were, we do not know. It would be best humbly to consign vocations to the undeserved goodness of God's mercy and charity.

Nonetheless, we would be wise to be conscious of the working of God's providence in the case of each individual religious vocation, for he has in mind his own divine purposes in choosing each one of us. Under that providence we may be the means to guide a particular soul; the example which a certain young heart will follow. Also—and here lies the point, which because of its pertinence we would like to stress—for some poor sinner, our prayers may make the saving difference and secure the deliverance of his soul from eternal damnation. From the beginning of time God's eternal planning may have directed our assignment to a particular place, to work with a particular group, or to convert a particular isolated sinner. Mindful always of these preconceptions forced by faith upon the consciousness, we must strive unceasingly to bring forth Christ in the lives of all—including even sinners, even when our only means of reaching them is the separated, distant way of prayer. It is a strange vocation that banishes sinners from its care; sinners, who have been created by God, live in God's world, and were destined for God's heaven.

Our attitude toward sinners must follow the example of St. Theresa of Lisieux. If we follow her example, we can acquire some of the great spiritual gains which were her own. Her solicitude for the sinner is portrayed in this pericope from her *Autobiography*.

From that day, the cry of my dying Savior: "I thirst!" resounded incessantly in my heart, kindling within it new fires of zeal. To give my Beloved to drink was my constant desire; I was consumed with an insatiable thirst for souls, and I longed at any cost to snatch them from the everlasting flames of hell.

In order to enkindle my ardor still further, our divine Master showed me how pleasing to him was my zeal. About this time, I heard people speak of a notorious criminal, Pranzini, who had been condemned to death for several horrible murders. He was impenitent, and in consequence it was feared he would be eternally lost. Longing to avert that greatest of misfortunes, a calamity beyond all repair, I employed all the spiritual means I could think of to obtain the ransom of this poor sinner; and knowing that of myself I could do nothing, I offered up the infinite merits of our Savior together with the treasures of Holy Church.

In the depths of my heart I felt convinced my request would be granted, but, that I might gain courage to persevere in the quest for souls, I said in all simplicity: "My God, I am sure thou wilt pardon this unhappy Pranzini, and I shall still think so even if he does not confess his sins or give any sign of sorrow—such is the confidence I have in thy unbounded mercy. But, because this is my first sinner, I beg for just one sign of repentance to reassure me."

My prayer was granted to the letter. Though Papa never allowed us to read newspapers, I did not consider it an act of disobedience when, on the day following the execution, I hastily opened the paper, *La Croix*, and looked for the part concerning Pranzini. What was it I saw? . . . Tears betrayed my emotion and I was obliged to run from the room. Without confession or absolution Pranzini had mounted the scaffold, and the executioners were dragging him towards the fatal block, when all at once, apparently in answer to a sudden inspiration, he turned round, seized a crucifix which the priest held towards him, and kissed our Lord's sacred Wounds three times!

The inspiring quality of this account should be readily apparent to all of us. While signs such as those vouchsafed to St. Theresa are restricted generally to our great saints, the sign ought not to be considered the important thing; of infinitely greater importance is the fact that because God is pleased at our prayers for sinners he will employ these prayers as the means of carrying out the redemptive work of his divine Son, that most beautiful task of increasing the Mystical Body. Since prayer for sinners ranks as high charity it should bring equally high perfection to the religious; the bond of perfection is charity and prayer for sinners is the most altruistic of charities. No one need ever know of this charity; even to ourselves no results may be visible. This charity gains no public plaudits, perhaps not even the esteem of associates. Its object is neither attractive persons, nor those who can "do things" for us; only pure love of God can provide its motivation and sustaining force.

But God sees and God will reward. Any charity of ours draws down upon us his mercies. "Amen, I say to you," are Christ's words in the Gospel, "as long as you did it to one of these, my least brethren, you did it to me." Certainly the generous flow of his assistance will enable us to forge ahead spiritually. Our prayer-life can anticipate better attention and deeper fervor, since the charity prepares us well for the times of prayer. Grace strengthens our resolution and renders our spiritual energy more adequate in accomplishing Christ's work. As a kind reward, God's goodness etches its marvelous design in the willing, cooperative soul, and a new and greater moral beauty is resplendent there. Cast upon the waters, our bread of charitable concern for sinners returns to make of self the greatest beneficiary.

Charity is particularly salutary for those engaged in classroom work. By the nature of our position we are forced to do a good deal of saying "no"; admonishing, correcting, some fault finding, and even denunciation of bad example and defections, simply must be part of our routine fulfillment of duty. Latent in such necessary activities lurks a real danger of growing over-critical and censorious. Unless we are careful, we may imitate the error of the Pharisees, and, tithing mint and anise, become forgetful of the larger law of charity. While at times we must lay burdens upon the shoulders of our charges, we would become like Pharisees indeed did we not lift a finger to lighten those burdens. Prayerful concern for all sinners and, in particular, for delinquents who may be numbered among our own classroom household, will serve to counteract any such tendency on our part and will happily provide our personalities with a balance wheel of charity.

This compassionate attitude truly reflects the compassion of the Church, when her children have succumbed to moral weakness and even fallen away. We may cite here the principles of the moral theologians of the Church, which govern sacramental absolution. Painstaking care prevails lest anyone properly disposed, no matter what his crimes may have been, be denied forgiveness. Even in cases involving habitual sin the approach remains a merciful one. Many very strict rules need to be fulfilled before any theologian would judge definitively that a penitent should be dismissed without absolution. Even then, the confessor is counseled to break such a decision very kindly and very gently and always to add the solace and encouragement that should the future find the situation or dispositions sufficiently altered, the penitent may return and receive absolution. Since this is the policy of the Church herself, can we be other than understanding and compassionate toward poor unfortunates?

Every school has its percentage of "risks," students who succeed in remaining—which may be good—but without righting themselves or permitting others to right them—which is bad. Any high-handed uncharitableness toward such students, may be just the straw that tips the scales in the wrong direction—perhaps for life. No right-minded person denies that, from time to time, the school has no alternative but to dismiss certain students from its ranks. There are, however, ways of dismissing students; the right way insists that the final separation be marked by understanding and kindness, which make clear that the question of dismissal has been the subject of our thoughts and our prayers. Every school likewise faces the prospect of some "bad graduates," those who later go morally sour. When they do so, we feel a certain natural sadness. But, how much more tragic would be that sadness, if, because of our past uncharity, they should suspect that we will not welcome them back and be eager to help them.

May we always welcome them, and all sinners, to our prayers. Much sin and delinquency have stained our world, yet it is still the world to which on Christmas night Mary brought the Redeemer. Mary's efforts to bring to all, including sinners, her infant Savior, are ceaseless; and so should be our own. Though it may appear hopeless, let us keep up our prayers for heaven's outcasts. Those prayers will sweetly soften our charity and aid our spiritual progress, as they help those who—no matter how sinful they may be—are not yet beyond help. Seeing our prayerful love for sinners, Christ will recognize in us a pleasing resemblance to his own mother. Perhaps, because of that resemblance, in heaven we may meet saints seeking to thank us for our part in their salvation. Happily, we shall know then that our own prayers to Mary finally shared her winning ways; winning ways which caused the exasperated devils—according to the highly imaginative medieval poet, Gaultier de Coincy—to complain that the Mother of God prevailed upon her Son to deprive them of sinners they had long awaited as their legitimate spoil.

> There's nothing she can do or say
> That he'll refuse, or say her nay.
> Whatever she may want is right,
> Though she say that black is white,
> And dirty water clear as snow;
> "My mother says it, and it's so!"

≈ 3 ≈

The Help and
Hope of Heaven

13

Revelation, Milieu
of Our Vocation

THE BLAZING SUN OF NOON WITH ITS WARMTH
and light symbolizes that revelation, which, as Christians, we
enjoy under the divine dispensation of the New Testament era.
For many centuries mankind knew only the limited truth mani-
fested through the angels, Moses, and the prophets; today, our
revelation has been received in all its sacred fullness from the
lips of the Son of God. Only partial foreshadowings graced the
moving messages of the prophets; Old Testament angels were
but agents accomplishing isolated tasks; Moses was a faithful
servant indeed, but only a servant. By virtue of the patent contrast
with those times and those mediators, we begin to appreciate
our great good fortune and to understand how all-important
Christ and Christ's truth must loom in our lives. When, quite
fittingly, Christ dominates those lives, they become pliant instruments of divine goodness, and through them his light and warmth
bless and cheer the entire world.

While these thoughts should enlarge our personal happiness,
nonetheless, despite such easily available happiness, we sometimes lurk in shadows and permit the sterling brightness and
radiant warmth of Christ to stagnate, activated neither in the

expression of our personality nor in the influence of our deeds. In our attitude toward everyday affairs we act, mistakenly, like Old Testament members of the human family. Each morning heralds our daily burdens: labors that must be faced; irritations remembered, and probably to be repeated; temperamental disinclinations, clamoring for their own way—all these, very humanly, we call to mind in the dawn's early light. Here indeed, without that warmth and light of Christ, a bleak prospect unfolds. So, too, at nightfall, as the day's books are balanced, failures seem to outweigh successes; sorrows crowd about trying to shut out our few modest joys. Unless the sight of Christ softens our gaze and solaces our heart, concerns seem all awry. If, however, we arm ourselves with the revelation of the New Testament, Christ's words offer encouragement: "These things I have spoken to you that in me you may have peace. In the world you will have affliction. But take courage, I have overcome the world" (John 16:33).

In all of Plato's writings, the passage most widely known and alluded to recounts the "Allegory of the Cave." Plato pictures a man so seated in this cave that his face looks upon the wall of the cave, while behind him lies the cave's opening. Light, flooding in, causes shadows to flicker across the wall—reflections of realities outside the cave, behind the back of its occupant. For the seated man, naught exists but these distorted images which he sees only in reflections.

Although the product of a pagan mind, this same allegory serves to illustrate the plight of the Christian religious who fails to look upon life through the revelation of Christ. Should a religious refuse to draw upon the full message of the New Testament, only shadowy images are visible and these compose a depressing picture overloaded by trials and difficulties which hamper her mornings and disquiet her evenings. Only when our evaluations possess the insight gleaned from attentive adherence to Christ's doctrine, do we properly picture our vocation and all its variegated aspects. To dwell upon the more harsh and trying circumstances of our vocation, and to separate those circumstances from the alleviating principles which neutralize and even sublimate them, is to follow the example of Plato's cave-dweller, and results in a distorted, disheartening picture, utterly unreal because essentially incomplete.

Viewed with faith, hardships reveal themselves as fragmentary, and recede before the supernatural; heaven unmasks the fraud of a solely earth-bound picture; Christ and Christ's truth place before our gaze the realities of grace, the eternal verities of our vocation. In this complete context, life's accidental disappointments appear rather imaginary, greatly fictionalized. How otherwise could we comprehend the Sermon on the Mount, especially its eight beatitudes? Only when sustained by Christ's strength-giving truth can we live as believers in his teachings: that the meek and poor in spirit are blessed; that our mourning will find comfort and our thirst for justice its fill; and, above all, that we should rejoice when we meet with reviling and persecution.

Christ must be brought to the day's beginning and the evening's close in a spirit of intense realism. When he holds the center of the mind's stage, how insignificant all else seems. We need that vision which St. John possessed on the Isle of Patmos as he looked back over the full day of life and salvaged with his aged pen what was all-important: "In the beginning was the Word, and the Word was with God; and the Word was God. . . . All things were made through him, and without him was made nothing that has been made. In him was life, and the life was the light of men. . . . And the Word was made flesh, and dwelt among us" (John 1:1, 3-4, 14). Our lives as consecrated religious can recognize no other context; any other context opposes God's plan for our vocation. From all eternity, Christ in the bosom of the Father knew the whole fabric of our lives; beyond history, in his glorified life, Christ awaits as our unceasing reward. If "all things were made through him," can we not include everything affecting us, every challenge and every suffering? If he "dwelt among us," what do our problems matter? In him, and in him alone, we must recall, is our life.

The central fact of the glad tidings of Christianity emphasizes our participation in the divine life itself, which makes us truly sons of God.

> This likeness consists, according to the Second Epistle of St. Peter, in an enrichment by grace, in a fulfilling and permeation of our being by divine and holy forces. We shall be made "partakers of the divine nature" (II Pet. 1:4). We win "a share in his sanctity" (Heb. 12:10). Therefore, man's end lies, not in mere humanity, but in a new sort of superhumanity, in an elevation and enhancement of his being, which essentially surpasses all created powers and raises him into an absolutely new sphere of existence and life, into the fullness of the life of God. God shows himself most luminously as the absolute Personality, sufficient for himself and independent of the world, in the fact that he reveals himself personally to us, as one person to another. And he shows that he is absolute Goodness in the fact that he reveals himself to us as our Friend, nay, as our Father, so that by the power of his love we become his sons and may cry "Abba, Father."
>
> (ADAM, *Spirit of Catholicism*, p. 205)

How can this precious exaltation captured thus in Karl Adam's moment of insight, be perpetuated? How can it be decoded and its message spread in a practical fashion over the routine events of day to day? Faith in Christ and the glad tidings of his revelation distills this exaltation into a practiced program of Catholic action. In the fullness of our faith we draw near to Christ with true hearts; then, our lives quite naturally—in a supernatural manner—become Christ-centered lives.

When, in this way, faith serves as the basis for our activities, all that we plan and do, even our evaluations of the results of those plans and activities, have their starting point in principles which are grand and holy because available only through revelations which Christ granted to those who were his companions and to those who would be his companions. One does not possess such dominant faith easily, but it more than rewards the most extravagant efforts expended in its pursuit; once possessed, it leads to high perfection, for high perfection is quite obviously the lesson of Christ's example and his teaching. Should this starting and sustaining strength, powered by faith, be missing, our spiritual acceleration will sputter and remain ever in vacillation; one day it will soar meteorically, the next day it will capsize. Bedrock faith in the words and deeds of Christ, alone makes possible enduring, constantly progressing virtue.

Ascetical writers have borrowed from philosophy the axiom, *arte perfecta non deliberat,* and in their examination of its implications they have sought to clarify the essential role of faith in the quest of holiness. Just as perfect art does not deliberate, neither does spiritual perfection. The working habits of a great artist become second nature to him; almost mechanically or instinctively the right stroke crosses the canvas. In the same way, firm faith surveys, almost automatically, every vocational problem from the viewpoint of the supernatural. Daily irritations, vexations, and disappointments, are softened by the very gaze of faith; the right response to the opportunities of grace offers itself almost without thought.

Temptations do not surprise and overcome; rather they spend their force in the nullifying context which receives them—an unwavering faith. Victory does not hinge upon a sudden resolution, a vigorous impulse of the moment, a frantic rallying. Virtue's triumph springs from habit, the extension of the whole integrated personality, the outcome of faith. Such souls require little antecedent deliberation because their faith in what Christ has told them in the New Testament concerning God's dealings with man is so rugged and pervasive that it precludes deliberation, thinking it an extra, superfluous, step. Faith, so firmly braced and placing Christ so luminously before the soul, is more than a quality of the mind; it has the fullness and power of life.

When the faith within the marrow of our souls is of such caliber, it contains an antidote to any discouragement. Such faith imparts the realization that everything we do, is done for Christ;

seeking his will, we simply do our best, leaving all results completely to him. With faith of this sort, it is hard for us to establish rational grounds for discouragement; or, turning the sentence around, when we are discouraged it must be on the natural level alone; there is no discouragement when the natural and the rational are supernaturalized, elevated by faith.

The age in which we live has been termed an age of anxiety; in all walks of life people seem entangled in personal fears, enmeshed in doubts, hauntingly preoccupied with the weaknesses of self. In varying degrees, complexes destructive of personality hamper the concentration which our problems require and sap the determination which their solutions demand. Such instability of soul and such paralysis of achievement are rooted fundamentally in a lack of conviction with regard to what is important in life and what are the means to obtain what is important. In brief, there is a lack of conviction that God has given answers and that they may be found in the New Testament of Christ's glad tidings. Only such conviction makes possible strong starts and staying power in the spiritual combat; without it, a pessimistic troublous defeatism agonizes our consciousness. Indeed, it is not impertinent to inquire whether the fullness of faith of the religious community itself has not been swayed by the subtle undertows sweeping round it.

When we cringe before difficulties, perhaps we do so because we have been influenced by the temper of the times. Should every proposed new effort find us counting the cost of cooperation—not only carefully, but even craftily—it may indeed be so. If we aim low perpetually, are content with mediocrity and even less, well may we ask ourselves the why of this reaction. If we quit repeatedly, sometimes just before the call to battle has sounded, we should be disturbed with self. Answers to these inquiries will point up a lack of conviction and the need for a strengthened faith.

Such false attitudes, when they are discovered in the religious community, present a sad picture to the true religious; and the picture grows sadder as that religious ponders over the contrasting scenes of former years. Looking back makes it hard to resist the temptation to become a *laudator temporis acti*—a praiser of the days of old. Yet, what inspiration we can drink from these earliest days of religious communities in the New World.

The vast, rolling plains of the West as well as the teaming, toiling cities of the East knew no nobler pioneers. Misunderstanding, opposition, even persecution, met them at every turn. Hardship touched their living quarters, their food and clothing, their every duty and their challenging opportunities. But, they were rich and strong in deep religious faith. No known ideals ever outmatched the supernatural faith of a religious devoutly dedicated to Christ. How doubly true becomes the following tribute to the pioneers, when it is applied to pioneer religious:

> It was hard to trace
> The slow sure growth of convictions from the seed
> Till they harden and are like armor—and yet, it happens.
> And when it happens . . .
> You have a force in the world.
>
> (s. BENÉT, *Western Star*, p. 123)

There was a force in the new world—a divine force firing the hearts of leaders such as Frances Cabrini, our first citizen-saint, and her dauntless daughters. How paltry the hardships of our modern age, when, from the distant past, memory recalls the kind of hardships they had to face. How resolute our predecessors in religion—shaming us at times. May their unextinguishable faith kindle ours in its bright flame. May their determination and courage somehow graft themselves to our own faith. Then, with our own indomitable faith, following their example, and, above all, with Christ's help, we shall follow bravely today's paths to spiritual glory.

Faith faces life courageously and conquers it, today just as in former times. Yet, examples of this sort have not been as widely or as fully emulated as they might be in our cautious and jittery twentieth century. Among the mental sicknesses doctors are

concerned with today is paranoia. Often it has among its components this very failure to face life and grapple manfully with
its realities. In such pathological cases, the victim separates himself from reality and lives in an imaginary world of his own creation. Sometimes these persons imagine themselves to be Napoleon, Churchill, or some other notable. As they attempt to act
out their imaginary personalities, their words and actions appear
so foolish as to evoke laughter from those who behold their antics.
We ourselves would be equally foolish to live in a make-believe
world; and we do just that when the added dimension of faith
does not dominate our lives. A religious who lacks realistic faith
lives in a world of make-believe, a world of unreality. For the
religious, the world of faith embraces reality; any other world
will soon be found false, and, unless that discovery is quickly
made, such a concept of the world will destroy the life of the
religious vows. Should a religious, quite unthinkingly, plan and
act on a purely natural level—a level quite apart from faith—
the life of that religious is just as silly as the life of any paranoiac
who imagines himself to be Napoleon. It is no more nonsensical
for a shoemaker to act as though he is Napoleon than for a religious to act out the daily life of the rule and the self-sacrificing
duties of the religious state on an exclusively natural level, unin-
spired and unsustained by faith. Answering the question, "What
is life?" we either include faith or we abandon the aspirations of
our religious vocation.

To acknowledge that the perfect living of the rule of the
community means accepting a hard task, marks the height of
sensible realism. That task unaided by faith gradually waxes impossible. Often the obstacles confronting us are so sizeable that,
in the natural order of things, we cannot, of ourselves, be vic-
torious. Our plight in such situations resembles that of Judas
Machabeus when he was threatened by the hosts of the powerful
Timotheus. So formidable was the strength of the enemy, Machabeus had not the slightest chance of victory. Not in the armed
might of the Jews was his trust placed; he consigned the battle

to the goodness of God, and in a spirit of deep faith asked divine aid. He received that assistance; he gained the victory—a victory clearly the work of God and the reward of faith. Faith likewise holds the key to our own victories. Faith's world is truly God's world; faith reminds us that his knowledge and his power are omnipresent and omnipotent. While Christ remains at our side we should not be discouraged; we will not be defeated.

New spiritual vistas open in the wake of faith; trials and hardships, previous sources of discontent and discouragement, change to accepted, even welcome, opportunities of reparation and expiation. Acknowledging, in accordance with the dictates of faith, our need to link our daily lives to the Savior who expiated our sins in the laver of his precious blood, willingly we permit the drawing of our own blood in the many sacrifices inextricably bound up with each day's efforts to share in the work of redemption. In doing so, our faith rejoices to see us grow more Christlike.

At morning Mass we experience a potent rekindling of the fires of faith. During the day our reliving of the morning Mass, especially its remembered voluntary offering of the chalice, solaces and hallows the burdens of lengthening hours. Our personality, revealed in its judgments, affections, and determinations, becomes stabilized and strengthened by this active faith. The purification of the spirit attendant upon such faith renders much less formidable temptations from either the world, or the flesh, or the devil. Faith separates us from the attractions of the profane, and gradually molds us into completely dedicated instruments of divine goodness. That is the meaning of holiness and sanctity—lives transformed by faith in Christ and utterly given over to him.

Today we enjoy life in the fullness and brightness of New Testament revelation; opportunities, unknown to those dwelling in the shadows of the Old Law, are realized. While only glimpses were caught by them, our privileged possession of Christ rejoices because "we know that the Son of God has come and has given us understanding, that we may know the true God and may be in his true son. He is the true God and eternal life" (I John 5:20). Only as members of the Mystical Body of Christ, suffused with his warmth and light, can we properly appreciate our vocation.

Only through faith can we properly appreciate the context of our vocation, namely the whole world around us; the whole world as revealed by faith, the world as seen from the eminence of the truths of the New Testament. This world of faith ranges far wider than the world of sight and sound. It embraces heaven as well as earth: the faithful angels, true messengers of God to man; and the faithless devils, slavish subalterns in Satan's wiles to ensnare us. This world has inhabitants other than ourselves: the blessed above; the damned below; the souls suffering in purgatory. As well as force and motion, it includes the action of grace and the realm of the supernatural.

This supernatural realm of asceticism has God as its focal point, and views everything in relation to him. Everything that exists can be traced back to his power and is sustained only because of his goodness; whatever happens falls under his permissive will; the heart of the individual, as well as the pulse of the universe, is in the hollow of his hand.

Only these dimensions added to our workaday world can provide the insights necessary for an ascetical life, a life truly not of the world. Without the insights provided by faith, how can we ever recognize various deordinations in our own lives? Many things are regarded by the world as perfectly acceptable; faith must insist, however, that they be purged. How many attachments exist to places, persons, and things; attachments which the world judges to be perfectly natural. And indeed they are perfectly natural; one needs the illumination of faith to understand that they are not perfectly supernatural and that supernatural perfection requires us to wean ourselves away from such attachments.

We need the help of faith to make us understand the great harm of pride, the inevitable obstacles it places in the path of any ascetical ventures which the sincere soul attempts. Faith has exposed the wicked pride of the angels, the kindred pride that shattered the paradise of our first parents, and the pervasive taint which has remained to trouble fallen human nature. The greatest antidote to pride, a sad awareness of our personal sins, so offensive to a loving Savior, stems from divine revelation. Only faith reminds us of the New Testament lesson for any herald of Christ—"He must increase, I must decrease."

To become a religious should mean to dedicate oneself to the hidden life. But the hidden life makes no sense to the world; all the motivations of the world and all its drives move in the opposite direction. That God was born in the poverty of a stable, was known as the son of the lowly carpenter Joseph and the unknown Mary, and shared with them the simple life of their obscurity for thirty years out of thirty-three, remains unintelligible without faith. How can anyone be convinced of the wisdom of the *Exercises* of St. Ignatius when, for example, he holds before us the ideal of choosing poverty rather than wealth and of turning aside from honors and reputation, unless deep religious faith is brought to these wonderful pages of high spirituality?

Any practice of the virtues is likewise deeply steeped in faith. Against the savage assaults of temptations which threaten holy purity, a strong faith must be had to power our resistance. Human nature and mere natural reason alone will not suffice to keep us always strong. In the last analysis, there must always be a deep love of Christ born of faith.

The world's pity and man's natural goodness can rise to a certain humanitarianism, but for the practice of heroic charity in dealing with our neighbor, we need to see him as a member of the Mystical Body of Christ. He has to be accepted as one who is truly Christ's brother. We need to believe that what we do to one of these little ones, we do to Christ. We need to love him because we love Christ. Only then can we faithfully carry out the works of charity as well as we should.

Fruitful faith means that we succeed in fulfilling the exhortation: "Let that mind be in you which was also in Christ Jesus." Once faith is achieved as our true state of mind, we should move steadily and unerringly to holiness. Christ will be on our tongue in prayer, in the innermost desires of our heart, in the power of our will. Our whole nature begins to feel that here we have the only emphasis that counts, that in this one word has been synopsized all that we hold dear. Briefly, here is the result of faith's acceptance of the New Testament, in the words of a modern convert who is speaking to unbelievers: "You cannot understand how much we love Christ and how much he means to us. He is always before our eyes; his hand is ever on our shoulders. When we work or when we rest, when we eat or when we sleep, when at home or when abroad, Christ is always within us. A Christian who knows what he believes lives in the presence and the company of Jesus Christ" (August Cochin, *Espérances Chretiennes*, p. 339).

Faith accepts, and then lives in accordance with, that fundamental advice Christ gave to his followers: "Abide in me, and I in you. As the branch cannot bear fruit of itself unless it remain on the vine, so neither can you unless you abide in me. I am the vine, you are the branches. He who abides in me, and I in him, he bears much fruit; for without me you can do nothing" (John 15:4–5).

Emboldened by faith, prayer fructifies in the most intimate union with God. We have learned from our personal life and from our reading of ascetical theology what a wonderful experience prayer can be; how at such times God can delight the spirit with moments of supreme happiness. If the lives of those who have followed Christ are thoughtfully examined, we see that their prayer brought frequent solace of soul to them, and at times even enraptured their whole being.

In short, there can be no doubt that prayer makes possible such exultation and exaltation. There can be no doubt either, unfortunately, that sometimes barriers, for which we must accept responsibility, prevent advances in prayer. Such a self-erected barrier, hampering our prayer life, arises from a lack of complete, powerful faith. We are compelled in all honesty to acknowledge that our faith has failed to penetrate as deeply as it might the wonderful mysteries of Christ. Concentration upon his passion and death seems to have been the special focus of the prayer of the great mystics; their own writings testify clearly to this. They tell us in these written revelations, that Christ himself inspired the direction of their prayerful hours. Christ's own words contain the same stress: "And I, if I be lifted up from the earth, will draw all things to myself" (John 12:32).

Our concern with the cross, therefore, a concern which flows from our faith and is joined to our prayer, goes far beyond mere acquiescence to the limitations inherent in our perfect allegiance to the rule of a religious institute; our concern with the cross and with everything in our life bearing its imprint, signifies a bold aspiration for union with our crucified Master who "humbled himself, becoming obedient to death, even to death on a cross" (Phil. 2:8).

To the Jews, the cross of Christ was a stumbling block, to the Gentiles it was folly, and they rejected it. To the religious the way of the cross is neither, and has been accepted as the path to paradise. This must be the ultimate significance of our vocation, our loftiest response to the call "come follow me." A mounted cross, spiring to the sky of heaven, told of Christ's love. Love wrote his Gospel; its criterion, "Greater love than this no one has, that one lay down his life for his friends" (John 15:13). Such love remains still the quintessence of the following of Christ, and following Christ remains the quintessence of the religious vocation. In the fullness of revelation the New Testament dispensation assures us that even where we find the cross, because we also find there Christ, we possess present happiness and the beginning of eternal happiness. Resplendent in the warmth and brightness of his love, even the cross, and therefore all things, viewed by the deep faith of the devout religious, loom as guide-posts to heaven.

14

Faith, Its Proper Dimension

TO CALL TO THE ATTENTION OF THE RELIGIOUS community the wonderful treasure of faith lying within its walls, can be a very real service. Unquestionably, we are aware of faith without anyone calling it to our attention, but being aware of it is one thing, it is another to be as fully aware as we might and as deeply appreciative as we should. Any intensification of our effort in that direction, prompted somewhat perhaps by the words of this chapter, will be a real service to self.

Dealing as it does with the infinite majesty of God, his sublime attributes, his deep mysteries, the relationships—unfathomable in their fullness—of divine goodness to human weakness, faith can be ever-evolving in its fruition; no limit or point exists at which we can say, now we need go no further. On the contrary, we must press on to develop our faith during our time on earth, when we see only in a dark glass; no amount of attention, can be regarded as superfluous or sterile.

We may begin by examining the degree of joy we feel in our faith, for because of faith alone, religious should be joyful people. Happily, the joyfulness of religious is often commented on by the outside world; non-Catholics particularly are impressed, although a bit puzzled, by the natural, graceful laughter welling up from the heart, which they have noted when they chanced to share the company of Catholic sisters.

Examining things somewhat more closely, however, the fact is that these outside observations have generally been made under ideal conditions; the sisters were momentarily enjoying a little freedom from their day-to-day cares; they were on holiday to some extent, their problems and tasks far away on a deserted work desk. By dint of circumstances, their best faces, so to speak, were put forward. It is of more moment for ourselves, of more serious concern, to determine what habit of joy, what deeper inner characteristic, marks our lives.

This joy will be in proportion to the richness of our faith, for, while joy is a fruit of faith, both joy and faith are closely intertwined and mutually nourishing. Faith makes possible a much fuller life, adds to existence a whole new dimension, renders audible to the soul the more rarefied decibels of joy. This joyous faith wafts us above earthbound cares. Not that we deny their existence or fail to come to grips with them, but they have been deprived of the power to overwhelm us; they disturb us much less. Instead of letting life center about such cares, we keep the modifying, consoling values of faith uppermost in our minds; because of faith, joy remains essential, and gnawing cares become peripheral. The case is simply this: deep faith preserves the proper hierarchy of values. Perhaps the above seems somewhat negative in approach: positively, faith also imparts joys to the down-to-earth business of daily living. Faith so presents people, situations, and events to us that we react with confidence and reassurance; we do not meet them exclusively in their sometimes depressing earthly contours.

Occasionally, one has to deal with people who seem repellant or with others who certainly would not be deliberately chosen as companions—and let us honestly concede that such estimates can be quite unbiased and accurate. The supernatural dimension of faith maintains—however things may be on the natural level—

that these people are children of God; Christ is their brother and his divine redemptive blood has been shed because, despite their faults, they are beloved of heaven.

Any sacrifices we make for the students committed to our care are sustained by more than that concept of "service" which professional persons, including the teacher, subscribe to; ours is the infinitely more glorious concept of helping to save souls for Christ. Various situations we encounter seem quite difficult, even desperate, from the viewpoint of their visible, tangible ingredients, but faith provides the supersonic helps of the supernatural. "More things are wrought by prayer than this world dreams of," is the solid encouragement of faith. God's grace, faith assures us, can yield amazing achievements where natural abilities alone reap only bleakest failures.

These faith-inspired counsels should protect our joy, preserve our peace of soul, and sustain the tranquillity of our prayerful inner consciousness, which we have reserved as a sanctuary for our hidden life with God. Here lies the hearthstone of our spiritual joy, that joy the world cannot give nor take away.

People who have no faith are generally lacking in joy, in the absence of its light a fearsome darkness characterizes their relationship with life. Many of them, even though wishing to lead good lives, seem unable to achieve certainty about right and wrong in essential matters. What a trial for the aged to have to approach death with only fear of what lies beyond. The young, unstrengthened by the lofty and unchanging principles which faith alone can provide, find themselves overwhelmed by ubiquitous examples of licentious living. Among all groups, when financial distress or enduring sickness renders daily living harsh, if faith does not ease the burden, how hard, and finally how despairing grows the struggle. Has not the want of faith contributed to today's fabulous sale of sleeping pills and to the current obsession to lie on psychiatric couches?

These mixed-up, star-crossed lives rebuke us for taking our own faith so much for granted. No spiritual life would be even

possible without this priceless gift. Content with, and sure of,
the permanent, fundamental values supplied us by faith, we are
inclined to forget that not everyone shares them. Although the
earth at times may spin dizzily, faith remains an ever-available
and always-effective stabilizer. Faith starts our life at a point
thousands will have to struggle to reach; at a point that other
thousand will never reach.

This fact sometimes goes unrealized, or is not as fully realized as it ought to be, even in the religious community. Before
entering religion many of us had the happiness of enjoying a
faith-filled environment. Many may have had little acquaintance,
by and large, with that other world of men who have no faith.
Personally, perhaps we met little contrast or challenge. The experience of others may have been different; varying samplings
of that other world may have infiltrated their lives. But, such experience, now long past, frequently fades into an unremembered,
distant dream. We have lived so long with faith and so close to
faith, that, paradoxically, it has become difficult for us to value
our faith precisely because of our faith.

In this we resemble those exuberantly healthy people who
have never had an ache or pain. They almost have to sit down
and go through a determined reasoning process to realize there
is an empire of hospitals stretching over the land with hundreds
of thousands of suffering patients. Being grateful to God for our
faith is not something that is going to come to us naturally and
spontaneously; it has to be a conscious, deliberate effort on our
part. It is an effort, however, that we ought to make sincerely
and often, and with all humility. Conscious gratitude for faith
will always be a quality that marks real depth of faith; it is an
intensification of faith, particularly of the joy of faith.

Deep faith, too, will have no admixture of worldliness in it,
for worldliness is an insidious corrosive of faith; there must be
no failure on our part to realize that the struggle between the
world and the followers of Christ, which he himself warned of,
continues unabated in our own times. Between the values sym-

bolized by the star of Bethlehem and the pleasures of the world, advertized in neon lights, there cannot be compromise; we need ever to be forewarned and forearmed. We have turned our backs on the pagan values of the world; for solutions to life's problems our faces must remain turned fully toward Christ.

Worldliness strives to cozen our faith: "Be practical," "Take it easy," it advises. Worldliness stresses that today is the era of the thirty-five-hour week. It whispers that Christianity, after all, is a corporate endeavor; one person alone is not expected to perform miracles. Saints, it tries to persuade us, are very unusual people; let us be content with a down-to-earth, run-of-the-mill spirituality. In effect, it attempts to delude us into believing that full allegiance to Christ is mere stargazing.

Worldliness seeks also to flatter us. In the matter of reading we are cajoled to be rashly "broad-minded," for this is the twentieth century and we are not mere children. It reassures us that we are more than able to sift out any rough passages from even the worst best-sellers. As for our conversations, were they not made for relaxation? In them we are not expected to be angels, always charitable and elevating. Our lives are not lived in a vacuum, we hear and see evil things, and so, reasons worldliness, why not be frank and talk about them? Under the guise of broad-mindedness, worldliness remarks archly that our rule is substantially all right, but its details—well! certainly no sensible person can be reasonably expected to pledge allegiance to anachronisms concocted in the Dark Ages.

These are some of the contests intermittently taking place between worldliness and faith. The religious cannot live as a man on a seesaw, shifting first to one side, then to the other. Inevitably, the man on the seesaw falls off. And, inevitably, the religious who jeopardizes faith through worldliness, allows that faith to become a rather neutral, nondescript sort of thing; for all practical purposes its greatest possible usefulness is destroyed.

True faith ought also to be endowed with complete confidence in Christ. Yet, even among Christ's most intimate followers, the apostles themselves, that confidence was sometimes absent. Instances need not be multiplied—sad to say they were frequent and are familiar—the account of their fears during the storm at sea, although Christ was in the ship with them, is typical. A confident faith casts all its cares upon the Lord in obedience to his express directive: "Let not your heart be troubled. You believe in God, believe also in me" (John 14:1). And this confidence yields deep peace, a spiritual calm honeycombed in the recesses of the soul: "Peace I leave with you, my peace I give to you. . . . Do not let your heart be troubled, or be afraid" (John 14:27).

Satan sometimes strikes in this area of our faith, for a trusting faith is a strong faith, which Satan hates. When faith is weak, when spiritually we backslide a little or remain idle, then the enemy is worldliness. But when, on the contrary, faith is strong, when things go well and we inch ahead in our spiritual progress, then faith becomes a target for the machinations of Satan himself. Satan menaces the trustfulness of such a faith. Alien, harmful thoughts rush in upon us to disturb our deep joy; scruples may seek to overturn that cradle of true prayerfulness, our calm of soul; Satan stimulates and simulates doubts, worries, fears—apt weapons of sabotage. In such trials we need to recollect quietly that Christ remains just as close to us as he was to the apostles in their storm-swept ship. At such times we can trustingly recall that the winds and waves are subject to him, and any perils, no matter how threatening, ought only serve to move us closer to Christ.

A barometer of the condition of our faith may be provided by an assessment of our good works. Faith without good works, we know, is dead, for Scripture has warned us to be doers and not hearers only. "What will it profit, my brethren, if a man say he has faith, but does not have works? And if a brother or sister be naked and in want of daily food, and one of you say to them: 'Go in peace, be warmed and filled,' yet you do not give them what is necessary for the body, what does it profit? So faith too, unless it has works, is dead in itself" (James 2:14-17).

We may think that the zeal and self-sacrifice productive of good works ought to be predicated of us automatically, by the very fact that we have undertaken the life of a religious. In truth this should be so, but, regrettably, it is not necessarily so. Only by stirring up in our own souls the potencies placed there by faith will our good works shine forth.

In one of his lectures, an elderly priest-teacher urged the religious teachers who made up his audience to be generous and zealous in their teaching apostolate—and for their own good. Then he drew a word-picture of a religious who was not.

This fairly young religious was pictured as sitting in a rocking-chair by the radiator, a heavy shawl wrapped around her, gazing listlessly out the window. At the time, it had seemed to many in the audience that anyone in religion, because of the heavy teaching schedule and the other duties imposed by rule, could not help being zealous. However, as the talk continued, the speaker's penetration showed that it could be a question of attitude.

A religious can complete the full day, but in such a way that a good deal of it is merely going through the motions. Toward classwork there can be a studied devotion to short-cuts which short-change both school and students, combined with an unwillingness to take cognizance of anything that could prove troublesome. When another teacher asks for assistance, although not refused, it will be given in such a fashion that both foresee that the request will not be repeated. Toward those emergency assignments which a harassed superioress may occasionally have to levy, there will be no outright disobedience, but a sort of shrewd passive resistance. Tasks accepted with the air of a resigned martyr will be completed grudgingly.

And so it will eventually happen that a person of this sort will go one way and the community another. Such a religious does not live the dynamic, exciting life of full faith, but rather vegetates, becoming prematurely senile.

Suppose now, that we are quite unlike this religious who lacked zeal, that constantly we are faithful to all duties, and in a fashion both energetic and cheerful; that we have always genuinely helped fellow-religious whenever we could; that various superiors have found in us a providential resource in their needs; in fact, it is acknowledged that we have always been a hard worker. What about the results? Can it be that in spite of all our efforts, we sometimes appear to have achieved very little?

Faith helps us here by enabling us, for our own spiritual well-being, to understand properly the Kingdom of Christ. The workings of that Kingdom, faith recalls, Christ himself explained in the parables he told his followers. In them he outlined its nature, rules of operation, and its progress through human time and earthly space. Quite deliberately he employed parables, so that the measure of faith would be also the measure of understanding.

One such parable, that of the cockle and the wheat, indicates to us that much of our work can be expected to be oversown with evil and seem barren; somehow, evil grew up to dwarf the wheat we laboriously tilled. Although in our work apparent failures and ungrateful reactions insinuate that we have reaped nothing, the parable disagrees. Christ paints on a canvas that is eternal; time alone cannot disclose, even to ourselves, the beauty of our Christlike achievement; our kingdom, like Christ's, is not of this world. Finite eyes may not immediately perceive this, yet in the light of faith it is clear.

This lesson of faith is a lesson which must be borne in mind by the religious dedicated to the teaching apostolate. To offset discouragement we need, periodically, to return to these considerations. In addition, we have to be quite realistic about our work with the students and—*per accidens*—at times with their parents. Some cases yield wonderful results it is true, but almost inevitably there will be others which give us little or no satisfac-

tion; and there are times when particular results seem very bad
indeed.

As you doubtless know, a fallacy exists in the minds of many
outside the school system, to the effect that the school is responsible for any evil done by students. These people forget that
the pupil may be but one of fifty in a class, is in school for only
a fraction of the time he or she is outside of it, and arrives on the
first day of school already rather firmly formed along certain
lines of character. Furthermore, family development of the young-
ster continues on the most intimate basis during all of the years
spent in educational institutions.

These observations are not presented to diminish zeal in any
way or to commit us to a sort of fatalism, but we do owe it to
our own spirituality to recognize that discouragement can be a
very formidable trial. If, foolishly and needlessly, we permit it
to get the better of us, our progress in holiness will unquestionably suffer. It is a matter of record that discouragement of this
sort, in an exaggerated form perhaps, has been a factor contributory to regretful departures from religious life. Such discouragement might have been averted by a strong faith, for
perhaps previously there was too much reliance upon the natural
order, upon purely natural means, and upon purely natural evaluations of results. Should we feel ourselves so tempted, the memory
of another parable descriptive of the Kingdom of Christ, that
of the mustard seed, may be helpful; it illustrates God's ways
among the children of men.

Like that seed, our contributions may appear small. So also,
much of the effect of what we have done remains hidden; we cannot trace roots which often spread great distances underground.
In the nature of things, we see only our own small effort, the
contributory efforts of others often escape us. The grown tree,
the cumulative effort of the work of all the religious and priests,
however, stands tall. We plant, Apollo waters, and God, according to the measure of his wisdom and in his good time, gives
the increase. The yield is always for the future, and although

we cannot now see the future, our faith must ever be aware of it.

These considerations reach deep into the nature of our religious vocation itself. This religious vocation must always be viewed as one of the most precious fruits of faith, from which it is inseparable. It represents a refinement or intensification of faith, for without faith not only is a vocation an impossibility, it is a huge mistake. We always act unwisely when we contemplate our vocation or attempt to analyze it in isolation from the concerns and values of faith; faith alone can properly measure its dimensions and accurately weigh its achievements. Any analysis lacking faith yields only false, misleading answers. From faith, too, derives the happiness that is its hallmark.

Precisely because of strong faith, we desired to love God and to serve him as fully as possible; herein lies the root of our vocation. Doing God's will is the essential way of serving him, and the degree of success is found in the extent of the union of our will with his. Vocation's great value consists in this: it specifies for us exactly what is the will of God. In faithfully carrying out the duties of our vocation we cannot delude ourselves or go astray, for we follow an inerrant road-map to perfection. Focusing as it does the light of the star of faith directly upon Christ, our vocation illumines a straight, sure path to our Savior; we cannot fail to be successful and happy, because, without any question, we are doing what God wants us to do and we are uniting our will to his.

Good people possessed of an equally strong faith, who have remained living in the world, often have this as the central problem of their lives: they, too, wish to do God's will, but they are troubled about what exactly is God's will for themselves. Repeatedly, some of them have to ask if what they are doing is what they should be doing, whether or not there may be some other activity that would be more pleasing to God. For this very reason, Christopher career schools are crowded today with men and women possessed of well-paying jobs but possessed also of grave doubts about whether those jobs are meaningful. Some of them consider taking up other pursuits, pursuits that might help to change the world. Others attempt to supplement the routine of their current occupation with tasks promising a more Christian fructification: some join groups that recite parts of the divine office; some contribute to the social justice efforts of the Association of Catholic Trade Unionists; some belong to Catholic Action cells; some sponsor projects in interracial charity. But the pattern is clear, people are searching for a surer way to Christ.

In spite of the wonderful zeal present in these dedicated lives which continue to be lived in the world, there has arisen in some instances, a canker to mar their work—the fear lest even subconsciously or unintentionally their previous way of life may have been serving self instead of Christ.

We are fortunate in possessing in our vocation the perfect antidote to this universal obstacle to perfection. Already, decisions have been made by us excluding all else but Christ; complete dedication is presupposed by our very presence in the convent. All of our tasks are performed under obedience to superiors and to God, whom they represent. Our acre to plow has been given us; it has come through a series of hands that reach back to Christ's own. In the vow is our consummate surety; our faith, our vocation, the legitimate decisions of ecclesiastical authority have localized Christ for us with the exactness of precision instruments. We are spared the world's intellectual vacillation, its self-wearying of the will, the gamut of its indecisive emotions. Firmly following faith, all we need do is get to work.

But the best wine, the reward of faith, has been saved for us till the last, that moment when the tasks and trials as well as the glories of the classroom, and of all else, are over and we go to our final reward. During our mortal existence, faith, although indeed most wonderful, has been but a means; it helps bring us to eternal beatitude, and is no more. Why did we seek to deepen our faith? To please Christ. Why do we perform good works? To draw close to Christ. Why were we joyful and confident? Because we were eternally to possess Christ. Faith-inspired charity is the very life of the bride of Christ, the ultimate purpose of her religious vocation. Through faith we believe in the heavenly Bridegroom of our hearts, it remains now only to love him for all eternity. Her faith now consumed by charity, the faithful religious says simply, "I live now not I, but Christ lives in me." A fulfilled faith has redeemed its promise, "We shall see him face to face."

Thus, we shall experience at the end of life—what should, through faith, be the guiding principle of life as we live it now— that God is all truth, all goodness, all beauty, our only true happiness. All this lies too latent at times in our present-day faith. Surely from time to time we can remind ourselves of what a precious treasure we have. The suggestions made to strengthen our faith, to appreciate it more fully, are but salutary reminders of how rewarding will be any further efforts we make to live each moment of each day in the spirit of faith.

15

The Holy Ghost and Integrated Asceticism

THOSE WHO HAVE STUDIED LITERATURE FOR MANY years understand quite well that literary works contain vast stylistic differences—differences ranging from a simple style for narration of ordinary happenings to sublime prose anxious to recapture elements of grandeur with fitting loftiness. In music, too, varieties of compositional approach move from mere catchy tunes all the way to Beethoven's thunderous symphonic crescendos. The purpose of offering these examples is to illustrate something similar in the spiritual life, for there, too, different approaches or styles appear just as they do in literature and music.

Individual religious noticeably differ in their ascetical efforts; while some religious, quite unimaginatively, may tread the plain, competent road which leads to a serviceable spirituality, others who live beside them are daring the high, winding, narrow path which leads to a magnificent holiness. In the case of the first group, the attitude to duties, to self-denial, and to prayer may be somewhat halfhearted, may center too much on self. The second group, on the contrary, have adopted a more formidable spiritual approach, have chosen a more generous, fervent asceticism which centers not on self but on God. To overemphasize the importance of this spiritual attitude or approach seems impossible, for herein lies the difference between a saint and the merely good religious. When we aim at composing simple refrains, we cannot expect to produce symphonic masterpieces; when we aim at journalese prose, we cannot expect to become Miltons. In things of the soul this same law holds true; if our spirituality remains self-centered, then we cannot expect lofty perfection; only when the greatness and power of God become our fulcrum are we able to move not only the world but heaven itself in the same way the saints have done before us.

A spiritual outlook of this latter type characterizes those religious whose lives have been devoted to the Holy Ghost. When we emphasize the role of the Holy Spirit in our souls, when we give free rein to his shaping of our spirituality, there results an unhesitating willingness to place all in God's hands—ascetical progress, daily work, the over-all goals of a particular position, indeed all problems and successes and disappointments which coalesce into total human life. Such reliance upon the Holy Ghost commits us, in turn, to a self-abandonment characterized by an obedient, sensitive harkening to divine inspiration. As long as we concentrate upon the indwelling of God, our quest for perfection soars to the heights; for true devotion to the Holy Ghost, absorbing human weakness, invites the soul to spiritual greatness.

A great mystery of religious life is this: by what process is the saint singled out, what forces produce the saint in the community? Is there any reason, any rules whereby one person arises like the sheaf of Joseph and towers above the others who must then pay willing, happy homage to sanctity? Why the saint on the one hand and simply the good religious on the other? In the business world, the world of art or sport, individuals also rise to eminence, but here the phenomenon is clear and understandable; their personal qualities and accomplishments make it evident that they could do so, desired to do so, and actually did.

The genesis of the saint in the community, however, remains a unique and hidden process. Exteriorly, few differences are observable; the routine, the tasks are the same. All the others, as well as the saint, get up at the same time in the morning, make the same meditation, attend Mass, receive communion, and join in the same prayers. All teach similar subjects to similar pupils in adjacent classrooms. Superficially, the sisters seem like so many peas in a pod, but from them emerges "the" saint, generally not a community of saints.

Wherein lies the difference? In all likelihood, as far as these things are humanly discernible, the difference lies in the degree of union with God. The saint brings to all of her activities a deep spirit of recollection; throughout the day God's presence in her soul looms in her consciousness as a strong dominating reality. Her activities flow from a high level of contemplative prayer which nourishes and sanctifies. The intention with which all activity is powered has been completely purified; failures, as well as accomplishments, proceed under the impetus of sanctifying grace. But it is the Holy Ghost who is the wellspring of this interiorized way of life; the spirit of the saint becomes so immersed in the Third Person of the Trinity, it acts only under the divinizing shadow of his wings.

Because the saint's soul is knit to God in a close bond, her consciousness becomes so overawed, so overwhelmed by this presence, that her attitude toward venial sins, faults, and imperfections has to be consistently that of a perfectionist. Against this backdrop venial sins appear dreadful things indeed, are avoided at all costs, and, should unguarded moments of surprise yield concessions to these faults, they are immediately and deeply regretted. Does this not point up a vital sphere of separation between the saint and the simply good religious?

Another area winnowing out those who have not yet attained the resplendent holiness of the saint, is that of humility. For many this is the great stumbling block. Many religious perform all sorts of good deeds, but when their lives lack a necessary humility, the end product, spiritually viewed, emerges as a tainted product. All sorts of time can be likewise devoted to prayer, but again, when salutary humility fails to filter out self, progress will remain limited. God reserves his richest graces for the truly humble. Yet, this humility, so basically needed, may be termed an almost natural by-product of deep devotion to the Holy Ghost. Self is shunted off into rightful insignificance; self seems but the puny light of the firefly lost in the blazing glare of the sun itself. Where an intimate, accurate, generous realization prevails of the sheer perfection ensconced within the core of the spirit, a proud self becomes an utter impossibility.

Masters of the spiritual life are in emphatic agreement that the degree of charity we bring to our daily work is of prime importance. We find it a means of greater spiritual advancement to perform a limited number of works done out of charity than a whole host of such works done without charity. Our devotion to the indwelling of God is decisive, for it fructifies by the happy coloration of all our works with a burning charity. Devotion to the Holy Spirit yields such an awareness of God's love that our daily actions become fully charitable ones.

This obviates the danger of our actions being rather mediocre products of a careless use of theological charity, for the deeper our devotion to the Holy Ghost, the greater the intensity of our self-sacrifice. Thus, the saint's life approximates a perpetual adoration of God. She simply takes for granted the worthlessness of self; any thought of self is consumed in the loving acknowledgment of the goodness of Almighty God. The holocaust of self, naturally so repulsive to human nature, is looked upon as desirable in the light of and under the affection of God's love. She can even understand the fourth station of the cross. At that station Christ and his mother meet amidst painful conditions; so painful that the human mind asks how could such extreme suffering be chosen or endured? Only saintly insight into the wonderful lovableness of God, for love of whom these and all things are willingly accepted, offers an answer. If such is the measure of how lovable God is, can we have any thoughts apart from him, any desires not centering upon him, as we increase our devotion to his indwelling in the soul?

These are admittedly very lofty concepts, although this constitutes no indictment of their validity. They have their counterparts on a more earthly level—considerations rooted in and mixed with the worldly milieu. The devotion of a religious to God's indwelling can be seen in her approach to the most routine tasks as well as to the most unusual or extremely important ones. A laudable zeal always obtains, but somehow it always succeeds in remaining a detached zeal. Overpowering emotions, either of fear or trepidation, when the attendant difficulties are great, are not present. There is a quiet joy if the assignment is particularly desired, and if it is executed well, a modest contentment; any lack of restraint, any lack of self-control is absent.

This attitude maintains its even keel even when success is loudly and widely acclaimed by others. Approximately the same reaction is secured when failure strikes; failure registers, but it does not conquer. In all of these eventualities the detachment, the preservation of the inner sanctity of the soul, is identical. Like a high mountain half hidden in the peaceful clouds but still discernible in the affairs of the surrounding earth, the saint, while moving busily amidst many daily concerns, retains in her inner soul this devotion to the Holy Ghost. Her sacred union with God, peaceful and unmoved, remains steadfastly unperturbed by the wind and storm of surrounding human fluctuations.

Faithfulness to God's Spirit must be an essential condition for highest spiritual advancement. The character of our present-day environment has intensified this idea. More than ever before the world is too much with us, and its values today are terribly perilous. Worldliness, if we may so phrase it, is today more worldly and more persuasive.

The atmosphere in which we live, saturated with pleasure-seeking and naturalism, almost blocks out the supernatural. Like weary pilgrims we plod through the desert of worldliness, but because it surrounds us constantly, we can easily come to accept and feel at home in it. Christians who lived in pagan times had some advantages over us; in such times, at least the line of demarcation between what was pagan and what was Christian remained sharp and clear with the result that mistakes of identification were rare, and more rarely excusable. How different today: everywhere we face deception. Today, even those seeking to champion Christian values sometimes find themselves unwitting tools of this insidious paganism; no longer sharp and clear, the line of demarcation has become terribly blurred.

All this makes our dedication of self to the Holy Spirit invaluable. Dwelling within us, the Holy Ghost—if we are sufficiently conscious of his presence and sufficiently amenable to his inspirations—enables us to see this line clearly, to differentiate accurately the things of the world and the things of the spirit; we possess a divine measure for any and all events crowding into our lives. Our vision, guided by God's enlightenment, cannot fail to be thoroughly spiritual, and, following this vision to be incisive in seizing upon sound supernatural values. Aided by God, we are not likely to compromise with the world or to be cajoled by its blandishments, but will rest secure in Scripture's promise: "And as for you, let the anointing which you have received from him, dwell in you, and you have no need that anyone teach you. But as his anointing teaches you concerning all things, and is true and is no lie, even as it has taught you, abide in him" (I John 2:27).

How revolutionary would be the effect on our lives were we to meditate, with prolonged penetration, upon whom we have dwelling within us. Thus enthroned in our souls, what knowledge does God possess? All knowledge. He is all truth, the beginning and end of all conceivable knowledge. And the whole process and fruit of human knowledge, what does that amount to? Simply feeble gropings searching out in insignificant degree the truth already in the mind of God. We look all around us for truth, but Truth already abides within our souls. All the hours of labor—the reading, observation, study, and so forth—are at best mere attempts to reach the threshold of the knowledge in the mind of God; efforts to partake of the knowledge whose fullness is his.

The soul was created by God; the intellect, the memory, and imagination, the senses which are the initial avenues of our knowledge, are all ours because he gave them to us. Whatever powers of discernment and absorption they boast, depend completely upon his sustaining power; without him, they would vanish. Whenever these faculties are enlightened, when they grasp truth keenly and accurately, God has aided that achievement. The faculties have been effective precisely because, and only inasmuch as, they have siezed upon pitifully small fragments of divine truth.

And the object of our knowledge? Whatever the field of endeavor, it must deal with things of God or things created by God, things whose innermost nature he alone fully comprehends. Should the knowledge deal with events, they have been known to the mind of God long before they occurred; they occurred only after his permissive will decreed that they might.

Much of our valuable knowledge, spiritually speaking, is directed to ourselves—self-knowledge—and is the necessary groundwork prefatory to all the spiritual activities we put in motion to save our own souls and to help save the souls of others. A lifetime of the most intelligent self-knowledge achieves but a tiny fraction of knowledge when compared with the ocean of his knowledge of us. And this is an inadequate comparison; inadequate, because it falls short of contrasting properly our poverty before the infinite richness of the knowledge which God possesses.

Because, among us, spiritual concerns are foremost, we need to be alert to discover any knowledge which would helpfully apprize us of the devil's machinations. For the same reason, we also need a knowledge of the world in order to eschew worldliness —to see through its values, to reject its subterfuges, to recognize its maxims and bewitching examples. This, too, is all known perfectly to the mind of God. The devil's most clever maskings are utterly transparent to him; the devices of the world merely point up its utter nakedness before his all-seeing eye. When we dutifully practice our devotion to the Holy Ghost, he will enlighten us, and we will be able to understand clearly these temptations which attempt to entrap us. When we place our knowledge and our trust in the sacred keeping of the divine Maker, we need not fear any temptations from the world and the devil.

The very pinnacle of the quest for knowledge on the part of the religious should, of course, be a knowledge of heavenly things: *Nostra conversatio est in coelis*. But surely, any knowledge of high spiritual matters, of the profoundest truths of the Christian religion, of the secrets of the Sacred Heart of Jesus, must begin with fervent prayer to the Holy Ghost, the Spirit of Wisdom. Either this divine enlightenment is secured, or all our labor is in vain and is utterly foolhardy.

This knowledge possesses a very special character. It is a mysterious knowledge in the original and deepest sense of the word, *mysterium*; the knowledge of Jesus Christ and him crucified. Far above the patterns of the merely-human knowledge process, this knowledge involves boundless faith, indomitable charity; aided by God, we approach God.

We are most privileged to receive the Holy Spirit. When the Paraclete was promised, Christ made it clear that the promise was made not to worldlings but only to his followers: "The Spirit of truth whom the world cannot receive, because it neither sees him nor knows him. But you shall know him, because he will dwell with you, and be in you (John 14:17). But do we, despite our very privileged status, permit this *spiritualis unctio*, this sweet perfume, as our hymns term the presence of the Holy Ghost, to penetrate our lives? Are we grateful for, or even adequately aware of, our blessings? Quite possibly we go for days without adverting to the presence of the Holy Ghost, although in theory, we consider this presence the most important single factor of our existence. For this spiritual unction fully to penetrate, demands a concerted effort on our part so that the indwell-ing of God's Spirit may dominate our consciousness. When we make that effort, and succeed, every item of our lives and every corner of the world with which we are concerned, feels the result. So dominated, our spiritual life cannot but move forward con-stantly to the loftiest goals, and an uninterrupted universality— quite different from sporadic sallies after isolated virtues—then characterizes our holy gains. Devotion to the Holy Ghost achieves the perfect integration of our asceticism. Under his influence, such is our transformation that it defies depiction. Even the cele-brated effort of St. Basil to describe this transformation must be considered inadequate. He employed the comparison of metal heated by intense fire; just as the metal takes on properties of brilliance, heat, and radiance, until it seems swallowed in flame, so also our soul grows inflamed with God's love.

Devotion to the Holy Ghost aids the religious in many ways. No matter what type of work the community superioress assigns, this divine aid is always near. It does seem, however, that the devotion is suited pre-eminently to those assigned a teaching apostolate. In the encyclical on education the Holy Father in-sisted that there could be "no true education not wholly dedi-cated to man's last end." Since we are dealing with man's last end, a supernatural end, our concern in education must be not only with nature but also with grace. Teaching efforts focus upon the minds and hearts of the young, but the reactions of the young are repeatedly elusive. What lurks in those minds and hearts? Even the wisest of teachers cannot say with certainty. Yet those minds and hearts hold the key to admit, or to lock out, all our attempts to influence. Human skill alone cannot grasp that key, much more is needed—the help of the Holy Ghost.

Despite attempts stretching over centuries, the available books concerned with adolescent psychology and educational principles offer only partial help. Our knowledge of those com-mitted to our care does not partake of mathematical certitude nor is it of a sort that can be diagrammed; we have no way of telling, either surely or accurately, how the smallest example we have given may affect the young. We are the blind leading the blind, unless, under the guiding inspiration of the Holy Ghost, we happily choose to perform examples fruitful for the supernatural development of our charges. Gravely limited of ourselves, we cannot boast a prophet's preternatural foresight, and the futures of our students remain hidden. Yet, our greatest contributions are principles, examples, and considerations which provide the answers needed for those future moments when their turning to evil or good hangs in the balance. We can but ask the Holy Ghost to shape our present training of the young so that, providentially, our students may remember the right answers when trials burden their young lives.

Generally, those who teach live a busy existence. For this reason, religious assigned to teach find it doubly difficult to keep supernatural evaluations and purposes uppermost: grave temptations arise to boast of a high number of passing students, even when the cold facts belie their proficiency in our subject; how difficult also do we find it to block out all favoritism from our professional judgments; fund-raising, a necessity we cannot ignore, is a legitimate task, but at times strange methods suggest themselves; certain stage plays may succeed in attracting large crowds, yet achieve nothing but the large crowd; charity and justice may be sacrificed on the altar of our rivalry with other schools in athletic and intellectual competition; in brief, our vision once turned away from the Holy Ghost, may define success as the world does.

Here we can learn from the example of wise and spiritual bishops who guide diocesan institutions and who make certain to have among those institutions groups given to contemplative prayer. They do this because they realize that any successes credited to their institutions, to be worthwhile and lasting successes, must be within the realm of present grace and future glory. Success in schoolwork should not be excepted, it requires measurement by identical norms. No matter how efficiently and systematically our human planning realizes all possibilities, such planning must be guided by those same supernatural norms; we must yield ourselves and our plans closely and fully to the promptings of the Holy Spirit within us. As more and more our thoughts, judgments, and actions accord with the inspirations of God's sanctifying Spirit, more and more those entrusted to our care will also think, judge, and act in obedience to supernatural values. More successful, too, in the achievement of eternal awards, will be the record of our institutions.

The following excerpt, written by "A Carthusian Monk," makes this point in rather striking fashion.

> Msgr. Lefebvre, Bishop of Cochin, China, perceived this clearly, when, immediately after his consecration, being filled with the light of the Holy Spirit, he formed the resolution to found a convent of Carmelites at Saigon. The governor, hearing that this was the bishop's first decision, remarked that one should not think of luxuries before having a house to live in, and received the answer, "What you call a luxury is, in my opinion, the first necessity of our Christian ministry. Ten religious who pray will help me more than twenty missionaries who preach" (*The Contemplative Life*, p. 36).

One would have to add that much would depend on the prayer-life of the missionaries, but the anecdote has an illustrative value for our purposes here.

Do not object that the above recommendations are not consonant with acceptable pedagogy. These suggestions, on the contrary, represent the soundest pedagogy. Manuals of education continually urge us to use well whatever space is at our disposal, to get the most out of the type of building which is ours, to employ to capacity the classrooms and other facilities we have at hand. Because as religious teachers we are architects of souls, what unspeakable folly we should be guilty of were we to omit from our planning—although we have utilized all else—the indwelling of the Holy Ghost, our greatest asset. That this is so, a little reflection should convince us.

God is Pure Act; his wisdom is the most active of all active things. How then can God's Spirit be present within us without his intending to make his indwelling active, effective, and flowing into our daily lives? How serious the failure when, through neglect or carelessness, we permit this indwelling to lie fallow. How contradictory, to be pleged in theory to a life all for God, and in practice to be forgetful of his presence within us. God's activity, his missions, can never be purposeless. If the Holy Ghost is sent to us and his mission is in vain, the blame must fall on ourselves.

God's purpose has divine strength; his indwelling bestows upon our souls additional forces, powers, energies, and special helps. On our part, we must use these helps. These special aids, generally referred to as the infused virtues, elevate and perfect our natural faculties. Faith, hope, and charity give a sweeping supernatural orientation to our lives and spread out our actions from an integrated life of grace. Among these special aids we number also the infused moral virtues, whose apt task it is to order sweetly our reactions to concrete situations involving ourselves and our neighbor.

This unction of the Holy Spirit which happily overshadows our own personalities in our dealings with others, can likewise affect the teaching process. In the classroom we want to give our young scholars the necessary array of facts; this is basic. Further, we want to give them a real understanding of the substance of the various subjects; that, too, is a requisite of worthwhile instruction. But we want to be sure they acquire also, during their sojourn with us, a knowledge of, and a love for, virtue; otherwise, the sacrifices which made possible our Catholic schools is superfluous.

Apart from the religion class and the various devotional exercises which form part of the over-all training of the student, motivations toward a life of virtue can be found in the personality and example and *modus agendi* of the teacher. Although not programed as such, this, too, is a very definite form of teaching; sometimes, as far as essential values are concerned, it is a good deal more important than the labeled, scheduled courses. A teacher, so devoted to the indwelling of God that both personality and life breathe this devotion, teaches a very high knowledge, the goodness and greatness of God; and that knowledge is somehow imparted to the pupils so that it kindles the beginnings of holiness in their young souls.

The influence which the Holy Ghost activates and effects in our own souls and which flows into our daily lives, is the same influence that radiates out from us into the souls of others to help transform their lives. We cannot put boundaries to this divine activity; it does not stop at the spiritual contour of our own selves. Thus, under the aegis of this *spiritualis unctio* hallowing the center of our souls, we communicate mysteriously to others a desire to sanctify life.

It seems reasonable to expect, although admittedly one would be hard pressed to document the details, that drawn to such a teacher, the prayer-life of the students would be either inaugurated or increased. (This, of course, means a prayer-life usual for those of a certain age group and condition. Perhaps even the phrase "prayer-life" cannot avoid being something of an exaggeration. Obviously, the meaning intended here is not a state equivalent to that secured by a contemplative monk. It does, however, suggest the influence at issue.) So too, as a consequence, the sacramental life of the students may well achieve increased earnestness and fullness. These aspects of their lives should be affected, because, positing their training, such avenues are the normal outlets for the impetus which has been imparted to them toward a life more pleasing to God.

The good teacher, or to phrase it clearly, the holy teacher, who is completely amenable to the inspirations of the Holy Ghost, becomes an instrument of God's sanctifying power in the world, and in this fashion is the greatest force for the promotion of true "school spirit." Today, a great deal is made of a school's high rating in the matter of good "community relations." It seems that these relations to the community on the part of both the individual student and the school as a whole, swayed by the example of such holy teachers, should approach closely to the ideal.

Students, thus fortunately led, should in turn be the means of bringing to the corners of their own environment the redemptive fruits of Christ. In their own way, by their zealous actions, they promote the cause of the Kingdom of God. They, in their own proper proportions, help to build up the membership of the Mystical Body of Christ. Thus, even teen-agers, in the values they make important in their homes, in the example they give in the busy exciting life of the streets, in their work and recreation, constitute a human extension of the hands and feet of the holy teacher. The Holy Ghost, the Spirit of Wisdom, reaching out from the soul of the saintly sister engaged in the teaching apostolate, pours forth upon the world that wisdom which reaches from end to end ordering all things sweetly.

As friend and guest, the Holy Ghost dwells in our soul. He is our best friend, because he is Love itself. "Love" is the personal name that belongs to him and it symbolizes perfectly all he means to us.

Our response in turn should be one of love, a love that will ennoble and sanctify us. Conversations, companionships, and friendships, can be uplifting, we know, among persons of steadfast character; hence, how much more so, when the object of the companionship and friendship is God. St. Thomas points out that, since love of the truly good betters and perfects the one who loves, our greatest betterment, our supreme perfection, comes from loving God (I–II, q. 28, a. 5). When we are drawn by affection more and more to the object of our love, we become assimilated to that object. An abdication of self is brought about, for our concern fixes only upon the one loved; happiness becomes measured by the well-being, not of ourselves, but of the beloved, effecting a kind of identification. Our love of the Holy Ghost within us brings us close to God, makes us mindful always of the divine will; any egotism or self-centeredness melts away. As increasingly this love becomes the axis of our world, sanctity prevails.

In merely human love, separation sometimes intervenes because of business, or travel, or war, or death. Separation reduces that human love to a love that can be only affective and moral; affective internal acts in remembrance of the beloved are repeated, but for the time being real union has been lost. The Holy Ghost, however, remains always with the soul that lives in the state of sanctifying grace. There is no separation, there is always real presence, real union; this union, nothing can separate, neither business, travel, nor death. As God and the soul converse and live together, we can sing those blissful accents of the Canticle of Canticles: "I found him whom my soul loveth; I held him: and I will not let him go."

How wise is the religious whose spirituality centers on the indwelling of the Holy Ghost. In time, perhaps only through slow steady progress, that religious will surely realize the truth of the words of Pope Leo XIII: "This wonderful union which is properly called indwelling differs only in degree or state from that with which God beatifies the saints in heaven" (*Divinum Munus*).

16

Mary's Fiat, Our Blueprint

A BEAUTIFUL PASSAGE FROM THE WRITINGS OF
St. Ambrose presents an ideal departure point for a discussion
of our religious vocation in the light of the life of the Blessed
Virgin. Perhaps the fact that we celebrate his feast on the eve of
December eighth, the day on which the liturgy honors Mary's
Immaculate Conception, hints at the Church's recognition of
his many splendid tributes to the Mother of God. In free trans-
lation the particular passage we have reference to reads:

> It is fitting that you take your way of life—as does the
> pupil who seeks to copy the skill of a great artist—from an
> example teaching what to correct, what to retain, and what to
> stress. If, in learning, the greatest incentive is the nobility of
> the teacher, who could be a more noble teacher than the Mother
> of God? Who a more radiant example than she who devoted
> her entire self to Goodness itself? Who more chaste than she
> who generated a body without the contagion of the body?
> Virgin in spirit as well as in flesh, no shadow ever tainted her
> sincere affection. Humble of heart, grave in action and prudent
> in thought, she always was; zealous in meditation, but sparing
> in speech. Not in the uncertainties of riches, but in the prayer
> of the poor, she reposed her hope. Devoted to duty, yet modest

in its accomplishment, her judgment sought the approval, not of man, but of God. Opposing no one, wishing well to all, properly deferential to high authority and not envious of equals, she fled vain glory, followed reason, and loved virtue.

Sentiments similar to these prompt our holy liturgy to begin each year with Advent—Mary's time of preparation for the coming of Christ. Because the Church proposes that during the year the faithful have as their goal the bringing forth of Christ in their own lives, we are given Mary as model. To the religious vocation, since it is designed to bring forth Christ in the soul of the devout religious and to increase the Mystical Body of Christ through the ministrations of that vocation, Mary furnishes a flawless prototype. At the outset, or Advent, of our own vocation we cannot have a more worthwhile blueprint for our future holiness and happiness than the preparation of the Blessed Virgin for Christmas. Accordingly, our acceptance of our vocation means that we become understudies of the Advent role, heavenly awarded, of the Blessed Mother.

"The Holy Ghost shall come upon thee, and the power of the Most High shall overshadow thee." Could not these words of Gabriel telling Mary of her divine call, be applied to our own vocation? Surely, in the beginning it was in response to divine inspiration that we first examined even the possibility of a vocation. As our vital affirmation took on the driving force of conviction, some of our strength, we can be certain, like "every perfect gift," was from above. "Now we have received not the spirit of the world, but the spirit that is from God, that we may know the things that have been given us by God" (I Cor. 2:12).

In a minor way, we have shared the overshadowing of the Holy Ghost promised to Mary's vocation by Gabriel's words. Her months before Christmas found parallel in the months of our own arduous novitiate; during them we strove for the configuration of Christ in the depth of our souls. So great was Mary's humility she could not but voice wonder at the greeting which saluted her as blessed among women. Pondering the honor that has become ours—for who are more blessed than those chosen to be the brides of the Lamb—must inspire in us kindred feelings of humility at God's great favor; wonder, too, and continuing gratitude that, despite personal weaknesses and natural proneness to failings, we have been sustained in our holy way of life; not —we must conclude—without the fruits and gifts of God's sanctifying Spirit.

Sometimes it almost seems that gratitude is a virtue which comes only with old age; speaking generally, the young cannot advance a strong claim to its possession. As we grow old in the religious life, however, and then look back, we do not elect to be grateful—the avalanche of remembered blessings literally forces gratitude upon us; we have no choice but to be grateful.

A certain rashness marks the bold gaze of the young, with its temerity of leveled, challenging eyes—even when the spiritual is looked upon and a vocation's future measured. Perhaps it is good that this is so, else Mary would have very few pledging themselves to follow her and to echo her response, "Behold the handmaid of the Lord; be it done to me according to thy word." How much did the mother of our crucified Savior pledge in those few words; how much also the youthful religious.

At vocation's threshold, the religious looks upon the spiritual life and sees an inviting lake, calm and beautiful. But after the soul has launched out far from the shore, there are times when rough winds lash the surface; angry, mounting swells cascade over the bow; flying spray stings the tautly drawn lines of that face which earlier had smiled in easy confidence. At such moments of our religious life how terribly distant seems the safe shore; how lonely and fragile the bobbing craft; how small and powerless the human hands clasped fearfully in prayerful supplication.

There are such moments of trial as the spiritual life advances; in intensity, in frequency, they may differ, but in some fashion they are there, at one time or another, for almost all of us. Humble in heart, we must still respond in Mary's words, "Be it done to me according to thy word," and we must mean them just as much as when we first spoke them. Those words, through our fidelity, have become words of pure gold. We must treasure the example of our Heavenly Mother's faithfulness to such fateful words as we try to live out her example in our own lives; her true children follow willingly where she has led so lovingly.

One painful but commonplace trial of religious life parallels Our Lady's journey to Bethlehem. Made in obedience to the mandate of Caesar Augustus, that journey, from the natural point of view, was a difficult and unwelcome one. We find a very similar trial in our periodic transfers from one post of duty to another. Such a folding of our tent and silently stealing away, grows to be routine in our closely disciplined way of life; but so, to a certain extent, is it routine to have a tooth extracted. Yet, the fact that everyone has teeth pulled, and that at one time or another must expect to have teeth pulled, is of little solace to one who is undergoing the painful process. Unless the toothache was particularly unbearable before the operation—which can sometimes happen—our self-discipline receives quite a testing.

Both the welfare of our own soul and the welfare of those entrusted to our care, require that we develop a proper attitude to these transfers. While a transfer is a personal thing, it is, even more so, a social factor. Should a religious determine to harbor resentment over a disagreeable assignment, such resentment bears fruit in testy, frigid, uncharitable thoughts, words, and actions— all of which are directed eventually against the fellow-religious who are our day to day companions. Life cannot but be un-pleasant also for the students who, although they are blameless and have no way of understanding the whys and wherefores of the case, remain duty bound to attend the classes of such a reli-gious. From this victimized group, future vocations would indeed be rare triumphs of God's grace over needless obstacles. The teaching process, beclouded and slanted in the hands of such a maladjusted personality, can scarcely hope to attain a maximum efficiency; indeed, it is doomed to become patently inefficient.

How the personal spiritual life of such a religious can possibly survive in a self-created atmosphere of frustrated, obdurate discontent, and even potential serious disobedience to God's will, is very hard to comprehend.

The example of Our Lady should lead us away from such tragic reactions and light the salutary path of obedient acquiescence. Those who wish to be her true followers cannot pick and choose among the paths she trod. Does not the degree of our perfection depend upon the degree of our resemblance to Mary? That resemblance becomes particularly marked when it has the courage to follow the *via dolorosa*, the sorrowful way. Such a sharing of the life of Our Lady provides the acid test of our love for her.

In its externals the journey to Bethlehem could not have been a pleasant one. To travel those roads meant days of difficulty, exhaustion, and danger; and, even as the journey drew to its end, there remained the added trial of seeking chance hospitality among utter strangers in an unknown town. But these bleak prospects, while unappealing, represented God's will, and for Mary that was all that mattered. For ourselves as well, let it be all that matters.

It is necessary, by way of parenthesis, to insert a word of caution here. The principles we have been dealing with represent general principles and, as such, are meant to cover average situations. The qualification that there can undoubtedly be transfers giving rise to situations plainly impossible to live with must be insisted upon. Appointments of this type are, presumably, rare, but quite logically they call for a different plan of action. If a particular transfer to more arduous duties falls to a religious in poor health, and if medical opinion urges the termination of the assignment, then quite clearly these inescapable facts, clamoring for the sister's retransfer, should be presented to legitimate authority with the humble request that the medical recommendations be acted upon. However, this case, and equivalent cases, as has been stated above, are by way of parenthesis, by way of exception to the general rule.

After the trying, unexpected trip to Bethlehem, Mary brought forth Christ. As you know well, the surroundings of the wondrous birth were poverty and cold, an isolated hillside and an abandoned cave. But in bringing forth Christ, Mary transformed her surroundings. Surroundings became quite secondary, almost insignificant, so concentrated was her loving gaze as it riveted itself upon the Savior of mankind. For the religious also the supreme concentration must be ever on the divine presence of Christ in the soul; surroundings must be placed second; no matter what shiftings our surroundings undergo, forming Christ in our soul remains the changeless life work. Thoughtful devotion should keep reminding the religious that cooperation with the working of the Holy Ghost in the sanctuary of the soul to bring forth Christ is all important, the first of all religious duties. Without Christ, no duty can be performed as well as it might be. No matter what her assignment, each religious will be judged according to the fullness of Christ in her soul.

God's grace, given free play, achieves much in any surroundings. Drawing upon that grace, and through loyal cooperation with it helping to fill up the Mystical Body of Christ, the religious will obediently imitate the spiritual maternity of Mary who, in the spiritual order, is mother of all mankind. Although the Virgin of virgins, Mary appeals to us also as the most fruitful of mothers. To give life is a characteristic of God himself, and God wishes to see this characteristic mirrored also in his dedicated followers; never did God intend virginity to be the road to atrophy. Just as virginity, far from abandoning womanhood, devotedly consecrates womanhood to God, so also physical maternity is overshadowed by spiritual maternity. Spiritual motherhood must be described as very real, but a motherhood of the supernatural order, sublimated and transfigured under the guidance of God. Through the order of grace, on the plane of the supernatural, the religious, in emulation of Mary's spiritual motherhood of mankind, dispenses abundant life.

Mary's motherhood of mankind aims at uniting human nature to God. Just as during the days after Christ's death she helped to keep his first disciples loyal to her son, today Mary strives to keep his twentieth-century followers close to him. Is not this the basic explanation of the everyday active life of the religious? Do not our tireless endeavors seek to bring those under our care to Christ, that they may admire him and love him and imitate him? No other purpose provides an ultimately satisfactory explanation of our schools or of any other of our institutions. Because she knew him so well, Mary could tell her children all about Christ. Hence, in order that the religious may also speak eloquently of him, Christ must be her ceaseless study.

So great was Mary's love for Christ that her children were always drawn to him; her aim was not to draw them to herself. When the religious leads her charges to Christ, she imitates Mary; should she seek instead to draw them to herself, she follows Eve. Self-seeking is ever the great spoiler, a blot on spiritual motherhood. Like Banquo's ghost at the royal banquet, self-seeking ruins the entire spiritual feast which the religious institute tries to place before the palate of the young. Because of the unpleasantness inflicted by Banquo's ghost, all the guests had to be dismissed—the joyful evening ruined. Self-seeking, too, as history so conclusively shows, marks the quickest road to ruin for any religious institute.

In any religious vocation, preoccupation with self must be forgotten, for that vocation is a concern of all humanity rather than a merely private affair. When Mary and Gabriel spoke together it was not in discussion of a private matter—the whole world hung in the balance; redemption of the world was the outcome. Such is, or should be, the outcome of the religious vocation; nothing less satisfies its sublime and lofty purpose. After God had decreed that the Second Person of the Trinity would become flesh, Mary's consent presented human nature in order that it might be so elevated. The religious, in following Mary, model of all vocations, continues to present and prepare the members of the human race for that same union which Christ still seeks. Undoubtedly, a sin-enmeshed humanity can sometimes obdurately resist that union and, as a consequence, the task of the religious enjoys little tranquillity or ease. Nonetheless, to win humanity to accept Christ's redeeming merits continues to be the ever-present duty of the vocation we have freely accepted.

It is not incompatible with our vocation, and we must clearly understand that it is not, that the task of bringing to the crucified Christ those whose welfare is in our charge, may at times mean traveling the way of the passion and standing grief-stricken at Golgotha. Never does the religious cooperate more fully in the work of redemption than when she stands close to the cross, the font and symbol of redemption. Since one of Mary's titles addresses her as Queen of Prophets, she clearly knew the consequences of her acceptance of her vocation. In the temple the aged Simeon further told Mary of the sword of sorrow destined to pierce her love-filled heart. But Mary's consent to the way of the cross and the cruel climax of Golgotha, had already been given when she spoke to the angel at the Annunciation. Our similar consent was pledged at our own profession; may we remain close to Mary and loyally live that consent.

The matchless redemptive cooperation of Mary found her at the side of the Infant of Bethlehem, watchful of the child's footsteps at Nazareth, attentive in the crowd that heard the Prophet of Galilee announce his new gospel, dispensing silent encouragement at Calvary. As Bossuet beautifully points out, the fact that Mary gave Christ to the world represented God's providential ordering of things. Since God once so decreed, that same order of things remains; God does not change. Today Mary still offers Christ's graces to the waiting world. Near her Son's side at heaven's treasury of graces, our happy, generous mother smiles as those riches pour down a delightful balm upon the thirsting souls of this barren earth.

As more and more the living of our vocation molds us in the likeness of Mary, the more generously will her Son open the treasure-trove of grace at our bidding. We have been separated from the world, not to forsake it, but that the world may become a better place. The cloister separates the mother from the children, that through the sacramental life and prayer and penance of the convent, the mother's heart may become a more holy heart—like Mary's heart. The mother's heart becomes also a grace-giving heart, for in response to such a sister, God will grant his graces—and to give grace is to impart the highest form of life.

Father Scheeben, the celebrated nineteenth-century German speculative theologian, speaks frequently in his writings of the "bridal motherhood of Mary." In this way, apart from the divinity of her Son, Mary's motherhood is distinguished from every other motherhood; for in Mary the mother is at the same time inseparably the bride of her Son. Those who have come to the convent to form their lives in the likeness of the Blessed Virgin, are likewise repeatedly termed the brides of Christ by the liturgy of the Church. This the *Roman Pontifical* makes clear, most beautifully and most insistently, in its ceremony for the Consecration of Virgins. Already, we have seen how the devout religious seeks to emulate the spiritual motherhood of Mary. Adapting this concept of the bridal motherhood, the saintly religious, desirous of coming as close as possible to Mary, now discovers new glory, new horizons in her wonderful vocation. Prayerfully she can offer God that bridal vocation in these inspiring words Abbot Guéranger once wrote of the Church:

> Remember thy bride . . . and support her during her earthly pilgrimage, until the number of thy elect is filled up. She longs to possess thee in the eternal light of the vision; but thou hast given her a heart with such mother's love, that she will not leave her children as long as there is one to save, nor

cease to save until that day comes when there shall no more
be a militant Church, but the sole triumphant Church, inebri-
ated with the enjoyment of the sight and embraces of her God.

(*The Liturgical Year*, I, 256)

17

Community Charity and
Christian Individualism

DOES THE RELIGIOUS COMMUNITY, WHOSE ES-
sence lies in being communal, find itself confronted with a riddle
when it attempts to live that essence in the midst of a society
which is individualistic? Many think modern civilization has
gone too far in its individualism. Speaking in his capacity as
president of the American Psychiatric Association, Dr. Karl
Menninger traced much of this unfortunate imbalance to a widespread overconcentration on self. There are other signposts, too,
testifying to this excess of individualism. Quite evidently, for
instance, a growing group of novels, plays, and movies exalt an
unpardonable self-expression; unpardonable—not that self-expression or individualism within proper limits is wrong—because
at the expense of the Ten Commandments, which, instead of
enjoying the dignity of commands, have come to be regarded as
bowling pins to be knocked any way whatsoever by the whim of
the moment. Perhaps this distortion of proper individualism
explains also why a percentage of modernistic art appears in-
telligible only to its creators. In any event, there are unmistakable
indications, which could be multiplied at will, that a wrong,
twisted individualism is a characteristic of the modern milieu,

and it would be unrealistic to presume that the religious community entirely escapes the impact.

For its happiness and well-being the religious community needs to boycott any individualism that amounts to plain selfishness; it requires that we give consideration to the group as well as to ourselves. The closeness of living in society is, in general, multiplied infinitely in the religious society; living in so compact a community we put ourselves and others under a magnifying glass. If we do not look through that glass with forbearance, with understanding and charity, we can create a distorted and disturbing picture; and it will be a nightmare that will haunt and hamper our efforts to thrive in the spiritual life.

Strangely enough we can sometimes very easily forget obvious and fundamental things, such as the truism that our religious community has basic human nature as its raw material and that, as a result, there must be a reflection of those varied human temperaments that make up human society. Actually, we ought to welcome this as a good thing because harmony and beauty, following out St. Augustine's classic definition, derive from a splendid order amidst variety. A religious community, or anything else, for that matter, were it absolutely monolithic, would be indeed most dull; committed in a way to the absence of life, it would resemble a tomb. Yet, that diversity of temperament also needs to beware of courting the other extreme, a chaotic individualism; live and let live remains the irreducible minimum of charity.

By way of example, pause for a moment to envision two types drawn from the scale of possible temperaments: the effervescent and the reserved. There is nothing wrong with a bubbling personality. There is nothing wrong with a sedate one, either. But it requires a mellowness of understanding for the ebullient on the one hand and the phlegmatic on the other hand to admit this and to concede it to each other. Even in a group joined together for purposes other than spiritual ones—for example, the secular office of an industrial company—this mutual understanding becomes quite necessary. People who work together must submerge individual differences in group achievement if only for self-defense and the efficient carrying on of business. In the religious community, however, we hope that the charitable attitude is more positive. How wonderful it would be to observe in every religious group an eagerness to seize upon these differences of temperament as a valuable gold mine for the exercise of kindness and self-discipline.

In our religious household we can find the mellow wisdom of those who view problems and triumphs with a veteran's eye. Also present we find the neophyte who observes all things with a zeal for getting things done quickly. Unless a careful self-restraint rules us, the veteran may charge the neophyte with impatience, intemperance, radicalism; in reverse, the neophyte may assail the veteran on the score of inertia and obscurantism. Place must always be made for freshness of outlook, but likewise place must ever remain for the lessons that experience has validated. The larger community resembles the smaller community of pastor and curate; both pastor and curate look at the same parish, yet both have approaches that differ at times to common problems. Certainly the parish needs the new ideas of the curate; no less certainly the parish needs the many service stripes that the pastor's priesthood has accumulated.

Any factionalism, separate groups with individualistic ideas, always spells death to achievement, as the great heroes of our nation have repeatedly warned the American republic. Washington, in his Farewell Address, cautioned that it would distract and enfeeble, that it would agitate the community with ill-founded jealousies and false alarms, that it would enkindle the animosity of one against another. Before the Civil War, Lincoln, with prophetic vision, quoted the words of our Savior, "A house divided against itself cannot stand," a truth which does not limit itself to history.

Our work in the religious community can be viewed as an extension of our personalities. Often, we so project ourselves into whatever becomes our particular task that we identify the position with ourselves; hence, here too we must beware of individualistic excesses at the expense of common achievement. In the community, duties differ, and not without effort do we realize the value and the extent of the tasks of others. It seems to be a fairly serviceable caveat that no one exactly appreciates the work of another until one performs the other's duties.

The experience of listening to a group of graduates discussing the careers upon which they have launched their young lives, may point this up. Each regards his or her own career as very, very important and grows rather manifestly disdainful of the other fields of endeavor; only after the conversation has run its somewhat stormy course, do they acknowledge, not without some chagrined surprise, their blindness in demeaning the other person's occupation. Just as the teen-agers acknowledged their blindness, perhaps we ourselves have some revising to do of attitudes that have crept into our estimate of the positions held by our fellow religious. "A little child shall lead them."

The religious community possesses specific weapons for effectively withstanding the spirit of individualism. One such a weapon is liturgical prayer. The liturgy primarily, of course, represents a communal, social manifestation. We are able to see this in the forms of liturgical prayer. "We," not "I," says the liturgy, and there is a valid symbolism in the broader pronoun; preoccupation with "I" often betrays that narrowness of outlook which characterizes excessive individualism. Since life is largely the product of outlook, such an outlook reaps its own type of life, life overbearing in its assertiveness, life wrapped up and sealed in self, a small, thin, stingy life.

How different the life powered by liturgical prayer! Liturgical prayer looks beyond self, beyond even the physically present congregation, to the entire body of the faithful; unlimited by time, its horizon reaches out to eternity; nor is it limited to the human alone, it invokes Divinity. By the addition of these dimensions, those whose actions flow from a love of the liturgy lead a life enviable in its fullness. In the face of a genuine love of and devotion to liturgical prayer, it is difficult to see how a harmful individualism can persist in a religious community. The corporate spirit of liturgical prayer presents a clear analogue to true community spirit. Like true community spirit, liturgical prayer inspires a certain softening of inordinate independence or unregenerate self-sufficiency; each religious then contributes not only as a worthwhile entity but also as a cohesive part of the unified group.

Extreme individualism may be symbolized by the Tower of Babel; the communal spirit of liturgical prayer by the dialogue Mass. A while after the deluge, the descendants of Noah, unable to live together in peace and harmony, essayed to build the Tower of Babel. But God said: "Let us go down and there confound their tongues that they may not understand one another's speech." As a result their disharmony accomplished only confusion. In the dialogue Mass, on the contrary, the voices of all are perfectly attuned in the same words and sentiment; as one group, at communion time, all receive the same Christ. This epitomizes both the spirit and the fruit of liturgical prayer. At the eucharistic banquet of his modern disciples, Christ prays the same prayer that he prayed during the first eucharistic banquet: "As the Father hath loved me I also have loved you. Abide in my love." "This is my commandment, that you love one another as I also have loved you." "That they all may be one, as thou Father, in me, and I in thee: that they also may be one in us." "I in them, and thou in me; that they may be made perfect in one."

The harmonizing of a proper individualism and true community spirit must have, of course, as its beginning, middle, and end, the keystone virtue of charity. Charity is the life blood of a religious community, and should its flow cease, or even flag, there can be no ideal life within. A person who is a religious, although she may be an individual admirably accomplished in any number of ways, must first possess charity, otherwise the words of St. Paul, "I am nothing," represent an understatement of her worth to the community. What a godsend it would be to religious communities, were someone to invent a machine capable of measuring the amount of charity in the hearts of those seeking admission. To have people already within the gates and then discover all too late that they lack charity, gives rise to the most lamentable predicaments.

When an adequate reservoir of charity can be drawn upon, communities can weather the worst of storms. However, no matter how well things go, if charity is not numbered among the available possessions, life cannot be other than miserable. A religious community without charity involves a contradiction—like Christianity without Christ.

It is not enough to have some charity—a selective charity extended to most of the members. That is a wrong, individualistic "charity." The excuse that those to whom it is denied do not deserve any charity, is an obvious fallacy, completely unworthy of our vocation and contradictory of our enlightened spiritual training. One of the prime realities we must accept in this life on earth is the weakness of others. People, by their very nature—a fallen one—are not perfect. To draw our own private line of demarcation barring those we label imperfect, means we want to live in some sort of never-never land—to which, incidentally, not being perfect ourselves, we could not even gain admittance.

These very weaknesses, interpreted in a Christian spirit, should constitute an invitation to our charity, a reason for its constant exercise. Precisely because people are weak, and those in religion have weaknesses too, they have great need of charity. Our fellow-religious need our charity. It may well be that nameless and numerous vocations owe their survival, under God, to Christ-like community charity.

Failings in others which irritate us may be merely manifestations of deeper problems agonizing their lives; hidden problems which lay a heavy cross upon their shoulders. We can have no appreciation of this interior struggle silently endured. Observable failings may represent occasional defeats; the many victories that have been won we know nothing of. An uncharitable reaction to one such defeat may be the last straw that ends the will's fight for survival.

By what right do we, amidst our own faults, demand angelism of others before we will allow them to play on our team? This is an erroneous individualism of the most selfish sort, and it makes day to day human relations the province of canonized saints, who, as matters stand, are found exclusively in heaven.

Some vocations have been termed "borderline vocations"; they may come to splendid fruition, but also they may be lost. Our charity has a grave obligation here, and a particularly difficult one, because in this matter charity must "fly blind," that is, it has no means of knowing that in the case of a particular individual such is the actual situation. Strong vigilance, consequently, needs to be exercised lest we be uncharitable, for we cannot adequately measure the potential harm. The possibility that our past uncharity may have done such harm and we were not even aware of it, is a haunting thought. To put it bluntly, our lack of charity may quite possibly contribute to the wrecking of a vocation. With our left hand we may be taking from Christ what we give with our right.

How much time and effort religious communities currently expend in their attempts to foster vocations by the attractive and forceful presentation of the religious life. Can it be that side by side with these efforts a cold, weak charity in the community itself causes us to lose vocations, or at least potential vocations, actually within our grasp?

Surely in our nightly examination of conscience it becomes all too evident that we ourselves have our "moments." We ourselves can be irritable, proud, vain, cantankerous, and so forth. In the depth of our soul we know this; such an awareness should be the climate of opinion into which the faults of others are received. When we do so, we will be able to muster the humility necessary to deal kindly with the routine failings of those who share our common life. In point of fact, this is no more consideration than we expect for ourselves. It is a just concession to the individualism of others.

To need charity is a very human thing. Our whole being craves affection; that is the way we are made; the heart is essentially an instrument of love; love to be given and love to be received; an unloved and unloving person is an unhappy person. This reveals itself in very simple things. Men and women who live alone regularly keep some sort of pet. It may be only an animal, but at least they do not come home from work night after night to four unfeeling walls. The homecoming, amid joyous barks or tail-wags, makes a difference—something, if not someone, is glad to see them.

Troubles, disappointments, and rebuffs, are rather standard fare in this life. While some of us may be able to bear all of these things with deep resilient spirituality or a sort of stoical equanimity, most of us find them occasions when we require a bit of consolation. We should not feel shame or embarrassment about this fact; it is a perfectly normal reaction. It can even be good for our souls to seek out necessary consolation. In its ultimate reduction, this simply means we seek that charity which others should willingly and generously provide; a charitable balance essential to the proper adjustment of the individual to the group.

Nor is this in any way an insincere thing. It does not mean we must be agreed with when we are clearly in the wrong. Nor, just for our benefit, should the unpleasant facts of a difficult situation be distorted. Truth has its rights and deserves to be appraised accurately and then acknowledged. That we have been at fault can be stated, if need be, plainly and fully. None of these things is incompatible with the tendering to us of helpful sympathy and the making of a real effort to emphasize available cheerful aspects so that our melancholy may be lifted and our state of mind buoyed up. As a result, we will be better able to keep pace with the inexorable demands of routine living.

Encouragement qualifies as a valuable form of charity. Encouragement helps us to hold to the even tenure of our ways even when things go well enough. Apart from this, the need of encouragement at particular times in life is an experience so universal as to constitute an integral part of existence in this vale of tears. On our part, when we see that it is needed by our fellow-religious, we should give it gladly. True charity develops a keen sensitivity in its detection of this need, and imparts the helpful balm with a tactful delicacy that enables it to be welcomed rather than resented.

In allegiance to our high spiritual aims we have tried to eliminate pride and vanity from our personalities, and our measure of success in this regard offers a good index to the actual progress we are making in the spiritual life. However, to desire an occasional bit of praise for our accomplishments, should not be regarded as a complete evacuation of that spiritual position. Justice, as well as charity, concerns us here. We owe it to each other to recognize our valuable contributions. Certainly, to withhold due praise is an indefensible form of uncharity and one which hampers the work of any community. Not that contributions are made merely to receive praise, but when contributions never receive the slightest acknowledgment, human nature being what it is, we find it that much harder to go on making the sacrifices which make achievement possible. The end result of uncharity of this sort will be a lowering of the level of community accomplishment, for it may well disappoint and embitter those very ones who are most capable of doing fine work for the cause we have all espoused. Praise, undeniably pleasant and agreeable, also contributes powerfully to personal happiness and equilibrium of character, both so basic to a successful acceptance of the rigors of living fully that real asceticism preliminary to holiness. Our fulfillment of holy aspirations becomes easier and the spirit is refreshed for new, loftier thrusts. The individual is helped to be a better individual.

Private families dwelling in the world utilize these aids to contented living by offering them freely as a matter of routine.

In the religious family, which becomes our second and no less true family, we play our full role only if we extend these normal manifestations of the virtue. Indeed, the more such charity is exercised, the more a genuine family spirit prevails and the happier are its members.

When the matter is given deep thought, we realize that even for our own well-being we need to exercise charity. We have been created with affections which naturally seek after their proper object; our heart, unless its reactions are totally unnatural, wants to offer love. It would be dangerous to stop up these wellsprings of charity. What would we become? It is difficult to say; possibly some sort of unfeeling robot, the dried-up outer-crust of ourselves. At any rate, not a religious of warm attractive qualities drawing others to Christ; rather, one who would repel others from the beauties of religion—the poorest type of apostle.

Our very presence in religion testifies that the greatest desire of our lives is to love Christ. How can this be reconciled with a lack of charity toward others? Charity toward others represents the proving ground of our love for Christ. We deal constantly with our neighbor; the opportunity to be alone with Christ is far less often offered to us. Consequently, charity marks the normal means of expressing our love for Christ; in our neighbor we must find his presence. St. John warned us quite accurately: "If anyone says, 'I love God,' and hates his brother, he is a liar. For how can he who does not love his brother, whom he sees, love God, whom he does not see? And this commandment we have from him, that he who loves God should love his brother also" (I John 4:20–21). We have also Christ's words: "Amen I say to you, as long as you did it for one of these, the least of my brethren, you did it for me" (Matt. 25:40). The great lesson of community charity is that the other individual is Christ.

An invaluable asset in religious life, but one not always met with, is the ability to maintain a calm objectivity in estimating our fellow-religious. We live so close to each other, and

so many community affairs involve us personally—and this
on a twenty-four hour basis day after day—that our feelings
become involved. Our attitude toward others, toward their viewpoints and doings, grows emotionally charged. Intellect and
judgment may easily be blinded by a bit of bias; past happenings
may have prejudiced us. Sometimes, too, alliances are formed
within the community and there arises an interest for some
projects and a disinterest for others. If we only had complete
objectivity and with a fair mind quietly analyzed things, how
could we escape the essential conclusion that Sister X, despite
her failings, is a good religious? That is the main point, the
focus of evaluation; any irritating foibles which X may possess
should be consigned to the periphery. In this way we emphasize
the central fact—X is a good and deserving religious to whom it
is an honor and duty to be charitable. We see X not as an
individual, but as an individual religious.

Unless this balance of mind is persevered in, our dislike
of certain aspects of the character of X begins to snowball. Then,
we begin to concentrate upon her faults; they are made the context of all we see and hear, they form the frame of reference for
our judgments. Thus, uncharity receives free rein; to look for
and pounce upon any failings becomes almost a preoccupation.
Paradoxically, we experience the temptation to elevate to the
status of duty or virtue what is in fact a calculated, extensive
program of uncharity.

In the end this will establish a relationship of hostility between two people who *ex officio* are spouses of Christ and sisters
in religion. When that situation exists, experience testifies too
well that it inevitably becomes known to the others in the
community, and may become a matter of serious scandal. Some
will follow the bad example and choose sides. What this does
to the unity of community spirit and the efficacy of community
work, need not be spelled out in detail.

Further strength for our charitable assimilation into the
community, with no sacrifice of our proper individualism, comes

to us from the self-knowledge imparted by religious training. This fosters a praiseworthy individualism, the true individual as that individual is seen in her relation to the Creator and to eternity. The accurate lineaments of that individual emerges from her weekly confession, which provides such marvelous insight into the very core of the soul. In the humbling context of sorrow for sin, we accurately see ourselves, our strengths and weaknesses, our progress and our problems; a vision which quickly kills vanity, or conceit or self-aggrandizement.

In addition, this soul-searching provides a lever for spiritual direction, which otherwise might not find *entrée,* and which represents one of the intended benefits of the sacrament. Commenting on the canonical legislation pertinent to the confessions of religious, Wernz-Vidal point out that, historically, one of the reasons for establishing the post of Ordinary Confessor was to achieve a unicity of spiritual direction. While Diocesan Statutes often urge this effort, some groups remind him that his post is confessor; each will choose her director. But all will agree with St. Bernard who once said that whoever constitutes himself his own guide becomes the disciple of a fool. On the other hand, any individualism molded by the spiritual direction of the sacrament, is one far removed from modern worldly fallacies, one that need never worry us. Such is proper individualism, pleasing alike to God and man. The individual is thus truly the image and likeness of God, as was destined at the instant of creation; now that image is developed by divine providence and is beautified by sanctifying grace.

Regardless of the varying philosophies which attract the world, the bedrock approach to life, both social and individual, for the true religious, ever remains the precious doctrine of the Mystical Body. While this doctrine finds its place in the hearts of all the faithful, surely it should be especially treasured by the religious community. With Christ who is the Head, we the members form but one person, the whole Christ; all labor diligently for but a single end—the continuous sanctifying of the members of the Body for the glory of God. All have the same motive, the will of the Father, the wish of the Savior, the inspiration of the Holy Ghost.

Pondering the doctrine of the Mystical Body, we understand that the more we become members close to one another, become members mutually for one another, the more intimately we are united with Christ. Also, the more ardent the love that binds us to Christ, our divine Head, the more we are united to each other in the bonds of charity. Here lies the test of individualism. If it meshes with the doctrine of the Mystical Body it is laudable; if it is incompatible with the doctrine, it must be destroyed.

Most grave and most sacred is the vocation of the religious community in the light of the doctrine of the Mystical Body. Since our Savior does not rule the Church directly in a visible manner, he wills, for the carrying on of the work of redemption, the assistance of the members of his Body. Although the responsibility for continuing Christ's apostolate rests primarily upon those in sacred orders, nonetheless, the Fathers of the Church, in their writings on this matter, make it also the concern of all those who, following the evangelical counsels, pass their lives either actively among men, or in the silence of the cloister, or who aim at combining the active and contemplative life according to their institute. In exemplification of this, Pope Pius XII has specifically praised those religious women advancing the Kingdom of the divine Redeemer and has further emphasized their obligation to build up and increase this Body.

Our vocation perfects our individuality. Though humbled in ourselves with the self-knowledge fostered by spiritual training, we proudly realize our importance as faithful religious. Submerging any selfishness, we pray with our community our most sublime prayer of the liturgy, the Mass. At the eucharistic common table Christ perfects us as members of his Mystical Body; joined there to Christ and those to whom Christ has also joined himself, we dedicate ourselves each day to the increase of that

Body. Our redemptive labors with the youthful, for whom God yearns, firmly fix them in their place as members of Christ. From dawn to dusk in inspiration and perspiration we form the whole Christ; and the by-product—we become Christlike.

DATE DUE

MAR 20 '63			
JUN 2 2 '63			
JY 16 '63			
JUL 3 1 '63			
AG 14 '63			
AG 26 '63			
JE 25 '64			
JY 1 3 '64			
JY 27 '64			
AG 3 '64			
JE 24 '65 4			
JY 8 '65			
JY 24 '65			
AG 5 '65			
AG 1 4 '65			
NO 10 '65			
OC 24 '88			
GAYLORD			PRINTED IN U.S.A.